CRICKET'S
—GREAT—
ENTERTAINERS

Henry Blofeld

Hodder & Stoughton

Copyright © 2003 by Henry Blofeld

First published in Great Britain in 2003 by
Hodder and Stoughton
A division of Hodder Headline

The right of Henry Blofeld to be identified as the Author of
the Work has been asserted by him in accordance with the
Copyright, Designs and Patents Act 1988.

1 3 5 7 9 10 8 6 4 2

A CIP catalogue record for this title is available from the British Library

ISBN 0 340 82728 9

Typeset in 11/15.5 Berling by Servis Filmsetting Ltd, Manchester
Printed and bound in Great Britain by Clays Ltd, St Ives plc

Hodder and Stoughton
A division of Hodder Headline
338 Euston Road
London NW1 3BH

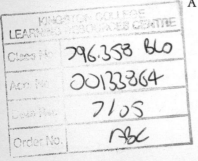

For Bitten who managed to stumble through this one without so much as a backward glance, and whose advice was as sharp and to the point as ever, with much love.

CONTENTS

PART THREE

1946–1966

PART FOUR

1967–1987

PART FIVE

1988–2003

CONTENTS

Part Six
A Watching Brief

PHOTOGRAPHIC ACKNOWLEDGEMENTS

The author and publisher would like to thank the following for permission to reproduce photographs:

Colorsport, Patrick Eagar, Empics, Getty Images/Hulton Archive, Marylebone Cricket Club, London/Bridgeman Art Library, Popperfoto.com, Popperfoto.com/George Beldham Collection, Popperfoto.com/Reuters, Press Association.

All other photographs and illustrations are from private collections.

ACKNOWLEDGEMENTS

I would, as always like to thank my editor, Roddy Bloomfield, for his considerable skills as a literary guide, counsellor and general signpost. In particular, I would like to thank him for a typically erudite luncheon at one of his better clubs when the whole idea was mooted. Writing a book without him at the helm would be not unlike batting against Allan Donald in a pea souper. It would not have been possible either, without the unfailing craft of Maggie Body who, as copy editor, has managed, against all odds and for the third time, to turn my original and largely indecipherable drafts into something cohesive, coherent and, I would like to think, compelling. My thanks to everyone else for their noble work at Hodder especially Lucy Dixon whose cheerful voice and non-stop enthusiasm makes the process of tapping the general public on the shoulder and saying, 'What about this,' both highly successful and great fun.

AUTHOR'S PREFACE

I HOPE that anyone who reads this book will want to argue violently with me.

An arbitrary selection of forty-three cricketers labelled *Cricket's Great Entertainers* can only raise hackles. Everyone will have their own idea of who cricket's greatest entertainers really were and none of them will agree with me.

I make no apologies for my selections and if it should be felt that one or two modern players are lucky to get in, I felt it was important to show that the contemporary game does produce its own characters. I fear though that it is those whom I have left out that will bring me the greatest earwigging. Why no Derek Randall for a start?

Why not even one of the famous three Ws from the West Indies? I can only come up with the answer the Yorkshire supporter gave to Neville Cardus one day at Scarborough. The supporter and his friend, who were sitting near Cardus, picked their side for the next Test match. They solemnly and at length, after much discussion, chose all eleven of the Yorkshire side. When they had finished, Cardus could not resist leaning over and saying to them, 'But you've left out Jack Hobbs.' They looked at each other and then anxiously back at the list of names on their piece of paper before one turned round to Cardus and said, 'Aye, but how could we get him in?'

There were a number of others I couldn't get in, too. Who would be a selector? If I have got it all wrong, so be it, but I have had an awful lot of fun while erring in my ways. I hope you'll forgive me and just say, 'Well, I suppose he did his best.'

Henry Blofeld
North Farm, May 2003

PART ONE

1830–1914

ALTHOUGH cricket was still highly recognisable as the game the peasants and then the aristocracy, in their unquenchable urge to take money off each other, had played in the eighteenth century, it was on the move by the mid-nineteenth century. The nobles had stopped trying to take large purses off one another, although gambling and the bookmakers were still a part of the game. The best players, the professionals, were no longer being employed by the nobility in their efforts to pull a fast one over their neighbours. The game had settled down more. County clubs were being founded, Thomas Lord had moved his ground, for the second time, to its present venue in St John's Wood, and William Clarke of Nottinghamshire had set up the game's first professional troupe. His All England XI would travel round the country playing sides against the odds, taking on, for example, the twenty-two of Bristol in the days before the massive invasion by the family Grace. Twenty years later Old Clarke might have needed twenty-two of his own if he was to take on even eleven of Bristol. Clarke was nothing if not an old rogue. He paid his players miserably and was a complete autocrat, causing much concern to the MCC, who had evolved from the White Conduit Club back in 1787. This was the year in which that itinerant Yorkshireman Thomas Lord had founded his first ground in London, on the spot which is now Dorset Square, just north of the Marylebone Road. Old Clarke's players were not available to play for MCC. He was challenged by John Wisden of Sussex who set up his own United England XI and for some years these two were locked in blood-thirsty opposition. It was not until 1835 that the MCC, then as now, the law-makers, decided to legalise round-arm bowling, although before that many had been testing the existing law to the limit in this respect. Cricket was beginning to leave its medieval beginnings behind.

The game was altered irrevocably by an unnoticed event in July 1848 when Mrs Martha Grace, the wife of a Gloucestershire doctor, gave birth to her eighth child, who was christened William Gilbert. In 1864, as a sixteen-year-old, he began to buckle on his pads with earnest intent and immediately began to score runs in previously unheard of quantities. By the time he retired in 1909, WG had scored almost 55,000 first-class runs, mostly on terrible pitches, and had taken all but 3,000 wickets. During the course of those forty-odd years, WG almost single-handedly steered the game from its rustic beginnings into the game we know today. He was the first batsman to score runs with equal facility off both the back and the front foot and his murderous treatment of bowlers caused them to rethink their method of attack. For example, sheer pace alone was now no longer enough. WG saw to it that it had to be controlled if it was to be successful.

Long before the Old Man had finished, Test matches were being played between England, Australia and South Africa and a new generation of players were coming through who were to take the art form he had so developed a stage further. The Ashes had come into being as a result of Australia's victory in the Test match at The Oval in 1882. Overseas tours to Australia and South Africa had become regular events on the calendar. The first to leave these shores, in 1859, had gone to Philadelphia where a good standard of cricket was played and Barton King bowled as fast as anyone had yet managed – WG himself went on two tours to America. He later twice visited Australia where his disdainful, not to say contemptuous, behaviour brought upon his shoulders considerable colonial dislike. In spite of his high-pitched, squeaky voice, WG had definite ideas about almost everything and anyone who ignored his views did so at their peril.

At home the County Championship was increasing in size all the time and each county acquired a considerable following. At the age of forty-seven, in 1895, WG had his most remarkable season of all when he became the first batsman to score 1,000 runs in May. By then, the Golden Age was under way and all those glorious, hirsute characters in their funny, slatted pads to go with their new-fangled strokes were taking the game by the scruff of the neck. The state of the world may have been becoming increasingly shaky but cricket strode along an uninterrupted path of glory until Kaiser Wilhelm became too big for his boots in 1914. By then another immortal figure, Jack Hobbs, had been taking English cricket by storm for nearly a decade as he began to steer the art of batting down new and untravelled paths.

Meanwhile, the MCC had recovered its authority, even if the committee, as usual, had more than its share of old farts whose natural home was the House of Lords. That self-appointed guardian of the game's morals, Pelham Warner, who had begun life in Trinidad, was very much a feature of the game. He captained England and Middlesex and was a regular in the committee room at Lord's. For all his apparent virtues, he probably got a better press than he deserved and at times became extremely adept at putting the telescope to the blind eye. Generally speaking though, the game moved forward on an even keel and took the shape that is still recognisable today. Contemporary players, in particular, tend to chuckle a trifle cynically at stories of the past, but cricket in the fifteen or twenty years leading up to the Great War was probably as entertaining a game as it has ever been.

It acquired a huge popularity and it was played by some real characters who could not help but leave their mark. In the following pages I have looked at a few of them. I think it is more than possible to see, with people such as these involved at the top level of the game and steering it further forward, why it made such an impact on the country at that time. Beating Australia was as important then as it is now, although somewhat easier. South Africa were beaten quite comfortably, although after Bernard Bosanquet, the father of the ITN newsreader, Reggie, had invented the googly early in the twentieth century, the technique spread rapidly to South Africa. Their exponents of this particular art caused problems to the well-being of both England's and Australia's batsmen. By the time the Kaiser began to get above himself, the inventions of WG and his successors had been incorporated into the game forever.

ALFRED MYNN

ONE of the most engaging and attractive characters, and near enough a prototype for WG, was Alfred Mynn from Kent who was as 'kind and manly' as William Jeffrey Prowse's much-quoted epitaph says. In the 1830s and 40s, Mynn was as much an institution as WG was to be three decades and more later. Mynn was an even bigger man, seldom weighing in at less than twenty stone, and Richard Daft marked him down as twenty-three stone. Small wonder that on a pitch that had not been properly prepared, he dug a huge hole with his front foot in his delivery stride. Mynn bowled round arm and he was uncommonly fast. As a batsman, his scoring was remarkable, considering the cart tracks on which the cricketers of those days generally played. He was the first cricketer to catch the public imagination with his ability to make runs and take wickets. With his genial personality he won the hearts of everyone. Huge crowds turned up to see him wherever he played. He had a commanding presence, but with it came an unusual gentleness. A visiting Frenchman who, as Mynn's regal figure strode on to the field of play, exclaimed to no one in particular, '*Voila, le grand Mynn*', summed him up to perfection. It was exactly how they all felt.

Mynn came from a family of yeoman farmers who were known not only for their sporting ability, but also for their size. In addition to his considerable weight, he was two inches over six foot tall. The family genes had worked overtime on his frame, but had hardly bothered to hand their sweater to the umpire when it came to distributing the grey matter. One problem he clearly never had the brainpower to sort out was how to make enough money to keep himself afloat. He was perennially short of the readies. The only thing he was any good at was cricket, but that was, financially speaking, never more than a mixed blessing because he played as an amateur. His wife and children seldom got their two square meals a day, although his father chipped in when it came to keeping the cricket going. But being the sort of chap he was, Mynn would happily have kept going with last year's bat if it meant that roast beef and Yorkshire pud would be on the dining-room table for the next few Sundays. When the old man put his cue in the rack even this option disappeared. He was forced to take the plunge and turn professional and although this produced a benefit game or two, it did nothing for his social standing.

He was no stranger to bankruptcy, but his shortage of funds never seemed to worry him. It did not affect his cricket, which he continued to play in a brilliantly stimulating fashion. It was the one thing he was apparently able to concentrate on even though the bill collectors were knocking the door down. It called for considerable coolness under fire. One can only think that during the lunch interval he was a serious rival to Mr Mike Gatting when it came to having second helpings, finishing off the potatoes and generally grabbing the calories. This would have made an evening meal less of a necessity. For years it must have been a hand to mouth existence for his family, for they would never have known where the bailiffs were lurking. There was a time when he joined his brother's hop business, but it was too much like hard work. His figure suggests that he enjoyed a pint or two of the product, even if he did buy it on tick.

On the cricket pitch he was magnificent. With that enormous body, which he must have kept in pretty good trim, he became probably the fastest bowler the game had so far seen. He had learned this aspect of his game from the famous John Willes who had been no-balled at Lord's for bowling round arm – whereupon he promptly stalked off the pitch, got on to his horse and, in high dudgeon, rode out of Lord's and out of the game forever. Mynn coming in to bowl must have put the fear of God into a generation of English batsmen. With all twenty-odd stone of him in top gear and those massive arms going like pistons, an awful lot of batsmen must have been treading on the umpire's toes at square leg. He must have been a truly inspiring sight as he approached the wicket. He had the smoothest of actions and his control was excellent. Relentlessly he pitched the ball on the leg stump before it snaked away to the off. A leg break at that speed cannot have been much fun to face. His hands were said to be the size of a leg of mutton and he put them to excellent use at short slip where he gobbled up everything that came his way. Looking at the shape of the man, it was predictable that he was labelled the most devastating hitter of the ball in the country.

He was as brave as a lion, too. There is a horrifying story told of him when he was playing a match for the South against the North at Leicester in 1836. He was hit a fearful blow on the leg in practice before the match began and was unable to bowl. He insisted on batting and in agony made 146 not out, which won the game for the South. He then went straight home, but the injury was so bad that he was forced to lie on the roof of the coach from Leicester to London. When he arrived back in Kent the doctors came close to amputating his leg, but Mynn gritted his teeth and refused to give in. Two years later he was back to his best form, but it had been a close squeak. Everyone loved Mynn for he was always good humoured and ready to laugh. He was generous to a fault and a cheerful, outgoing colleague who never tried to stretch the laws of the game in his own self-interest, as one has to admit WG made a habit of doing. No wonder he had such a big following and how sad it was that when he reached the age of only fifty-four his heart found it could not cope with that vast body any more. I would have liked to have heard him at the dinner table with the young WG. He may have been eternally bankrupt in one sense, but he was richer than most in another.

W.G. GRACE

Iᴛ can only have been typically stuffy Victorian prejudice that prevented Lytton Strachey from including W.G. Grace in his *Eminent Victorians*. No sportsman in the history of the world has had the actual and ongoing fame that has relentlessly pursued the memory of this deceptively mild-mannered son of a West Country doctor who is more of a legend than ever eighty-eight years after his death. He was dramatically conspicuous in his huge, bearded and idiosyncratic way both on the field and off it; he was benign and charming one day and then abrasive and downright bloody-minded the next; he was a paragon of virtue when it suited him, and a cheat when he wanted to be; he had the upstanding figure that seemed the prerogative of the gentleman and therefore the true-blue amateur and yet no one was more mercenarily orientated; his figure should have belonged to an aristocrat with a rich, cut-glass voice, yet he spoke in distinctive West Country tones which, to make it worse, were uncomfortably high-pitched. No cricketer has ever been more of an entertainer, whether scoring runs or taking wickets or just being WG. He could be petulant and infuriating as well, but then this was all part of the entertainment. You never knew what was coming next. His arrogant treatment of the 'colonials' on his two tours to Australia, where he made Douglas Jardine look like a close relation of the Archangel Gabriel, was insufferable. Like Jardine, he had it in for the Aussies whom he obviously felt were putting upon him.

The paradoxes are endless and although Lytton Strachey may

have turned his back on the doctor – if he had ever impinged on his consciousness in the first place – the MCC committee, in those days a selection of hereditarily ennobled dinosaurs, sucked up to him. On principle they objected to any innovation, however sound, that had burst upon the world since King Alfred had that unfortunate experience in the kitchen with the cakes. Nonetheless, they elected him as a member when he was still twenty-one. They knew which way their bread was buttered. The secret of WG was that he transcended the game of cricket in much the same way as the Colossus had once looked down upon the citizens of Rhodes – with a benign and untouchable disdain, which gave the impression of not being altogether averse to the odd pinch of skulduggery. The ultimate cricketing truth was that having WG on your side meant money through the gate and usually victory to boot. Human nature lent a hand in the MCC committee room just as it did everywhere else. One can only imagine the huffing and puffing that must have gone on at the committee meeting at which WG's election was agreed. It must have been a little bit like the one, 130 or so years later, at which the election of lady members was agreed. When an MCC committee swallows its pride, you can feel an H.M. Bateman cartoon coming on. The one compliment WG paid MCC was always to wear the yellow and orange cap, which became as much a part of him as his beard.

Everything was done on the grand scale. WG did not believe in keyhole surgery whether he was hitting a ball for four, indulging in sharp practice, negotiating a financial deal, putting an Australian in his place or telling an umpire to pull up his socks. The only occasions self-doubt entered the domain of WG were when he had to make a speech, something he detested, and this may have had something to do with his famously squeaky voice, and when it came to his dealings with women, with whom he was uncomfortably shy. When touring Canada in 1872, the England players found that there were beautiful ladies for the taking wherever they went, but WG's resolution was impressive as he let them all go past the off stump. It was on his return from Canada that he became engaged to nineteen-year-old Agnes Day, not that she had anything to do with his touring abstinence. She was the daughter of a cousin and she bore him three sons. Agnes was never allowed to get in the way of his cricket, or his shooting and fishing, except on the odd occasion in Australia and much to the annoyance of their hosts, which could have been the reason he allowed it. She spent her honeymoon, well provided for on the tour of Australia in 1873/74, and a second honeymoon there on another equally acrimonious tour eighteen years later.

Cricket was close to the heartbeat of the Grace family, yet even so the genes had concocted a powerful mixture when WG's mother, Martha, catapulted this particular squealing infant into the world in Downend on 18 July 1848. As soon as Martha and Dr Henry's eighth child could hold a bat it was clear that here was one to be watched. When WG began to play, the game was immediately recognisable as that which had, for example, been on view when the second Duke of Richmond's team took on that of Mr Brodrick of Peperharow in 1727, even though round-arm bowling had been a recent addition. Thirty-six years later, in 1864, overarm got the nod from the legislators and it was in that same year that WG made his first appearance in big cricket. Two days before his sixteenth birthday, he scored 170 and followed it with 56 not out for the South Wales Club against the Gentlemen of Sussex. Not many fifteen-year-olds have the determination to go on to 170.

Dates and statistics can assume a deathly pall. As far as WG is concerned they are essential to the understanding of the superhuman ability of the man, his entertainment value and even a social importance that was resoundingly ignored by those whose business it was to hand out accolades in the form of honours. But even his statistics do not go far enough, for they tell nothing of the appalling conditions in which he found himself playing. In his early days especially, he batted consistently on what were in all honesty not much better than cart tracks, yet his scoring was phenomenal. He played his first first-class innings in 1865 and his last in 1908 and in that time he amassed 54,211 runs with 126 centuries and an average of 39.45, in addition to another 45,000 runs in less significant cricket. He also took a small matter of 2,808 wickets at an average of 18.15. Just as important as these startling facts, he, almost single-handedly, leapt triumphantly across a nigh unbridgeable gap, taking the game from its advanced medieval condition to the game we would recognise today.

By 1908, Test cricket was flourishing between England, Australia and South Africa. WG had himself played in twenty-two Test matches against Australia and, but for the attentions of Mr Frederick Spofforth would have averaged more than 32.29. It would have been helpful, too, if he had been younger than thirty-two when he began his Test career, for he was then past his best. This was at The Oval in 1880 in the fourth match ever played between England and Australia. Nonetheless, he made 152 in the first innings, helping England to victory by 5 wickets. Small wonder that he became a universal hero, loved, admired and adored by people of all classes.

WG had not only taken the game into the modern age, he had also played it himself with an equal facility in all the stages through which he so quickly steered it. His own personal *coup de grâce* came in 1895 when, at the age of forty-seven, he scored 1,000 runs in May between the 9th and the 30th, reaching his hundredth hundred in the process. He was the first to achieve either feat. WG's statistics seem to go on forever and, with time, to become even more astonishing. Small wonder that as the popularity of the game increased, he became a good deal more than just a national hero. In England, perhaps only Queen Victoria was as instantly recognisable, although after her prolonged mourning and absence from public view after Prince Albert's death, maybe WG even pipped her at that particular post. The Marxist Trinidadian C.L.R. James, in that wonderful book *Beyond a Boundary*, links WG with Thomas Arnold, the headmaster of Rugby School, and Thomas

Hughes, who wrote *Tom Brown's Schooldays*, as being symbolic of Victorian culture. I don't know what WG, a simple soul for all his native cunning, would have made of that.

His entertainment value as a cricketer, pure and simple, was never in doubt, but WG's reputation would almost certainly not have survived as it has if it had not been for all those human qualities, both good and bad, which he had in abundance. The stories that have lingered long after the man himself have given him flesh and blood, even more perhaps than all those awesome statistics. The stories are legion and even if a few are apocryphal, so what? They are immensely good value. The extraordinary part about it all is that, although many of them do not show him in a good light, his antics never seem to have been held against him. His kindly nature, his generosity and his determination always to help the young, must in the end have won the day in an age that was quick to blame. His career as a doctor inevitably came second, but he was still much loved by his patients as he went about his business in a brisk, jovial and efficient way. After a difficult maternity case, he is said to have told his friends, 'Well, the baby's dead and I don't think there's much hope for the mother, but I do believe I shall pull the father through.' When instructing a mother to put her children, both of whom had high temperatures, to bed, he said, 'There's no need to call me unless they get up to two hundred for two before lunch.' He loved to tell these stories against himself. The poorer among his patients had no need to worry about calling him for a visit for the bills had a habit of not turning up. For all that, there was little time for doctoring in the summer months.

With a figure like WG's, which put one in mind of a rather squeaky cross between Henry VIII and Falstaff, he had either to be an entertainer or a kinsman of Machiavelli or both. For most of the population of Victorian England it was enough that he played cricket as it had never been played before, but if he had been small, demure and completely clean-shaven, I wonder if he would have had the same impact. It was roundly said that he was no fool and the more one reads about him the clearer this becomes. When Neville Cardus spoke to an old Gloucestershire pro who had played with WG, he asked him if he cheated. 'The Old Man cheat!' came the shocked reply. 'Why, 'e were much too clever for that.' He must have gone through most of his life with a sizeable tongue in his cheek, even if he grew an enormous beard to hide it. I am sure that in part this was true, but he was so much else besides. He was a self-publicist only in the way that his deeds spoke volumes for him. He would never have needed the assistance of one Mr Max Clifford or any other of his ilk. I do not for one minute believe that WG did not know exactly what he was doing and why he was doing it. The only thing that saddens me is that there is no evidence that he ever allowed himself a thoroughly good guffaw at the way in which he was having the lot of them on. Then there was the overgrown schoolboy in him, which was a large part of his charm and will have accounted for many of the things he got up to.

Nonetheless, he was, at times, staggeringly rude and this seemed to get worse the older he got. As the years went by he believed more and more in his own publicity. He did not like people who got in his way, which gave him something in common with Winston Churchill, Henry VIII and Bulldog Drummond. Yet there does not seem to have been any real side about the man; he was never caught blowing his own trumpet for he was too busy getting on with the next thing in his life, and he would have been terrific fun at a dinner party, particularly if there was plenty of champagne.

The tricks he go up to were too good to be true. At the age of twenty-one and with that Gloucestershire burr, he found that he had been elected to the Marylebone Cricket Club and all that implied. It was his genius as a player that had got him there and it was then as if, with a twinkle in his eye, he had said to himself, 'Right, I'll show them.' At the time of his election, the club supremacy was under threat from William Clarke's professional All

England XI, and the MCC will have felt they had to get WG on board to help ward off the challenge. But it was only a year or two later that he began to organise games for the United South of England XI for which he will have been handsomely paid. If there were murmurings in the committee room at Lord's, they were scarcely audible, even though that illustrious body must have realised that they had a professional within their ranks. Given an inch, WG was more than able to take twenty-two yards, and there was never a short run either. As his reputation grew, his confidence increased, often in step with his sense of humour. It was as if he spent most of that decade positioning himself while testing the ice here and there. He relied on his deeds with the bat, his huge free-range black beard and his ever-burgeoning figure, topped on occasions, especially in Australia, by a stove-pipe hat. But whatever he did, he was gilt-edged box office material – even Down Under where they have always loved to hate. On both his tours there he bent the rules to suit himself. He claimed catches after the ball had bounced, he was in constant conflict with the umpires, and off the field he did much as he pleased. Although he was hugely admired as the greatest batsman the game had ever produced, he received severe treatment from the Australian press and, in all honesty, he deserved it. Although he was paid £1,500 to go on the first tour and £3,000 for the second, he was always on the look out for ways of earning an extra bob or two. On both tours, the amateurs lorded it across the oceans and around the country while the professionals had to put up with steerage in every sense of the word and were not a happy bunch as a result. This was reflected in their play and WG had something to answer for here.

WG liked above all to win. It would be nice to think that rather than feeling that he was untouchable because of his position in the game and his unique ability to make any bowler look an ass, he behaved in a somewhat exigent manner for the hell of it. He was adored by the public who flocked to see him and those in charge of the gate would often double the entrance fee if WG was guaranteed to be among those buckling on their pads. He was worth a great deal to the game; he knew it and was determined to see that he was suitably rewarded and would let nothing stand in his way on the field or off it. He was a holy terror over expenses and yet county treasurers rubbed their hands with glee if they knew WG was coming to play.

In 1878, WG turned out for the South against the North. He was fielding at point when one of his opponents, Richard Barlow, a Lancastrian, played a defensive stroke and then obligingly pushed the ball towards him to save him the journey in to pick it up. Having done this, Barlow made a habit of scampering two or three yards up the pitch as if he was taking a run before turning round and going back to his crease. All good fun and smiles all round. At least, that was usually the order of the day and the crowd loved it. WG was not impressed and immediately appealed against Barlow for hitting the ball twice and the Laws being what they were, the umpire would have had no need to consult the third umpire had there been one. Barlow had to go. Was WG irritated that a lesser mortal than he should be taking the mickey out of him? Had his enthusiasm and his pursuit of victory got the better of him? Or, did he just think, 'Let's have a bit of fun here'? Or was it his competitive instinct? He will have had a word or two to say to Barlow as he departed, but he got away with it and curiously there is no indication that the North were deeply upset or that the crowd were tempted to throw bottles, cushions, insults or anything. They did not boo him, either then or later when he came out to bat, and I am sure they all thought that WG was at it again and everyone except poor old Barlow had a thoroughly good laugh. If they had sat next to each other at lunch, I wonder how the conversation would have gone.

There are plenty of similar stories about WG, usually constructed around his inbuilt reluctance to leave the crease when the umpire had indicated otherwise. When he ticked off umpires for giving him out saying, 'They've come to see me bat, not you umpire,' he was right. He was an institution and the huge crowds came hoping they would see him add to his mountain of runs.

One thing leads to another and each time WG did something like this and got away with it, he was unlikely to hold back the next time, no matter what the stage. Four years later, England were playing Australia at The Oval in the match that Australia won by 7 runs. It was the defeat that produced the leg-pulling obituary notice in the *Sporting Times* that precipitated the Ashes. In Australia's second innings, Sammy Jones who was batting at number eight, finished a run and, thinking that the ball was dead, made his way up the pitch to do a spot of gardening. WG had encouraged Jones to think that the ball was dead when he walked with it towards the bowler. Seeing Jones in mid-pitch, WG walked smartly back again to the wicket and had the bails off in a flash, and one of that, I am sure eminently trustworthy Bucknor and Venkatraghavan-like duumvirate of L. Greenwood and R. Thomas had no option but to raise the finger. There is no evidence of a hullabaloo afterwards in the papers, the Surrey committee room or anywhere else. Maybe, WG thought, 'I'll teach the whippersnapper.' Then again, he might have thought, 'This'll be a bit of a giggle'. Of course, as his reputation for these little idiosyncrasies increased, it will have become expected of him and, just as he did with his bat, he didn't want to let anyone down. In its way it was grand entertainment, although without end-of-day press conferences, mass media coverage, television and the wisdom of John Arlott, Brian Johnston *et al* on *Test Match Special*, very few will have been able to derive full enjoyment from it. But, my goodness, WG himself must have loved it.

While these are glaring examples of how the Old Man got up to it, he also played truant in other ways, if in a more minor key. In one match he ran 3 runs before the ball came back from the outfield whereupon it stuck in the top of his pads or his voluminous clothes. In those days the ball was not automatically dead when this happened and so, without a flicker of conscience, he called his partner and they ran another 3. Having done that, he refused point blank to give the ball back to the fielding side for fear he might find himself given out for handling the ball.

If WG had been playing in modern times, the moment he retired, some impresario would have offered him a fortune to go on the stage – shades of Tim Hudson, the English disc jockey from Los Angeles, who was keen to turn Ian Botham into a latter-day Errol Flynn. WG probably had too squeaky a voice to be much good as a singer and I am not so sure he would have had us all rolling in the aisles of the music halls for he was, believe it or not, a private and rather shy man. Without a bat or ball in his hands and that MCC cap on his head or, indeed, a cricket tour of Australia to run, he was happy with his own company. He would have left the pantomimes to others, even though there are so many parts that might have been written especially for him. Fee Fie Fo Fum and all that. Yet, how well he and Botham would have got on together and I daresay they would have taught each other a thing or two. One can only spare a thought for the poor unfortunate chap who might have had to manage an overseas tour with them both in the side.

WG went on three tours: one to Canada and the United States, in 1872, and then two to Australia. The opposition in Canada was a pushover and WG was at his most magnanimous. R.A. Fitzgerald's side was looked after magnificently, even though the amateurs were not altogether sure about the easy and immediate familiarity that came with the broad sweep of Canadian democracy. There was a lack of forelock-touching respect. It was on this tour that WG struck up a lifelong friendship with George Harris, later to succeed his father as Lord Harris. Harris was to recall 'the kindly, sympathetic consideration which characterised Grace's comradeship', saying that the tour 'commenced and cemented a friendship between us which I value at the highest'. In later life, when he presided at Lord's, Harris was a stickler for tradition and convention and a certain amount of WG's subsequent behaviour might have brought him eloquently to the boil, but he never wavered in his view that WG was 'one of us'. It may all have begun as a shrewd bit of arse-licking by WG in Canada, but a genuine affection must have followed.

WG who was initially surprised to find his reputation had preceded him across the Atlantic Ocean, was often asked to speak after dinner on that tour and he said more or less the same thing whenever he rose to his feet: 'Gentlemen, I beg to thank you for the honour you have done me; I never saw better bowling than I have seen today and I hope to see as good wherever I go.' The only variation was that on other occasions bowling became batting, fielding, pitches, catching, oysters and once, rather daringly, ladies. Canada also provided plenty of fishing and shooting and was a joy, apart from the perils of crossing the Atlantic, for WG was a hopeless sailor. In the eight matches he scored 540 runs with an average of 49.1 and the next highest scorer, Alfred Lubbock, made 146. WG was lionised from first to last and it was on this tour that he began to realise what he was worth. He had accepted Fitzgerald's invitation to go to Canada and the United States for the fun of it and without any apparent haggling over the terms.

Like the very best vintages, WG got better as the years went by. Sir Pelham Warner, a man not usually given to superlatives, or to seamless English grammar either, wrote in WG's memorial biography: 'Of all the feats I witnessed by WG, the one that most surprised me was a bowling one. It was in 1902 – he was then nearly fifty-four – against the Australians when Trumper was at his very best. The Old Man took the ball and I thought we were in for it. Instead the Australians were – 5 for 29; marvellously baffling, too, not a pinch of luck to help an analysis of which Tom Richardson would have been proud.'

Four years later, in 1906, WG saw a boy of eighteen batting in the nets at Lord's. He was told that it was George Challenor who went on to captain the West Indies. 'Take note of him,' the Great Man said. 'You will hear of him one day.' His eye never missed a trick. He was dismissive of the bookworm. He ticked off a fellow player who was always reading in the dressing room, 'How do you expect to score if you are always reading? I am never caught that way.' It was Ranjitsinhji in his *Jubilee Book of Cricket* who wrote of his batting: 'He turned the old one-stringed instrument into a many-chorded lyre.' Not bad for a chap who had himself turned it into the most delectable of sitars, but maybe without WG's example he would not have had the chance.

If anyone still has doubts as to whether or not WG was probably the greatest entertainer cricket has ever produced, he should learn by heart his incredible performances between 9 and 30 May 1895. He began on 9 May for MCC and Ground against Sussex. He made 13 and 103, his ninety-ninth first-class hundred, and then 18 and 25 for MCC against Yorkshire. Then it was down to Bristol where Gloucestershire were playing Somerset and he clocked in with a small matter of 288 and reached his hundred hundreds when no contemporary had scored even half that number. A visit to Cambridge produced one innings of 52. He next took guard at the Bat and Ball ground in Gravesend where he made 257 and a hectic 73 not out in under an hour in the second innings as Gloucestershire raced to victory against the clock. He had now scored 829 runs in May with two games to come, against Surrey and Middlesex. At The Oval, in front of a huge crowd, he had scored 18 when he was bowled by Tom Richardson. Now it was off to Lord's where he won an important toss and was able straight away to get down to the tricky business of trying to score 153 more runs. He had reached 58 by lunch and, in the words of *The Times*, 'There was all the old power in the drive and the cut, while few balls to leg escaped unpunished.' When he was out for 169, he had taken his aggregate for the month to 1,016 – and all this when he was well into his forty-eighth year. Like all the best in the entertainment industry, he trod his own particular boards almost to the end, which came on 23 October 1915. For one day WG even managed to get the Great War off the front pages and there have not been many who could have done that.

C.B. FRY

WRITING of C.B. Fry, it was Neville Cardus, whose principal love was music, who said: 'No living English musician, critic or performer of my acquaintance is half the work of art to look at and to experience as C.B. Fry. In himself he is a national gallery and a theatre and a forum.' In his prime Fry's batting average was seldom far short of 70 and this had to be blended with so many other achievements. There was a first-class honours degree in Classical Moderations at Wadham, he played football for England and represented Southampton in the FA Cup final in 1902, two days before making 82 for London County against Surrey at The Oval. He played rugger for the Barbarians and scored 30,886 runs in first-class cricket with an average of 50.22. He held the world long jump record (23ft 6½in) for twenty-one years; he looked like a god and was offered the crown of Albania while he was helping the Indian Princes Delegation after the Great War at the League of Nations. He was the kind of amateur whom John Buchan must have had in mind when he was thinking of Richard Hannay, and he scored hundreds in six successive first-class innings, a record equalled only by Don Bradman. The only outward and visible defect in Fry was his bowling for he was no-balled out of the game as a thrower by an umpire with no other claim to fame called Jim Phillips.

Fry formed a unique partnership with Kumar Shri Ranjitsinhji. Appropriately enough, they played most of their cricket together almost in the shadows of the Royal Pavilion at Brighton, which was only just down the road from the Sussex County Ground in Hove. It was a pairing of opposites. At one end was the Indian prince with his voluminous silk shirts buttoned to the wrist and a bat that weaved all sorts of intriguing spells and sent the ball deliberately in ever more eccentric directions; at the other, the quintessential Englishman whose progress was based on the front foot and the bottom hand. In time Ranji changed some of this, but for a while it was a stark contrast. Fry came forward and drove with a solid elegance, each stroke the product of logic and intense practice, while Ranji played back and, using the bat like a conjuror's magic wand, was prepared to tickle almost everything, no matter where it pitched, to fine leg. In the three seasons 1899–1901, Ranji made 8,692 runs and Fry 7,838 and bowlers everywhere – none more so than Yorkshire's – dreaded the journey south to Hove.

There were other contrasts too. Ranji was a Cambridge man who never achieved a degree; Fry belonged to Oxford. When it came to money, Ranji was a relentless spender, even when, in his early days in England, he had run dangerously short. When he at last came to the throne of Nawanagar, he gave the privy purse the fright of its life. Fry, who never had any family money behind him, arrived at Oxford with thirty shillings in his pocket and, while he always got by, he had to work hard for everything. In later years, with his monocle glittering, his stately progress by Bentley from Brown's Hotel in Dover Street to and from his box at Lord's suggested a plutocratic lifestyle. This was in large part the result of the generosity of the London *Evening Standard* for whom he wrote. He did wonders for their circulation. There were lobsters for lunch, an appropriate white wine, and the day would not end without Fry declaiming Herodotus.

Ranji went off to claim his kingdom in India without ever forgetting his great friend. Ranji, as Chancellor of the Indian Princes, was a member of the Indian delegation at the League of Nations. He needed Fry, or Carlos as he always called him, at his right hand. It was then that Fry was offered the kingship of Albania, provided that he had ten thousand pounds of his own to spend each year, which he did not, although he might have 'touched' Ranji. This story has never been accurately documented, but there is enough evidence to suggest that it did happen, although Fry loved nothing more than to perpetuate it. He was probably responsible for all the many variations for he loved to digress while telling a story. Christopher Hollis, a business partner of his, wrote that Fry 'had a great capacity for living a fantasy life'. While Ranji was easy-going and relaxed, Fry was wholly absorbed in himself. In all senses, Ranji was a romantic, Fry a stern, self-imposed classicist.

John Woodcock in his book *One Hundred Greatest Cricketers*, quotes Fry as saying, 'I really only had one stroke, but it went to ten different parts of the field,' and goes on to write himself: 'It was played off the front foot, mostly with the bottom hand, and was a form of applied science. As a conversationalist he had, as it were, a multitude of strokes, and was ever ready to air them – to those who could keep up.' Fry was always prone to hold court, as he did later in his life in his box at Lord's when the subsequent author, Denzil Batchelor, was his amanuensis. The Great Man would stride around his box dictating and gesticulating and Batchelor would write with fevered haste so as to miss nothing. The guests were always distinguished and any acquaintance Fry met on his way round to the box in the Grandstand would be gathered in. It is fair to say that Fry hardly drew breath from first to last. Alan Gibson, who met Fry on several occasions, wrote in his splendid book, *The Cricket Captains of England*, that it was only possible to get in a sentence, and a response to it, given three conditions. The sentence must be a question requiring an answer; he had just used the word 'however' with which he almost invariably ended verbal paragraphs; he was taking off his naval cap in which he kept his tobacco pouch, and was considering a pipe.

He was a captain in the Navy and had reached this rank because he commanded the training ship HMS *Mercury* on the River Hamble. He was inordinately proud of this and he and his formidable wife ran an uncompromisingly tough and unforgiving ship. Fry loved his naval uniform and wore it whenever he could, which prompted Crusoe Robertson-Glasgow to say that he looked 'every inch like six admirals'. One of his two great contemporaries at Wadham, F.E. Smith – John Simon was the other – came to visit him at HMS *Mercury* and was impressed, but ended by saying to the man who had once beaten him in a public examination, 'This is a fine show, CB, but, for you, a backwater.' Fry, three times an unsuccessful Liberal candidate for Parliament, replied, 'That may be, but the question remains whether it is better to be successful or happy.' What a man; what a life!

RANJITSINHJI

THERE was all the wonderment and inscrutability of the East in Kumar Shri Ranjitsinhji. He batted as if he held a magic wand in his hands and did things with it that were both incredible and distinctly heretical. By using his wrists which were as mobile as quicksilver, he took batting to new and hitherto undreamt of levels. At the same time he conducted a lifestyle of astonishing opulence. It was part of his charm that he could not afford to live as he did, but creditors pressed their bills less immediately than they would today and it is a matter of fact that, in time, all debts were repaid. Then, with his cricketing days all but over, he inherited the throne of Nawanagar, which had earlier been outrageously stolen from him by a ringer. In later life as the Jam Sahib, albeit without his right eye which he lost in a shooting accident in Yorkshire in 1915, he cut quite a figure. 'It may interest you to know,' he later wrote to a friend soon after the loss of his eye, 'that after the accident I continued shooting from the left shoulder and shot ten birds out of twelve shots.' He was never wanting for courage.

Ranji came to England for the first time in March 1888 when he was only fifteen. He went up to Trinity College, Cambridge for the Michaelmas term in the following year. In those days Indians were a rarity in England and for a long time Ranji was an object of considerable curiosity at Cambridge. It must have been an ordeal for a sixteen-year-old. For a long time he was not considered as a serious competitor to the university's recruits from the well-known public schools. While his early sorties on the cricket field will have been regarded with amusement, Ranji, who was an acute observer, was busily adjusting his game and refining his technique. Much of his early cricket at Cambridge will have been played, appropriately enough, on Parker's Piece, which is the nearest England comes to having a maidan of its own. It is on the maidans, or parks, in their cities that so much of India's cricket is played. Ranji was not slow to make his mark and there is the improbable story, vouched for by Ranji himself, of his scoring three separate hundreds on Parker's Piece in the same day. He scored his first hundred before lunch for his original team. He then walked over to another game and found the batting side was one short and made his second hundred before tea at which point he returned to his own game. His side was still batting. He again went for a walk and, finding another batting side in some distress, promptly made a hundred for them as well. In any class of cricket, he scored his runs at an extraordinary rate.

There can be little doubt that Ranji came up against a certain amount of instinctive racial prejudice in his early days at the university. It is against this background that his progress is made to seem even more remarkable. Alan Ross, in his excellent biography of Ranji, makes the point that his extravagant hospitality and generosity, as well as his determination to succeed as a cricketer, had much to do with his eagerness to break down social barriers. Not least of his intentions will surely have been to gain acceptance for himself. He was lucky that he had such a deep reservoir of natural ability at his disposal. In spite of all his innate handicaps, it seemed as if it was only a matter of time, therefore, before he made the jump from Parker's Piece to the adjacent Fenner's, the home of the university's cricket, but even now there were still problems. In 1892, the Cambridge captain, Stanley Jackson, had watched him play an innings of unorthodox brilliance on Parker's Piece and had not been particularly impressed. That winter Jackson went on a tour to India with Lord Hawke and it was only as a result of this adventure that he was prepared to take Ranji seriously the following season. It says a great deal for Ranji's character that he came through this prejudicial start unscarred. His subsequent progress is made to seem even more remarkable by all of this and it helps to give that magic leg glance, his own supreme invention, even more of a wondrous glow. Fortunately, Ranji himself had a great a sense of humour, which will have been a help in his early days in England.

Ranji won his Blue in 1893 and the following year made his debut for Sussex. Although he had been underrated at Cambridge, he soon made his mark on the County Ground at Hove where in 1895 he joined forces with C.B. Fry, beginning a close friendship that was to last until Ranji's death in 1933. Hove will never have seen anything to equal their batting and Neville Cardus put his finger on the spot: 'Who will ever forget the cricket ground at Hove in those days, salt tang in the air, and the deck chairs full, and a stand in progress between Ranji and Fry? East and West twain for hours, the occult and the rational.'

But still Ranji had not seen the last of the racial suspicions that had held him back at Cambridge. His continued success meant that the crusty old farts who ran the game were forced to consider the prospect of an Indian turning out for England. By 1896 when the Australians were again touring, he should have been an automatic choice for the Test side, which in those days was chosen by the county on whose ground the match was being played. The MCC chose the side for the First Test at Lord's, therefore, and Lord Harris, a former Governor of Bombay, was not in favour of playing someone whom he described as 'a bird of passage'. Ranji was left out and this caused a public outcry. In 1929, Ranji's nephew, Kumar Shri Duleepsinhji, played in the First Test against South Africa and when he was objected to by the South Africans, agreed to stand down for the rest of the series. There was scarcely an uneasy shuffle in the land and no doubt the Honorary Treasurer of the MCC, Lord Harris, will have thought Duleep's decision made excellent sense. Back in 1896, those who ran Lancashire's cricket were not so narrow-minded or prejudicial. Ranji was selected for the Second Test at Old Trafford in which he made 62 and 154 not out in a match Australia won by 3 wickets.

Wisden was in no doubt as to the quality of his batting in the second innings: 'Ranjitsinhji very quickly got set again, and punished the Australian bowlers in a style that, up to that period of the season, no other English batsman had approached. He repeatedly brought off his wonderful strokes on the leg-side, and for a while had the Australian bowlers quite at his mercy . . . It is safe to say that a finer or more finished display has never been seen on a great occasion, for he never gave anything like a chance and during his long stay the worst that could be urged against him was that he made a couple of lucky snicks.'

Ranji's two principal legacies to the canon of batsmanship were the leg glance and the art of playing predominantly off the back foot. It would be strange if no one had ever played the leg glance before Ranji, but in all likelihood it will have been played occasionally and only when the ball was fractionally outside or even on the leg stump. The opportunities to play it would therefore have been scarce. But moving across his stumps as quickly as he did, Ranji was able to play it to the ball pitching as far across as the off stump and sometimes even further. It took the bowlers, and, indeed, the captains of his time, a long while to appreciate what was happening and to set fields that were able to contain the stroke. Playing a ball from the off stump to fine leg was a bit like breaking half a dozen of the Ten Commandments at one go. It was as if his bat was laughing at the bowlers. They, in their turn, will have believed that heavenly retribution would be swift to follow. What they did not understand was that the suppleness of his wrists, the speed with which he was able to pick up the line of the ball, his fast and sure footwork, together with a wonderful natural sense of timing, allowed him to go on playing this stroke with safety. With this array of attributes he was able to obliterate almost all elements of danger.

When Ranji began to play cricket he had trouble in keeping his back leg still and, as a result, he had to have the offending right leg pegged down during his first two years at the game. This has been given as a reason for him being able to develop the leg glance as he did. He himself never gave any convincing reason as to why the stroke was to become such a major source of income. It is much more likely that it simply happened as his game developed and evolved. He had all the natural assets that were necessary and instinct took over. He will have gone along to the nets and found that it just happened. He is unlikely to have woken up one morning, clasped his brow and exclaimed, 'The leg glance is the way forward,' and rolled up his sleeves and buckled down to it. He was nothing if not an instinctive player.

A.G. Gardiner, who worked for the *Daily News*, wrote of what it was like to watch Ranji at the crease.

> There is extraordinarily little display in his methods. He combines an Oriental calm with an Oriental swiftness – the stillness of the panther with the suddenness of its spring. He has none of the fine flourishes of our own stylists, but a quite startling economy of action . . . He stands moveless as the bowler approaches the wicket, remains moveless as the ball is delivered. It seems to be upon him before he takes action. Then, without any preliminary flourish, the bat flashes to the ball, and the stroke is over. The body seems never to have changed its position, the feet are unmoved, the bat is as before . . . It is not jugglery, or magic; it is simply the perfect economy of a means to an end.

It was his perceptive nephew, Duleep, who had the greatest appreciation of how Ranji changed the art of batsmanship and the thinking behind it. Duleep went on to play twelve times for England before his health failed him and made 173 in his first Test, against Australia.

> It was Ranji who made the back stroke an attacking stroke. The idea of batting up until then was that the ball must travel back more or less in the same direction from which it came to the bat. He changed this by helping the ball in the same direction, more or less, by slightly deflecting it. This was the great difference between him and the others before

him. He used the forward stroke for attack and the back stroke for both attack and defence.

Perhaps the nearest modern equivalent to Ranji has been his fellow countryman Mohammad Azharuddin, for he, visually, conjures up something of the same picture that Gardiner and, to some extent, Duleep have painted. Any stroke that Azharuddin played was worth the journey and when he left the ball alone, he did it with panache. I am not sure, though, that he and Ranji would have bumped into each other in the bookmaker's. Of course, like his innovative contemporary Victor Trumper, Ranji often did not make as many runs as he should have done. He averaged 6 more than Trumper, almost 45, in fifteen Test matches, but sometimes showed an unbecoming frailty in county cricket that suggested, as it did with Trumper, that his mind was not always on the job in hand. But any runs that he did make will always have been enormously good value. Watching Ranji bat must have been not unlike watching Nijinsky dance.

Ranji did not play for England again after the Fourth Test against Australia at Old Trafford in 1902, only six years after he had made that unforgettable beginning against Australia on the same ground. He continued for a few years more to bat in that incomparable way of his for Sussex, each innings the expression of a unique personality. More and more his thoughts as well as his winter journeys took him back home to India. He still lived in England with the same extravagance and on occasions had to be at his most charming and persuasive with his creditors. Although he had been denied the throne of Nawanagar when it should have been his, it was always his destiny that he would one day be sitting on the gadi. When he had consulted his soothsayer in India in 1905, his palm had been read and calculations made. He received the following verdict a week later: 'If you do not sit on the gadi of Nawanagar on 11 March 1907, I will give two thousand rupees to charity and will give up my work.'

Soon afterwards the news came from Nawanagar that Jassaji, the twenty-four-year-old Jam Sahib, was seriously ill with typhoid and some weeks later he died. Now, after those concerned had ruminated for a long time, not least the English agent to the Governor of Bombay, the gadi was given to Ranji and he was crowned on 11 March 1907.

Although he had two more reasonably successful excursions to Sussex, in 1908 having nearly died from typhoid, and in 1912, his eye was slower and his figure had lost its youthful curves. Runs did not come in quite the same way. He was unwise enough, in 1920, to return without his right eye at the age of forty-eight for a final fling, but after he had played four undistinguished innings for his old county, he called it a day. It was a sad last attempt to bring back the days of his youth. By then, Ranji had spent a year on the Western Front before losing his eye while on leave, which put paid to any more active service. When the war was over, Ranji was co-opted as one of India's three representatives at the League of Nations and he wasted no time in acquiring the services of C.B. Fry to assist him. From the moment he set foot in England, Ranji was a committed Anglophile, and Fry was his greatest friend of all.

He was a great success as the Jam Sahib and did much to bring his tiny state, which covered 3,791 square miles and was approximately the size of three English counties, from abject poverty into some sort of financial independence. Ranji was much loved by everyone and no state could have had a more loyal ruler. His extravagant ways will have tested the state purse. Ranji had three palaces in Nawanagar and was building a fourth, which was ready in time to house the guests for his funeral. He also had an impressive hunting lodge from where he shot panther, as well as a palatial fishing lodge in Connemara and a house in Staines. But Ranji had not been the strongest of men and his heart gave out on 2 April 1933 at the early age of sixty. What would we have given to have been able to spend even half an hour in his company, let alone to have seen him play cricket?

GILBERT JESSOP

GILBERT JESSOP is the only batsman to have played an even more remarkable innings for England than Ian Botham's 149 not out against Australia at Headingley in 1981. In the Fifth Test at The Oval against Australia in 1902, England were left to score 263 to win on the third and last day. After twenty minutes they were 10/3, and the score was 48/5 when Jessop came out to join a confident-looking Stanley Jackson. Like Botham seventy-nine years later, Jessop went in at number seven. The night before at dinner he had offered odds of 10–1 against anyone reaching fifty and later 20–1 against anyone going on to a hundred. Thinking this was easy money his colleagues were quick on the uptake. As Jessop was walking through the pavilion the next day on his way out to bat, Archie MacLaren, his captain, said, 'I bet you don't make a century!' Jessop's instantaneous reply was, 'Done.' The wicket was made for the bowlers and yet Jessop reached his 50 out of seventy balls in only forty-three minutes with Jackson content to make the other end safe. It grew more hectic after that and one withering stroke after another took Jessop from 50 to 100 in the next twenty-two minutes. Four runs later he was out, having faced seventy-nine balls and scored off forty-one of them. With seven wickets down England still needed 76 to win, but George Hirst played a wonderful innings of 58 not out. He made the last 15 in partnership with Wilfred Rhodes when they famously did not get them in singles. Alas for Jessop, who was not a betting man, only small amounts of money had been on offer and he admitted that his winnings would scarcely have paid for 'a pot of paint'.

W.G. Grace and Jessop were both sons of Gloucestershire doctors who, as a breed, were a productive bunch. Jessop was his mother's eleventh child while WG had crept in at number eight. WG's family thought of little else except the game of cricket, but while father and mother Jessop had provided themselves with enough offspring to field a family eleven, there was no tradition of the game in the family. Nonetheless there was a strong sporting instinct and Gilbert and his four brothers played vigorous cricket in the small garden every Friday. This was fraught with danger because inevitably windows were broken and father Jessop, a huge man of almost eighteen stone, handed out 'lickings' to which Victorian prison governors would have doffed their hats. As Jessop himself said, this early confined cricket left its mark. 'On the leg side of the wicket lay safety; on the off, the surgery windows. Small wonder, therefore, if a pronounced penchant for the pull should have affected my batting throughout my days.' From an early age the strong, stocky Gilbert gave the ball an almighty tonk. He spent his first day in the Gloucestershire side, against Lancashire, in 1894 bowling twenty-nine overs. All he had to show for it was 1/70, but WG was full of praise. The papers the next morning did not confirm this and at breakfast he read, 'If Mr Jessop's batting is no better than his bowling and fielding, he is scarcely likely to become an acquisition to the western shire.' Batting vigorously he made 29 and 19 and WG, who had got him right, was again loud in his praises and the man who became perhaps cricket's greatest entertainer was on his way.

The value and the power of Jessop is perfectly illustrated by a look at the respective scoring rates of the best players. Victor Trumper and Frank Woolley, no slouches, clocked in at 55 runs an hour while Percy Fender and Percy Chapman both managed just over 60. Then we come to Jessop who, in all his 180 scores of more than 50, kept up a dizzy rate of 79 runs an hour. This meant that he scored at least as fast as the combined efforts of WG and Jack Hobbs who went along at 36 and 43 respectively. Only once in his career did he bat for more than three hours when he dawdled to 240 in 200 minutes, and there were only ten occasions when he was in for more than two hours. In all, he made fifty-three first-class hundreds and his average time for reaching three figures was seventy-two minutes. He made fifteen of them in under an hour. Then there was the bewildering fielding in the covers where he was a pioneer and the forerunner of Colin Bland, Jonty Rhodes, Clive Lloyd, Paul Sheahan and the others.

Apart from that formidable innings against Australia at The Oval in 1902, there are three or four more innings that illustrate the bewildering way in which Jessop hit a cricket ball. In 1900 a West Indian side, captained by Plum Warner's brother, Aucher, came to England. They played Gloucestershire in a three-day match at Bristol and on the first day, after a bad start, Gloucestershire made 518/7. Jessop made 157 in precisely an hour in what must have been the most staggering innings even he ever played. He reached 50 in twenty minutes, 83 out of 105 in thirty minutes, 102 in forty-three minutes and then, for good measure, added another 55 in seventeen minutes. Even then his rate of progress was held up by the antics of the fielders. The *Bristol Times and Mirror* stated that: 'Rarely did the ball travel twice in the same direction. Nobody enjoyed this wonderful spell of phenomenal scoring more than the coloured men in the ranks of the visitors. The bowlers who were being punished, and the fielders who were called upon to work as they had probably never worked before, were hugely delighted. One of them would lie down and literally shake with laughter after a big hit, and the next minute would be making a futile effort to save another four from being placed to the credit of the batsman. When fifty was signalled as Jessop's score, this particular player turned round, and asked one of the spectators, "Has he been in ten minutes yet?"'

In the same year there was some extraordinary hitting against Yorkshire at Bradford. In Gloucestershire's first innings of 269 Jessop made 104 in seventy minutes and in the second he nearly won the match for his side when they needed 328. He made 139 out of 182 in ninety-five minutes and both George Hirst and Wilfred Rhodes bore the brunt of this in a season in which Rhodes took 261 wickets. Jessop hit him for eight sixes in the match and in those days a ball had to be hit right out of the ground for the stroke to count six. There was another *tour de force* in 1907 at Hastings against the Players of the South. He made 191 reaching his first 50 in twenty-four minutes, his hundred in forty-two, and his 150 in sixty-three. Frank Woolley said he could remember Jessop's hands 'working' round the handle of the bat as he came in to bowl to him. Jessop was no role model. Stocky and of medium height, he crouched down low in his stance with bent knees. His bat was unusually heavy for the time, weighing about 2lb 9oz, and his peculiar grip made it impossible for him to cover drive in the normal way. His renowned square cut was almost a backhand stroke in which his bat was never over the ball. He also never hooked but lapped the ball to leg in the way that contemporaries sweep, although photographs show that he tried to play the ball behind square leg almost à la Denis Compton.

These prodigious scoring feats of Jessop's are unthinkable to cricketers playing at this level early in the twenty-first century. Obviously the game was different when Jessop played. Bowlers liked to attack and fields were set accordingly. Even so, there can never have been anything in cricket's history akin to an hour of Jessop. It is exciting to read about his exploits; one can only guess at what it must have been like actually to have been in the ground at the time.

VICTOR TRUMPER

WHILE there is something remarkably similar about the effect of Don Bradman on Australian cricket, and Field Marshal Bernard Montgomery (Monty) on the Allied forces in the Second World War, Victor Trumper was an astonishing mixture of Alexander the Great and D'Artagnan with just a touch of Florence Nightingale thrown in. The impact of Florence Nightingale could no more be measured by the length of the bandages she wound round gashed and bleeding limbs, or D'Artagnan by the number of sword thrusts he made than could Alexander the Great by the distance he traversed in conquering so much of the known world all those years ago. Between them they took compassion, a quick-footed search for honesty and the tactics and strategy of fighting prolonged military campaigns to new levels. They steered their chosen fields to new frontiers. In the same way, the impact of Trumper on the art of batsmanship could not be measured by runs only. He averaged a shade over 39 in forty-eight Test matches. Some of his contemporaries were far ahead of him. But while the others trod down a well-worn path, Trumper broke new ground and played a significant role in helping his art evolve. He did it, too, with panache, beauty and simplicity in a way that barely half a dozen have managed in the entire history of the game.

While that canny old Yorkshire pro Ted Wainwright complained that Ranji 'never played a Christian stroke in his life', he would surely have accorded Victor Trumper the same tribute if his features had not been so essentially Anglo-Saxon. Like Ranji and all the other great improvisers, the basis of Trumper's batting was the purest of techniques. It was from this base of excellence that he was able to weave his magnetic and implausible spells. Those who saw Trumper were convinced that the subtlety of his strokes was even more of a mystery than it was with Ranji. It was impossible to tell in which direction Trumper was going to hit a ball until it had left the bat and even then it was usually a matter of considerable surprise. Like Ranji, Trumper was never bound by batting convention, such as it was in those days. A ball pitching outside the off stump, let alone on the middle, would often find its way from the middle of the bat to the legside boundary, sent there by a delicate flick of the wrists at the last possible moment. Trumper could send a good length ball wherever it pitched to any point of the boundary he chose between square cover and square leg. The direction of the stroke was apparent to no one except Trumper himself. It goes without saying that he was the most perfect timer of the ball, which he never appeared to strike with violence. It was his ability to improvise that made him as good a player as 'the Master', Jack Hobbs, on the 'stickies', which provided so much entertainment in the days before the modern generation of humourless, bureaucratic, self-righteous, jobsworth administrators took over the running of the game. They have more to answer for than they will ever know as Trumper and Hobbs would have shown them more than anyone.

Ranji and Trumper were exact contemporaries and it was during A.E. Stoddart's tour to Australia in 1897/98 that Ranji first saw Trumper play. Early in what was a most unsuccessful tour for the side, as opposed to Ranji who scored masses of runs, they played New South Wales. Trumper made 5 and 0 and yet he greatly impressed Ranji: 'He seemed to be all there, and the confidence with which he played the bowling, although it was for a very short time, makes me firmly believe that he will be a very great batsman in this country, and at no very distant date. Indeed, I have seen very few beginners play the ball so well, and show the same excellent style.' It was an amazing assessment.

Trumper's feats on the cricket field were astonishing and yet perhaps they do not fall into their true perspective until they are aligned with his most unusual character, which we will meet in a paragraph or two. Trumper's second visit to England was in 1902, which was an extremely wet summer. The pitches were not easy and yet Trumper scored 2,570 runs, including eleven centuries. *Wisden* went into rhapsodies:

> Trumper stood alone among the batsmen of the season, not only far surpassing his own colleagues, but also putting into the shade everyone who played for England . . . It is safe to say that no one – not even Ranjitsinhji – has been at once so brilliant and so consistent since W.G. Grace was at his best . . . The way in which he took good length balls off the middle stump and sent them round to the boundary had to be seen to be believed . . . He was far indeed from being dependent on unorthodox strokes. His cutting and off driving approached perfection, and he did everything with such an easy grace of style that his batting was always a delight to the eye . . . He was not in the smallest degree spoilt by his triumphs, bearing himself just as modestly and playing the game as sternly at the end of a long tour as at its beginning.

His most remarkable innings of all came in the Fourth Test at Old Trafford when Australia won by 3 runs. Archie MacLaren, England's captain, was convinced that the pitch would become difficult after lunch as it dried out. As a result England's policy in the morning was to 'keep Victor quiet at all costs'. It was Trumper who had the last word, scoring a quite brilliant century before lunch when Australia were 173/1 with Trumper out for 104. This was the first time this feat had been achieved and only two others, both Australians, Charlie Macartney and Don Bradman, have equalled it in matches between England and Australia. In the years to come, MacLaren was ribbed a good deal about this innings. Soon after play had begun, Trumper drove two balls into the practice ground behind the bowler. 'I couldn't very well have a man fielding in the bloody practice ground, now could I,' was MacLaren's defiant retort.

Monty Noble, who captained Australia and Trumper, thought

that his best innings was the 74 he made on a 'sticky' at Melbourne in 1904 out of a total of 122. The two left-armers, George Hirst and Wilfred Rhodes, had the perfect pitch on which to bowl and yet Trumper reduced them both to bowling wide of the off stump in defence. Hirst had had trouble with Trumper when playing for Yorkshire. When Trumper hit him over the square-leg boundary, an indignant Hirst exclaimed to his captain:

'But look at his legs. Look at his legs, right in front of the wicket.'

'Never mind his legs,' came the reply. 'Look at where the ruddy ball is.'

There was an occasion when New South Wales played Victoria in Sydney. Jack Saunders, a left-hander, had taken 4 wickets on a wet pitch when Trumper came in. He was comprehensively beaten by his first ball. 'All right, Jack,' Trumper called down the pitch to him, 'I see what you are at. And I am an old friend of yours. It is either you or me for it.' Trumper was 71 not out at lunch and reached his hundred soon afterwards. Hanson Carter, Australia's wicket keeper at the time, described that innings as the best he had ever seen on a bad pitch and the 185 not out he made against England in Sydney in 1903/04 as the best he had seen on a good one. England had led by 292 on the first innings and Trumper then went to his century in ninety-four minutes.

The ticklish question that will always remain is: how did Trumper and Bradman stand alongside each other? Carter, who saw a good deal of Bradman and toured Canada and the United States with him, had no doubt: 'Put Vic way up there (pointing to the sky) and then you can begin to talk of the others.' Macartney, who had no small opinion of his own ability, made 345 in under four hours at Trent Bridge against Nottinghamshire. He was reading the local paper the next day. 'It says here that my innings was reminiscent of Trumper,' he called out. 'What rot! I wasn't fit to tie up Vic's laces as a batsman.' Jack Fingleton who wrote a biography of Trumper, whom he never saw bat, was certain that he was the greatest batsman ever to have played for Australia. That view has to be tempered by the fact that Fingleton, along with a number of other Roman Catholic members of the Australian side of the thirties all of whom were of Irish origin, always had it in for Bradman. Nonetheless, Trumper was a batsman who took his art to new frontiers. While Bradman may have rewritten the record books for all time, he did not help the evolution of the art in the same way. Bradman will have benefited from Trumper's example, but how much were those batsmen who followed on after Bradman helped by his legacy? Yet Trumper averaged a shade over 39 in Test cricket and Bradman left an average of 99.94 behind him after fifty-two Test matches to Trumper's forty-eight. Figures can be rum old things!

Now we come to the Florence Nightingale side of the man. There can be no doubt that while Trumper, the man, was a candidate for canonisation, Bradman, the man, did not take advantage of whatever measure of divine assistance was available. Trumper almost never thought of himself; Bradman as we shall see, almost invariably put his own interests first. Trumper was the most modest of men and he was completely without side, swank or arrogance. He could not do enough for other people and the stories about him in this respect are legion. One of the nicest comes from Monty Noble.

> Victor was not the sort of man to succeed in commercial pursuits . . .
> I could relate a score of instances to illustrate this side of Victor's nature, but one will do. Coming out of the London Coliseum one cold wet night, he saw a boy shivering in a doorway selling music. Victor broke away from the rest of us, bought the whole of his stock-in-trade and sent the youngster away happy. It all went into the dustbin.

His generosity went on to the field with him. On one of his tours of England a young Yorkshire collier was chosen to play for the county against the Australians. After Trumper had dealt forcibly with the front-line bowlers, the young man was given his chance. He was so nervous that he was all over the place. Trumper made no attempt to score off his bowling, explaining later that he didn't want 'to spoil that lad's chance of getting a living in an easier way than by heaving coal'. On one notable occasion, it is true, the iron entered his soul. Trumper was playing for Paddington against Waverley in the Sydney grade. One of the opposing bowlers, Tommy Rose, who was able to bowl effectively with either hand, told his colleagues that he knew how to get Trumper out. The Great Man got wind of what had been said and was ready for him in the second innings. When Rose bowled his first ball, Trumper was down the pitch and sent a low skimming drive back over his head for four. The next hit the fence on the full and the following four were hit out of the ground for six. He was on strike again for the third ball of Rose's next over. He pushed the first ball away without scoring and then hit the next three for six. He had faced ten balls and had reached 50 off nine of them in a fraction under six minutes.

When he ran a sports shop he would often take pity on his young customers. One day a boy went in with sixpence to buy a composition cricket ball. He came out with a couple of bats, pads and gloves, and stumps and bails, all for the sixpence. No wonder Trumper never made any money! When travelling with his fellow players he was always selfless. If there was an awkward and uncomfortable seat in a train he would take it. If there was a compartment over the wheels you would find Trumper sitting there. If a teammate liked a bat he was using he would give it to him. He loved to help children, who found him so easy to approach. During his testimonial match at Sydney he left the pavilion, went out of the ground through the Paddington entrance and walked round to the gate at the back of the Hill. He had a pocketful of threepenny bits, 'tray bits' as they were known, which was the charge for admission, and he handed them out one by one to the urchins who were waiting there for him. He had done it so many times before. Often when he returned home after making a lot of runs at the Sydney Cricket Ground, he would have a hit with the lads in the lane behind his house. They never thought that much of his batting because he let them get him out.

How cruel it was that such a wonderful human being should have died an unpleasant death from Bright's disease on Monday, 28 June 1915 at the age of thirty-seven. This was one occasion when the Almighty can fairly be accused of having taken his eye off the ball.

JACK HOBBS

IT would be difficult to imagine two more disparate characters than WG and Jack Hobbs, although they were both such pivotal figures in the development of the game. As we have seen, WG took the game almost from its medieval beginnings to the point where England, Australia and South Africa were playing Test matches on a regular basis. This was where Hobbs picked it up and even if the leap that he then made with it was not as gargantuan as WG's, all aspects of the game had changed considerably by the time he called it a day and, like WG, he had himself thrived at all the different stages he steered it through. In his years, the batsmen were constantly being asked to solve new problems by bowlers who were involved in a similar process of evolution. Although they could hardly have been more different in their approach to life as well as to cricket, there are many similarities in the performances of these two remarkable men, even if WG could not quite claim the sartorial elegance of Hobbs. First of all, though, they had one crucial common denominator: they were both brilliant technicians. Then, they both had long tenures of office; WG scored almost 55,000 first class runs and made 126 centuries while Hobbs amassed just over 62,000 and was the first batsman to go past WG's tally of hundreds and, indeed, took his own total to 197, scoring the greater number of them after the Great War, at which point he was thirty-seven.

Both these consummate technicians had their own *annus mirabilis* late in their careers. WG was forty-seven when he scored 1,000 runs in May, something Hobbs never achieved, and completed his hundredth hundred in the same summer, 1895. Hobbs was forty-two when he topped WG's number of hundreds and passed 3,000 runs in a season for the only time in his life. By a happy coincidence, WG was captaining the Gentleman of the South when Hobbs made his first appearance for Surrey in 1905. WG's first-class career had begun forty years earlier while Hobbs's more intense career lasted for the next thirty years, although four were, of course, lost to the war. He could never have gone on till he was a fifty-seven-year-old like WG because the game had become more demanding by the mid thirties. Hobbs last met WG in 1915, shortly before his death, when the old man came to Catford to watch a game in which Hobbs was playing on behalf of the Red Cross. WG was anxious to talk to him and to hear his views on a number of subjects even though there were a number of other former cricketers there who were nearer to his own vintage. WG was known as the Champion; Hobbs as the Master.

While WG strode out of the pavilion at the head of most sides in which he played, his figure and his stride made sure that he was just as recognisable even if he was not captain, but one of the pack. Hobbs did all that he could not to stand out. Whether playing for England or Surrey, Hobbs came out behind his captain in the middle of the group of his fellow professionals, almost as if he was trying to hide. It was Hobbs' very ordinariness that turned him into the folk hero he became. He never sought the limelight. He merely got on with the job he had set himself to fulfil and that was to perfect the remarkable talent with which he had been born and to make as many finely tailored runs as he could. One doubts that he ever went out to bat deliberately determined to outdo any other member of his side. He went out to bat always intent upon doing the best that he could. The fact that he was head and shoulders better than anyone else meant that, more often than not, he achieved more. No one would have been quicker to congratulate a colleague who had delivered when perhaps he himself had failed.

In the many photographs of the Master there never seems to have been a hair out of place or a single bead of sweat.

As a technician, he was impossible to fault. He was not, like many outstanding batsmen, known for one particular stroke. His repertoire was complete and from that modest, almost apologetic stance with his front toe slightly cocked, he was perhaps the nearest the game has ever come to a living coaching manual, to technical perfection. His popularity was universal and people flocked to watch him because they felt that he was one of them, that he was effectively their neighbour from next door. He never stepped out of line, he never pushed himself forward, he was courteous, impeccably mannered and modest to a fault. The combination was irresistible. It was extraordinary that he never allowed the adulation he received throughout his career to turn his head, even for a second. It was also worth the gate money alone to come and see him field at cover point. By all accounts he was probably the best cover fielder there has ever been. He was a superb athlete and, in the field, he would play cat and mouse with the batsman in the most engaging manner. He would allow a batsman to run a comfortable single or two when the ball came to him in the covers. Then, when he tried it again, Hobbs would pounce and time and again his throw would hit the stumps with the batsman well short of his ground. Of modern fielders, probably only South Africa's Colin Bland was able to throw with the same accuracy. The forty-six-year-old Hobbs pounced just like this and ran out Don Bradman in the Australian's first series in 1928/29, although in Hobbs' final Test series, in 1930, Bradman was himself to return the compliment.

Hobbs, the man, is summed up to perfection in one surprising story. The Third Test match between England and Australia in 1909 was played at Headingley. Australia were bowled out for 188 and early in England's reply, Hobbs, when 12, pulled a short one from Macartney. It went away towards the fine-leg boundary, but Hobbs suddenly realised that it was not going reach the fence. In starting to run, he slipped and his back foot hit the stumps and dislodged a bail. Hobbs' first reaction was to think that he was out and he set off towards the pavilion. It then occurred to him that he had knocked off the bail long after finishing his stroke, and he returned to the crease. The umpire assured Hobbs that he was not out, but Warwick Armstrong, who was not then captaining Australia, became incandescently angry and refused to accept the umpire's decision. Monty Noble, who was in charge, appears to have done nothing. The argument surged back and forth and Armstrong became angrier. Play was held up for a while and Hobbs, outwardly calm, was extremely upset at Armstrong's lack of sportsmanship. Eventually, Macartney continued his over and two balls later Hobbs walked away from his wicket and allowed himself to be bowled. One can only hope that this extraordinary and unnecessary piece of chivalry made Armstrong feel an utter cad. Australia won the match by 126 runs.

This Player who was every inch a Gentleman, was deeply appreciated wherever he went. He toured South Africa for the second time in 1913/14 and after he had made 72 and 80 against Western Province in the opening match, the following comment appeared in one of the local papers: 'Hobbs says he does not know what he has done to deserve the kindness shown to him. I think I know. He, first of all, lays us under an obligation by showing us the greatest of all batting without ever being in danger of requiring a bigger sized headgear. That's why we like you, Mr Hobbs.'

He was always true to himself and this was never better illustrated than when the Maharaj Kumar of Vizianagram invited him to tour India at the end of the 1930 season in England. At Hobbs suggestion, Herbert Sutcliffe was also invited and Vizzy, as he was later known when he became a broadcaster and a writer, did all he could to accommodate their wishes. This was fortunate because, in accepting to play in India, Hobbs had not realised that they played big matches there on Sundays. When Hobbs made his views known about this, the dates were rearranged and the matches were played on Saturdays, Mondays and Tuesdays. Like so much else, Hobbs kept his religious convictions to himself, but it requires no great stretch of the imagination to look at the way in which he led his life and conducted himself to deduce that he stuck pretty closely to true Christian principles. Hobbs never once played on a Sunday.

The start to his life in the game was as modest as the man himself. He was the eldest child of twelve children, which suggests a life of considerable hurly-burly if not disorder on the home front, although this all seems to have passed Jack by, for he was the most orderly of people. Being the eldest may have helped. His father was on the ground staff at Fenner's, bowling at the nets and doing some umpiring, when Jack was born, before moving on to become a groundsman at Jesus College. He too always stayed in the background, but will have been a source of constant encouragement to his oldest child who had a deep respect for his father. It was from his father that Jack inherited his gentleness and modesty. The Hobbses were a happy, well-disciplined family. It goes without saying that they were poor, although they seemed to live without undue anxiety within their means. For Jack and his father, cricket was the centre of their lives and they were in the right place to make the best of it. In his spare time Jack sang in church choirs, he enjoyed magic lantern shows and he had a pet kitten. There was nothing in the least remarkable or surprising about his early years. When he was nine he took part in his school concert when he blackened his face and sang 'I'm a little Alabama coon', and his headmaster was so impressed that he gave him a silver threepenny bit and turned it into his first professional engagement. Political correctness was not on the agenda in those days.

Jack was taken by his father to see the Australian touring side play Cambridge University in 1884 when he was eighteen months old. The baby yelled his head off throughout – the only time in his life Jack made an exhibition of himself – and one of the Australian fielders said to his father, 'Make a cricketer of that kid, old man.' Later, Jack helped his father at work when he could and managed to play his own form of cricket with the college servants at Jesus using a tennis ball and a stump. The wicket was one of the posts holding up a tennis net. A few years later, Don Bradman was to learn the rudiments of cricket by throwing a golf ball at a brick water tank and using a stump to hit the rebound. Both players found that this taught discipline for the eye and the feet and gave them both a sure foundation for what was to come. Jack tiptoed into the game when he played for St Matthew's Church Choir XI and then he assisted the Jesus College choirboys. In one of their games he made 90 when he was given out lbw, but in the local paper the next day it was down as 90 not out for the reporter had realised that he had been the victim of a poor decision – an early example of the power of the press to rewrite history. This innings gave his father particular delight.

He now graduated to Parker's Piece, a huge open space just across the road from Fenner's, which was named, rather strangely, after a respected college servant at Trinity although Parker's Piece is some distance away from that college. Although Jack never had an hour's coaching in his life, the way in which he had taught himself the art of batting was classical and foolproof. So correct was he that he never went through the prolonged bad patch that has from time to time brought down almost all the best batsmen. WG and Don Bradman were two others to escape this ignominy. In 1901 he consistently made runs on Parker's Piece and there was one innings of 36 not out that gave him particular satisfaction. The local side was a man short and they turned to Jack, who found himself playing in a charity match against a side that Tom Hayward, his hero, who was also from Cambridge, brought down each year. Jack's father was umpiring and admitted that his son had done quite well. Later that year he was selected by Cambridgeshire as an amateur for two matches. He played one innings of 30 that helped the county to victory but his average was a mere 8.75. The petals of his genius were reluctant to open out in those early days, but he did not let this worry him. Even as a young man, he was remarkably confident of his destiny. The next year he found himself a dreary job as a junior professional at Bedford School, but this gave him his first experience of London. He went with the Second XI when they played St Paul's and, although they travelled back the same evening, there was time for him to go for the first time to the old music hall theatre, the Tivoli, in the Strand, which was to become a home-from-home for him over the years. On that first evening he laughed so much that the rest of the audience laughed at him. This was the start of a lifelong love for the music hall.

Later that year he was offered his first professional engagement as a cricketer when Royston, a neighbouring county town, offered him ten shillings and expenses to play for them against the Hertfordshire Club and Ground. He made an excellent hundred which was much talked about locally. His father was delighted, but unhappily he was by now extremely ill and he died within the week. No one will have been more upset than Jack, but this was a personal matter and he never dwelt on it, then or later. It was now that a Mr F.C. Hutt, who scored for the Jesus College XI and was a friend of Tom Hayward's, lent a hand. He persuaded Hayward to come and have a look at young Jack who was given a twenty-minute net on Parker's Piece by Hayward himself and Billy Reeves, the Essex bowler. Hayward liked what he saw and muttered something about arranging a trial at The Oval the following spring. During the nerve-racking winter's wait, Jack applied for a job on the Essex staff just in case The Oval never came through, but Essex turned him down – one wonders who the excellent judge was. It did not matter for Hayward was as good as his word. Early the next year his invitation for a trial at The Oval arrived and Jack Hobbs made his way to London for the second time in his life. It all went well enough for him to be offered terms of thirty shillings a week in the summer and a pound a week in the winter. The only snag was that he had to live in the county for two years in order to acquire a residential qualification before he would be able to play for Surrey.

He moved to digs near The Oval, going back to Cambridge for the weekends and sending his mother as much money as he could afford. He was happy and enjoyed life away from cricket, which was one of his great strengths. He was a regular visitor to the music halls for he loved to laugh; he visited Madame Tussauds and listened to the band in Hyde Park. One evening he was taken to Soho for dinner where he remembered having eight courses for half a crown. In his first summer, 1903, he played cricket consistently and with success for the Club and Ground. The following year he again played for Cambridgeshire, scoring 696 runs for an average of 58. These runs included an innings of 92 against Norfolk after being warned that influential people from The Oval would be watching him. They were extremely impressed for he was at his best, although his 195 against Hertfordshire soon afterwards will have done him no harm. By a strange coincidence it was in Norfolk at Old Buckenham Hall seventeen years later that he made 85 before pulling a muscle in awkward conditions against the fearsome Australian opening attack of Gregory and McDonald. He considered this to be probably the best innings he ever played. Sadly, that pulled muscle kept him out of the ensuing Test series.

At the end of 1904 he played his first game at Lord's, for George Robey's XI against the Cross Arrows who, in those distant days, played on the main ground and not the Nursery ground, which later became their home. Players such as Tom Richardson, Gilbert Jessop and Johnny (J.W.H.T.) Douglas took part and Hobbs hit seven fours in his polished 55. On Easter Monday 1905, he made his first appearance for Surrey and, under the glare of WG from point, he opened his first-class account finishing with 18 in his first innings. In his second, he made 88 – he was 44 not out overnight and he took himself off that evening for a good laugh at the Tivoli – when he tried to hook at Walter Brearley and was caught at square leg. As he passed Brearley on the way back to the pavilion, the bowler said to him, 'I should drop that stroke if I were you.' 'I didn't drop it,'

Hobbs said later. 'I learned how to do it properly.' His first county match came on 4 May when Surrey played Essex. His 28 in the first innings was the second top score. In the second, he made 155 against good bowling and with a borrowed bat. He then finished off the match with a splendid catch in the deep and as the players walked off, his captain, Lord Dalmeny, awarded him his county cap. There cannot be many instances of that happening after only two matches. This remarkable young man took it in his stride.

That ultimate barometer of character and class on the cricket ground, Crusoe Robertson-Glasgow, wrote of Hobbs: 'He was the most perfectly equipped by art and temperament for any style of innings on any sort of wicket against any quality of opposition . . . I have seen Hobbs described as a frail man. Actually he had strength of thigh and forearm far above the average, a strength which was concealed in the art of method and grace of movement. His footwork was, as nearly as is humanly possible, perfect . . . To crown all, he had the gift of smiling quietly at failure and triumph alike.' When it came to handing out laurels of this sort, Neville Cardus never cared to be left behind. He wrote of Hobbs: 'The batsmanship of Sir Jack was like the man himself; a certain modesty could be felt even in his most dominating innings. He never demonstrated; his strokes were never rhetorical or brutal. He was perfect in timing a stroke . . . His technique was so well-bred that not once, during the many, many hours I saw him at the crease, did I see him commit a wrong, ungrammatical stroke.'

How did Hobbs see himself? In 1911/12, England toured Australia and the locals did not expect them to win a single Test match. As it turned out, they won the series 4–1 and Hobbs made three separate hundreds. He wrote a book about the tour called *Recovering the Ashes*, which happened to be the first cricket book I ever read and which I still have beside me. After losing the First Test, England won the Second having needed to score 219 in the final innings. Hobbs made 126 not out. He wrote:

It is quite ancient history to most people that we won by eight wickets, and there is no reason for me to write as to the manner in which we got the runs. Among those present was our Captain, Mr P.F. Warner, (he was taken ill soon after arriving in Australia and missed the entire series) who basked in the sunshine in a double sense, and looked the better for it.

In the Third Test, Australia were bowled out for 133 and Hobbs then made 187.

On the second day . . . I managed to stay in until nearly six o'clock, but was so very tired that I was not at all sorry to get out. My stay, however, was not perfect, for I gave chances in the slips off Mr Cotter at 116 and 118, and when I was 150 Mr Matthews might have caught and bowled me, but the last chance was fairly hard . . . I was naturally pleased at my own success – who wouldn't be? – and the best compliment I had paid to me was that contained in a newspaper paragraph, which ran: 'Hobbs jogged steadily along as smoothly as a well-trained hackney on a good road.'

In the Fourth Test, Hobbs made 178 putting on 323 with Rhodes, the best for any wicket in Test cricket up until then. Rhodes made 179. Hobbs again:

The weather on the second day was simply glorious, but I am afraid I cannot say very much about the cricket, because I was not an onlooker, excepting when Rhodes got the bowling, for he and I stayed together nearly all day, and it was not until just after five o'clock in the afternoon that I was caught at the wicket off Dr Hordern. We had a pretty good time, and thoroughly enjoyed ourselves, although, for my own part, I must confess that I got very tired towards the end of my innings.

While WG had kept the troops happy with a booming fortissimo performance, which stretched through the length and breadth of his career, Jack Hobbs performed his arias at the andante, which just occasionally rose to the allegro. In their different ways, they both brought the audience to their feet and over the years they obliged with encore after encore.

PART TWO

1919–1939

ENGLAND'S cricket was much more affected by the carnage of the Great War than any of her competitors and it took a number of years for it to recover so that on the field, it could again look Australia in the face. It was in the next twenty years that the game took on a greater international flavour. The West Indies, New Zealand and India all dipped their toes into the waters of Test cricket and, although, hardly surprisingly, they did not win very much, they made an important start and showed that as their experience increased they would come to play a worthwhile part in the general scheme of things. This was the era of two great cricketers, Jack Hobbs who, as we have seen, made an impressive enough start before the war, and Don Bradman. Hobbs was now to become the rock around which England were able to build while counting the cost of the recent war. Hobbs, the dasher, had now become Hobbs, the imperturbable, as he carried on his Test career until 1930 and his first-class career for four more years after that, taking his aggregate to more than 61,000 runs. No batsman at any time has had a more perfect technique than Hobbs and if the entire art of batsmanship was lost to mankind and then, hundreds of years hence, a film of an innings by Hobbs was discovered, it would be possible to divine the complete art of batsmanship from this one reel.

While Hobbs was both artistic and functional, Bradman was prodigiously functional. He scored runs at a pace and with a consistency that even WG could not have managed. Of course, the conditions for batting had improved out of all recognition and in that respect it was easier for Bradman. Nonetheless, the sheer weight of runs that poured from his bat was phenomenal. His non-stop strokeplay made the bowlers put their thinking caps on and inswing eventually arrived as a vessel of containment. Bradman had tuned his reflexes on his own at home as a boy and there was always something rather solitary and introspective about him, except when he had a bat in his hand. Like WG, almost his main interest was the relentless pursuit of money. This did not endear him to his team-mates and he became something of a loner. Later on in the thirties, when he took over the captaincy of Australia, he was often at loggerheads with the considerable Irish Roman Catholic presence within the dressing room. He was a complex character and this made it all the more remarkable that his success on the field faltered just once.

Before embarking upon the tour to Australia in 1932/33, the England captain, Douglas Jardine, realised that the only way in which Australia could be beaten was if Bradman could be neutralised. This led to the invention of Bodyline as a means of doing this, and it was successful to the extent that England won the series and the Bradman average was kept down to just over 50. For all that, it produced the biggest crisis the game had ever known and caused fraught governmental contacts to be made. There was even the implied threat that Australia might pull out of the Commonwealth. Harold Larwood never played for England again and Jardine called it a day soon afterwards. Bill Woodfull captained

Australia in England in 1934 and Gubby Allen, always a vehement opponent of Bodyline, took England back to Australia in 1936/37. Their skilful diplomacy did much to ease the strain between the two countries. Even now, though, on late, alcoholic evenings on tours of Australia, the conversation can still easily turn to Bodyline.

Bradman went on until 1948 and if he had managed to make 4 and not a duck in his last Test innings, at The Oval, he would have averaged a hundred in Test cricket. It was not surprising that a genius such as Bradman should have had such a profound effect upon the development of the game. The nearest England came to matching Bradman was with the somewhat enigmatic figure of Walter Hammond, who spent too much of his life in Bradman's shadow for his own good. At any other time he would have been way ahead of everyone else and with even better figures, although those he produced were not to be sneezed at. The other significant batsman towards the end of this period was George Headley from Jamaica, who soon acquired the epithet of the 'Black Bradman'. Headley, combined with the athletic histrionics of Learie Constantine, showed the world that it would not be long before the West Indies were challenging the best. His personal *coup de grâce* came in the Second Test against England in 1939 when he became the first batsman ever to score a hundred in each innings of a Test match at Lord's. Headley's example will have been important to Everton Weekes, Frank Worrell and Clyde Walcott, the famous three Ws, who were only just around the corner.

The conditions under which the game was played continued to improve between the wars. The pitches made life uncommonly hard for the bowlers, unless rain should work in their favour. Pitches were, of course, uncovered in those days and rain followed by sunshine brought rare smiles to bowlers' faces, especially in Australia where 'sticky dogs' eventuated. There were few batsmen who could cope with such conditions, although in Hobbs and Sutcliffe, England had the two best. The game was still run from the aristocratic committee room at Lord's, and the players, in

England, were a mixture of gentlemen and those without the luck to be born with a private income and who therefore fell into the peasant class. This meant that they stayed in inferior hotels to the amateurs, ate their meals separately and advanced upon the stage through a different dressing-room door. It was a situation that would cause a revolution today, but in those days it was accepted as a matter of course. I well remember going to see Harold Larwood when he lived in the Randwick, a suburb of Sydney, and hearing him lament the passing of the amateur captain who, he felt, brought an important independent spirit to the game. He would have died for Jardine whom he referred to, time and again, as 'my Mr Jardine'.

In the two decades between the wars, it was still a very different game from the one that is played today, even if it was in some ways moving perceptibly closer. It was, as always, badly strapped for money and the professionals who formed the backbone of the game and without whom it could not have existed in the form that it did, were still paid a pittance. Nowadays it seems remarkable that they should have been prepared to work as they did at the game and, in the context of their own times, achieve an excellence that enabled them to ply their trade with every chance of success against those who came from across the waters. They had fun, too, and, more than that, concocted from the situation they found themselves in, a rare and immensely valuable form of wisdom. Then, in 1939, just as Len Hutton, Denis Compton, Bill Edrich and countless others, both in England and overseas, were beginning to flex their muscles with intent, the Fuehrer marked out his long run on the other side of the English Channel

WARWICK ARMSTRONG

WARWICK ARMSTRONG was probably the biggest man ever to play Test cricket, larger even than WG and much larger than life itself. In fact, there was an awful lot of WG in him. By the end of his career, he clocked in at twenty-one stone. A normal weighing machine ran out of space at twenty stone and, unable to accommodate him, would come up clanking for air. He was known by his team-mates as 'the Big Ship' and it was seldom that he was not in full sail. Julius Caesar felt comfortable with men around him who were fat and corpulence often brings with it a humorous and genial conviviality. I am not sure what Julius Caesar would have made of Warwick Armstrong, but he would have wanted to have him on his side when the going was tough. He was a relentless opponent who never let go. His courage was there for all to see and he was the most determined of hard workers, especially when he was dealing with someone he didn't care for. He was a man of strong and unshakeable opinions and dislikes. Arbitration was no use to him unless he was the arbitrator. Irrevocably determined to have his own way, he was undoubtedly the most enormous fun and always interesting when he wasn't being infuriating. He loved a fight and was nothing if not irascible. Arthur Mailey rated him highly as a captain, although he felt he would have been greater still if he had always shown the toleration and understanding he developed later in his life. We have already seen how even such a mild-mannered chap as Jack Hobbs had felt the whiplash of the Armstrong tongue at Headingley in 1909. It was said, without fear of contradiction, that any ball Armstrong drove and any deckchair he sat upon, was never the same again. Edmund Blunden wrote that he made the bat look like a teaspoon and the bowling like weak tea. With a voluminous but clean-shaven figure that was almost as compelling as WG's, his following was huge and he did not short-change either his admirers or his enemies.

Armstrong was a formidable all-round cricketer. In a career that stretched from 1899 to 1921/22, he scored 16,177 runs with forty-five hundreds for an average of 46.75, and he took 828 wickets with his own curiously defensive version of leg spin, at 19.76 each. His batting was robust and devil-may-care and became more rakish and spectacular the older he became. In 1920, when he was in his early forties, and long past the age Australian Test cricketers normally retire, he began his season with innings of 157 not out and 245 for Victoria against South Australia. Then, in the First Test against England, he padded up when Australia began their second innings, drank whisky with his chums in the Members' Bar before going out to make 158 with some of the most remarkable driving anyone had seen. At one point Jack Hobbs, the Master at cover point, was forced to move back almost to the outfield. Then, just to make sure England had no chance of making the 659 they needed to win, Armstrong had Hobbs lbw for 59 playing for non-existent leg spin. On the way back to the pavilion Hobbs said to him with a half smile, 'Never again, Warwick.' In the Fourth Test, Armstrong persuaded Arthur Mailey to try and trick Hobbs in the same way and it worked. 'Got you again, Jack,' was Armstrong's grinning retort as Hobbs passed him this time. He took 6 wickets in the Second Test and in the Third, after England had led by 93 on the first innings, he made a furious 121 in Australia's second innings, which saw them through to victory. All this at the age of forty-one. While he batted in accordance with his character, his bowling was a strangely contradictory affair. He was an endlessly accurate leg roller. There was much more overspin than leg spin and he regularly defeated batsmen, as he had Hobbs, who were playing for spin only to find that the ball had the maddening habit of going straight on. In a Test match at Trent Bridge in 1905, Joe Darling brought him on to slow England's rate of scoring. In fifty-two overs, twenty-four of which were maidens, he took 1 for 67.

Being the man he was, he enjoyed his battles off the field as much as those when he was on it. Sometimes he used the latter to settle the former. Several of those he took on were people in a position to do him a fair amount of harm, but then Armstrong was a man of principle who feared no one. A particularly steadfast enemy was a certain Mr Ernest Bean who was the powerful secretary of the Victorian Cricket Association. He was responsible for dropping Armstrong from the Victorian side to play the Englishmen immediately after the Third Test in 1920/21 when Australia were three matches ahead. Armstrong had withdrawn at the last moment from Victoria's match with New South Wales in Sydney because of a badly bruised leg so as to make sure he was fit for the Fourth Test. He had a cast-iron case and of course captained Australia in the Fourth Test at Melbourne where he received massive support from the crowd. At the time, he was suffering from a recurrence of malaria and put himself lower down the order than usual, confident he would not have to bat until after the weekend. He ordered a couple of formidable measures of whisky, but then, to his horror, soon afterwards Australia were 5 wickets down for 153 and there was no escape for him. As he walked out he passed Mr Bean and his pair of waxed moustaches. The grin on Mr Bean's teetotal face seemed to say, 'I've got him now.' In just over three hours Armstrong put the innings to rights while making 123 not out. It will have done the Armstrong morale no harm at all when, on his return to the pavilion, he discovered that Mr Bean had taken to strong liquor and was drunk.

Although Australia won the series in 1920/21, 5–0, Armstrong was only chosen by the narrowest of margins to take the side to England in 1921. It was still held against him in some quarters that he was one of the six players who had refused to go to England for the Triangular Tournament in 1912 and he was the last of these still playing. When it came to autocracy, the Australian authorities in that period did not allow Lord Harris to have things all his own way back in St John's Wood. Having been given the captaincy, Armstrong proceeded to sweep through England like a tidal wave that was just beginning to mellow. First, he insisted on altering the programme so that the Australians had a rest day before the start of the Test matches. 'Stork' Hendry, the all-rounder, went on record as saying that the Australian cricketers owed a great deal to Armstrong for their rights and privileges. He would allow no one to stand in his way. The Australians played Kent at Canterbury just before the final Test on that tour. He used the game as batting practice mainly, in order to ensure that his bowlers went in fresh to The Oval Test. He refused to enforce the follow on and one of his own players, Nip Pellew, thought he had gone too far. He said years later, 'When we heard of his decision, I stood up to Armstrong – not an easy thing to do – and said, "You can't bat again, Warwick." he replied, "Can't I? You put the pads on."' Armstrong did not shirk the booing himself and went in early. It was when that Fifth Test match was petering out into a draw that Armstrong took himself off into the deep. After taking a catch there, he picked up a piece of newspaper that was blowing across the ground, sat down and began to read it. Years later, Arthur Mailey asked him why he had done this. 'To see who we were playing,' came the reply.

At the Imperial Cricket Conference that summer, Armstrong made the suggestion that the umpires should not be appointed until the day before a Test match. Lord Harris asked him why. 'The umpires are paid little for their services and, as there is a lot of betting on Tests, it would be wise to remove them from temptation,' he was told. After looking into it overnight, Harris said the next day, 'I can find no evidence of betting on cricket – people don't do it.' Armstrong pulled deeply on his pipe, leant across the table and said, 'You don't think so, my Lord? If you'd like £500 on the next Test, I can get it on for you.'

It was in character that Armstrong should have referred to the nine teetotallers in his party as 'the lemonade crowd'. His players held him in great respect as a cricketer and as a man too, and it was this that allowed him to get away with it when, during one match, he ordered his players to be in bed by eleven o'clock and yet he did not make it back to the hotel himself until one o'clock in the morning. In the Fourth Test at Old Trafford, Armstrong, presumably with his tongue firmly in the side of a considerable cheek, bowled consecutive overs on either side of a twenty-minute hold-up. Lionel Tennyson had declared England's innings when the rules forbade it in what had become a two-day match. The hold-up was caused by the lengthy debate that followed the declaration before it was decided that England had to continue batting. Armstrong versus Tennyson would have been a bit like Laurel versus Hardy.

Throughout his long career Armstrong never felt the need to watch the calories, but the only bad effect this had on his cricket was that it made it increasingly difficult for him to play good spin bowling. He went through particular agonies when playing against Mailey in the Sheffield Shield and the ensuing antics were said to provide an acceptable substitute for bear baiting. When the Australians were playing Hampshire at Southampton during a scorching hot June, Armstrong found as he strolled round the ground that a small boy was dogging his footsteps. He put it down to hero worship, but the boy was so persistent that he eventually turned to him and said, 'Here, give me your autograph book and I'll sign it,' to which the reply was, 'I ain't got one.' Armstrong now asked, 'Then what do you want?' The reply this time was, 'Please, sir, you are the only bit of decent shade in the place.' Six years later, after Armstrong had long since retired from first-class cricket, he was making his fifth tour to New Zealand. After one evening of considerable conviviality in Wellington, Armstrong and his side made for the ferry that was taking them down to Christchurch. After lowering his twenty-one stones on to a bunk, it was discovered that it belonged to someone else. The rightful owner said to the secretary, Hugh Trumble, that he wanted sole ownership ending with the words, 'Please get Armstrong out of my bunk.' Trumble looked at the rightful owner and then at Armstrong and said thoughtfully, 'Let's send for the army.'

LIONEL TENNYSON

'IN all ways of cricket and the world he was and is the perfect English Gascon, a gourmet of the whole feast of life which, for him, has been post-dated by a century and a half. He was cut out for the Regency. Lionel should have been the ancestor; Alfred the descendant.'

Rem acu tetigisti, as Jeeves would have said. There has been no one better at putting his finger on the spot, especially when writing about his contemporaries, than Crusoe Robertson-Glasgow. Lionel Tennyson, whose grandfather, Alfred, had been one of Queen Victoria's poet laureates, had been built when the Almighty was in one of his more generous moods. His frame was large, muscular and strong, but not outrageously so. It was when it came to the grey matter that God had been most particularly selfless and generous. Inside this robust and healthy physique he had formed a mind and a man who never considered doing anything by half and was a fearless as they come.

He was perhaps the most idiosyncratic of all the county captains. During his reign over Hampshire, from 1919 to 1933, he was very much the benevolent despot. One old pro was later to say, 'You never knew who was playing until you got to the ground.' Tennyson had bowled at a furious pace for Eton in 1907/08. Then he appeared to take five gap years, which went in step with his life-style, before first turning out for Hampshire in 1913. He had decided well before that that he was not going to make it as a fast bowler and turned his attention to batting. It says a lot for his ability that after one season with Hampshire he was selected to tour South Africa with the England side in 1913/14. Although he averaged only 16 an innings, he played in all five Test matches. One can only wonder how he hit it off on that tour with the great Sydney Barnes who was nothing if not austere and would surely have frowned at the aristocratic whippersnapper. Tennyson will, without doubt, have left an indelible mark in South Africa for he will not have failed to have been the life and soul of the party.

As you would expect, this living personification of Bulldog Drummond made light of a couple of war wounds and took over the captaincy of Hampshire when hostilities ceased. He was never able to resist a challenge – and probably a temptation as well – and he was soon to receive two. In 1921 a friend offered him odds of a thousand to one against him ever captaining England, which turned out to be an expensive misjudgment. The following year, when England were in a deep hole against Warwick Armstrong's Australians, the selectors, feeling the side needed spiritual encouragement, brought him back for the Second Test at Lord's. Although England lost by 8 wickets, Tennyson made a courageous and boisterous 74 not out in the second innings and the selectors, thinking him just the man they needed to give England a shot in the arm, made him captain for the Third at Headingley.

Sadly, after all too short a time in the field in Australia's first innings, he split his hand and Johnny Douglas, the man from whom he had taken over, was in charge for the rest of the match. Nonetheless, Tennyson batted in both innings virtually one-handed, but was still able to throw the bat with something of his usual vim and he struck 63 and 36 in a losing cause. He managed to draw the last two matches, with customary help from the weather at Old Trafford, although the match was not without incident. There was no play on the first day, which turned the match into a two-day affair, and on the second Tennyson tried to declare England's first innings at 5.50 p.m. with thirty minutes batting remaining. Armstrong was quick to point out that, as it was now a two-day match, Tennyson was not allowed to declare unless the side batting second had at least 100 minutes. The teams were off the field for twenty-five minutes while this was resolved. It was when play restarted that Armstrong became the only man to have bowled two consecutive overs in a Test match. At The Oval Tennyson made 51 at the end of the innings in which Warwick Armstrong read that newspaper while fielding. Off the field, Tennyson and Armstrong should have been like a couple of sailors on shore leave.

Tennyson's second challenge came in that incredible game at Edgbaston in 1922 when Hampshire were bowled out for 15 in their first innings. When they followed on they made 521 with George Brown making 172 and Walter Livsey, Tennyson's valet, batting at number ten, a small matter of 110 not out. Warwickshire were set 314 to win and were bowled out for 158. After they had been routed on the first day, there was a sizeable postbag in the Hampshire dressing room the next morning. The best of all was sent to the captain and it read: 'Tennyson – why don't you give up cricket and take your men to paint spots on rocking horses?' He, of course, showed it to the team and by way of an answer they came up with one of the most extraordinary results in the history of the game.

In 1937/38, Lord Tennyson – he had inherited the title on his father's death – took his own side to India. It was a memorable tour for the cricket and also for the hospitality that the assembled company of Indian ruling princes laid on for the side and particularly their captain. The Jam Sahib of Nawanagar, Ranji's cousin who had succeeded to the title, laid on a panther shoot for his lordship. There were a fair number of people who gathered in a rather palatial hide deep in the jungle soon after the sun had gone down, including one or two of the cricketers. The wretched tethered goat was standing in an opening in front of them when with a bound and a roar the panther leapt out of the darkness. His lordship poised and at the ready, took careful aim and fired, whereupon the panther looked up, obviously annoyed at being interrupted in the middle of dinner, and bounded back into the jungle. The poor old goat had taken a turn for the worse and lay slumped upon the ground, whereupon Alf Gover who was one of the spectators within the hide, broke the embarrassed silence with the immortal words, 'Good Lord, my lord, you've shot the goat!' Alas, the inmates of the hide did not realise their responsibility to posterity and failed to record the noble reply.

They did not make the same mistake at Indore when Tennyson hobbled out to bat, but unfortunately the prissiness of the censor allowed only a mild approximation. He had earlier been hit a resounding blow on the shins when fielding close to the bat on the offside and had leapt so high in the air as to give the impression that he knew a thing or two about the Indian rope trick. He stationed himself at the non-striker's end and was horrified to see Peter Smith, the Essex all-rounder, turn the next ball off the face of the bat to fine leg only to be given out lbw by an umpire who had already made four appalling mistakes. The batsmen had changed ends before they realised that Smith had been given out. His lordship who, on the boat out, had stressed to his side how important it was to accept poor umpiring decisions with a smile, advanced upon the umpire. Ian Peebles takes up the story: 'He made umpire Blunder a short address which blew him backwards, bow-legged. I cannot give you the exact text of that immortal message, that is umpire B's copyright, but stripped of its stupendous embellishments, it boiled down to a straightforward enquiry as to whether, having started blind, he was now also bereft of his hearing.'

Tennyson's general geniality and hail-fellow-well-met informality always hit the nail on the head in the West Indies. Once, as the Caribbean season approached, a cricket-lover was heard to ask in suitably humble tones, 'Is the Lord coming next time?' The last word also belongs to Robertson-Glasgow. 'He belongs more properly to the Regency. He would have questioned Brummel's cravat, flattened the hardest nuts at faro, and made a hundred in a single-wicket match after a thirty-six hour spell at Almack's [a gambling club].'

JACK MERCER

IN all the years I have watched cricket I have met few more diverting and engaging characters than Jack Mercer. When I came to know him he was Northamptonshire's scorer. He had swung the ball about for Sussex before the Great War, for Glamorgan between the wars and then had come to Northamptonshire first as coach and then, on retirement, he took up the noble position of scorer. As coach, the doctrine he followed was definitely *laisser faire*. Keith Andrew, the England wicket keeper, explained: 'I'd been there about three weeks when I said, "Who's that down there?" a smart chap with a suit and a trilby on. I knew he was a bit deaf because when you spoke, he never answered. "That's Jack Mercer, the coach. He doesn't do much coaching but gives the Colonel a lot of tips."' (Colonel Coldwell, a man of many parts, was the secretary.) Jack oozed good cheer and fellowship from perhaps the dingiest scoring box in the world, up the rickety old steps in the log cabin with the thatched roof that once housed the scorers and the press at Wantage Road. Jack was a big man who had to squeeze himself through the narrow door, but once there he held court in the most genial way. It was one-way traffic because Jack was stone deaf and in order to make sure that he heard something it was necessary to shout so loud that, if the window was open, the umpires thought someone was appealing.

With his verve and enthusiasm he turned scoring into a somewhat adventurous pursuit. It was always diverting to see him in action and accuracy was never a major concern. He lived in Sherlock Holmes territory in Baker Street in London and it was appropriate therefore that he should have been a member of the Magic Circle. A visit to the Northampton scorers, which was a bit like dropping into the Black Hole of Calcutta for a chat, inevitably produced a pack of cards or some coins from Jack's pocket, which would either disappear or multiply with bewildering rapidity. There was also a playing card that got smaller apparently without any outward assistance, and a handkerchief that seemed to have a mind of its own. He loved telling stories about the old days when he was playing and yet it was never easy to hear him. It was not unlike travelling down an interlocutory cul-de-sac. Two-way communication was out and one very soon lost the thread. It was never easy to tell when he had arrived at the punch line, but having guffawed enough to cover up one's incomprehension, Jack had the maddening habit of asking you a follow up question about the story. The shouting that followed would have had Dickie Bird holding up play and waving his arms about like a tick-tack man.

One of the best stories that, after long years of picking up a bit here and a bit there, I managed to piece together concerned his attempts to dismiss Jack Hobbs when he came down with Surrey to Swansea. Jack Mercer bowled at about medium pace and he would plug away at Hobbs, keeping him quiet and setting him up for the late outswinger. Before telling the story he would remind his audience that, in those days, the amateurs always fielded in the slips. The scene was set, over came the arm and the product was the perfectly placed outswinger. Hobbs played forward and the ball left the bat enough to find the outside edge. 'It would go at a nice comfortable pace and height straight to first slip. It would hit him in the tummy and as he bent down to pick up, it was the form to say, "Well stopped, sir."' Much raucous laughter followed and the square-leg umpire would again look round disapprovingly over his shoulder. Jack was one of the great men even if he has left many of Northamptonshire's career records in a state of mild shock and in need of hasty speculation. I never go to the Wantage Road ground without thinking of those eternally hysterical moments with Jack.

PATSY HENDREN

CRICKET leads naturally to humour because of its very timelessness, which can sometimes make the uninitiated feel they are glimpsing eternity. The genuinely funny man has time to play for a laugh without getting in the way of the game. There may never be a more humorous cricketer than Patsy Hendren who brought the house down in such diverse places as Lord's, Bridgetown, Kingston and Sydney and particularly in the IZingari tent during Canterbury week. No cricketer has proved more successfully that humour is a form of international currency. Hendren had the relative misfortune to be christened Elias, a name which may have been short of public appeal, and was not used for long. History has not handed down the time or the reason for this admirable change – for could he ever have been anything but Patsy? Whether it was done with parental approval or it was simply that the boys with whom he learned cricket and football in the London suburb of Turnham Green found they could not get their tongues round Elias and he became Patsy, sort of by default, remains a mystery. But Patsy he was and Patsy he always will be. As he so often did, Crusoe Robertson-Glasgow, for whose personal joy Patsy Hendren might have been specifically created, summed up the man better than anyone:

> Cricket, sometimes a rather solemn and calculating old bloke, will never forget Elias ('Patsy') Hendren. He played around cricket, and pulled at it, and called it names, and provoked it, and loved it. When he stopped playing for Middlesex, cricket must have missed its imp, its laughing familiar, as Lord's missed its hero. Hendren has been called a

clown; but he was more like the 'fool' who called Lear 'nuncy' and tried to keep the old man from going mad by a stream of talk that poured unmixed from the elemental humours of the earth.

Hendren was a natural clown and his humour was never out of place or embarrassing or over the top. Wherever he played, he brought joy and happiness to the crowds and to all but the most curmudgeonly of those with or against whom he played. He was small with thick shoulders, he moved busily about his job and he ran in a low-slung way that prompted laughter. A bland, impish face that always suggested a boyish innocence and a disbelief in his own eminence, topped all this off. Pomposity was anathema to him and there was a mischievous puckishness about all that he did. Neville Cardus, another devotee, wrote no less perspicaciously of Hendren: 'He represents democracy at Lord's in the same way that Lord Aberdare and his forward drive represented the aristocracy of the Pavilion and the Long Room. He is the idol of the Tavern – that rich part of Lord's where East End is West End and West End is East.'

When he was batting he seemed in more or less permanent conversation with the wicket keeper judging by the laughter on the faces of the close fielders. Whether batting or fielding at short leg or in the slips, his bottom stuck out in a pronounced, rather cheeky and ridiculous way. When he was on the boundary, where he made his name in his early days as an exceptional fielder, he never stopped talking to the spectators around him. He developed the habit, which always got him a laugh, of chasing a ball in the outfield and bending down as if to pick it up when he was still ten yards short of it. It was no surprise if the batsman fell for it and refused a safe third run. Hendren loved practical jokes. He tried one at the end of his career on his Middlesex captain, Walter Robins. When Robins was batting he used to charge down the wicket to the spinners and if he missed the ball he would carry on walking towards the pavilion without a backward glance. Once when Hendren was the non-striker, Robins rushed out of his ground to a spinner, missed and was about to continue to walk when Hendren yelled, 'Look out, he's missed it.' Robins spun round and threw himself headlong on a muddy pitch to get his bat into his crease. The crowd roared and Robins, got up, brushed himself down and then saw that the wicket was broken and the keeper, grinning broadly was tossing the ball from hand to hand.

There were so many similar instances and one of the best happened in 1929, when Alf Gover was playing for Surrey in his first game at Lord's. Hendren welcomed him fulsomely before the game began and asked him what he did.

'I'm a fast bowler,' Gover replied.

'Well,' said Hendren, 'be careful how you bowl at me. I'm not as young as I used to be, and I don't like fast bowling so much.'

When Gover had his bowl at Hendren, there were three balls left in the over. The first was a bouncer and Hendren hooked it into the grandstand. Gover thought it must have been a fluke on Hendren's part so he tried another, which went for four. He put everything into the last ball of the over, another short one, which was again unceremoniously despatched for six in the same place as the first. As the fielders moved positions for the next over, Jack Hobbs passed Gover.

'Why are you bowling bouncers at Pat?' he asked.

'Because he doesn't like fast bowling,' came the answer.

Hobbs was astonished. 'Who on earth told you that?'

'He did,' was the innocent reply.

'Then I am telling you,' Hobbs said with emphasis, 'that Pat is still as good a player of fast bowling as anyone I know.'

What enabled Hendren to play the measured fool as he did was his brilliant batting. Only two others, Hobbs and Frank Woolley, have scored more first-class runs than Hendren's 57,611, and Hobbs is the only one who has scored more than 170 hundreds. His strengths were many, although they were never in evidence until he had scampered that first all-important run with a startled nervousness. It was never a leisurely single, but a cramped prod into the covers or an uncertain push to leg. Then came a frantic shout followed by a frenetic race to the other end as if it might have been the last run he would ever score. This done, normality returned. Largely self-taught, he was as good a hooker (*pace* Alf Gover) as there can ever have been, thanks in part to his strong forearms and wrists. He also had all the other strokes at his command and he hit the ball a fearful crack. His fielding was exceptional and he only ever gave the impression that he was enjoying himself more than he could ever say, which was one of the reasons the crowds loved him as they did.

The only blemish on Hendren's career was his slow start in Test cricket, and it was thought when he first played for England that he did not have the temperament. On his first two tours of Australia, under W.H.T. Douglas and Arthur Gilligan, he made countless runs against the states but never put an innings together in the Test matches. It was only when he was well past thirty that he put this right and in such remarkable fashion that he finished with 3,525 Test runs for an average of 47.63. Douglas Jardine, never a byword for humour or laughter, refused to take Hendren on the Bodyline tour of 1932/33, although age may have had something to do with it for Hendren was then forty-three. But the little imp had the last word because he was back in the England side to play the Australians in 1934 and made a splendid 132 in the Third Test at Old Trafford when he was forty-five. But I can't, for the life of me, believe that Hendren would have countenanced Bodyline. One can imagine some marvellously humorous and pithy exchanges between him and Jardine for which it would have been a pity not to have had a ringside pew. Hendren would surely have tried to pull Jardine's leg and one can only wonder how he would have taken it. Probably with a chilling, autocratic silence.

ARTHUR MAILEY

I WONDER if cricket has produced a greater entertainer than Arthur Mailey? He was the first leg spinner to achieve the prodigious turn that we have become accustomed to in the modern era with the likes of Shane Warne, and he bowled a googly that was so well disguised that even Hercule Poirot would have had his work cut out to spot it. He was a brilliant cartoonist and in later life coped impressively with landscapes. Mailey began life in the slums of Surry Hills in Sydney in 1888 and fought his way out of squalor and deprivation. His journey took him to the Sydney Cricket Ground and on to Government House; across the world to London and Lord's; to a meeting with George V and Queen Mary; and across the Channel to Paris and Montmartre, always with an outrageous sense of humour and fun that never left him. He became a great Anglophile, he hobnobbed modestly and amusingly with the English aristocracy and was very much at home in their midst. It was all washed down with jorums of champagne which was for him the lifelong symbol of his escape from the slums and deprivations of Surry Hills. To put the final touch on an incomparable mixture, he was more Irish than the Irish. He chose cricket as part of an overwhelming desire to be himself and to do his own thing; he chose leg breaks and googlies because he discovered he had a natural aptitude for these things and he was, above all else, a romantic.

He bowled for fun and he loved to spin the ball. The seamer was anathema to him and his philosophy, which wouldn't do today, came straight from the Emerald Isle. 'I'd rather spin and see the ball hit for four than bowl a batsman out by a straight one.' He once said to Neville Cardus, 'If I ever bowl a maiden over, it's not my fault, but the batsman's.' Life, like cricket, was an unending adventure for Mailey and cricket was the vehicle he used. He lived the life of the unpredictable romantic and his cricket was the logical extension of this. His cheerful snub-nosed self-portraits were redolent of the boy who remained all his life wide-eyed with amazement at what he found each day after fighting his way out of those Sydney slums. He had longed for a comprehensive general education but it could not be found or afforded. But what he found for himself was wider and more comprehensive than anything he can have dreamt about.

His humble origins never left him with feelings of inferiority. When later in life he had taken to painting landscapes and country scenes, Queen Mary, together with her husband, stole up behind him when he was painting in the grounds of Lord Downe's country house next door to Sandringham, and cast her eye over one of his canvases.

'I don't think, Mr Mailey,' she said, 'you have painted the sun quite convincingly in this picture.'

'Perhaps not, your Majesty,' came the reply. 'You see, your Majesty, in this country I have to paint the sun from memory.'

One of his jobs as a young man was working for the Gas Board. He was still employed by them when he first played for Australia at Sydney. The teams were asked to Government House and the well-meaning Governor's wife said to him when he was introduced, 'I expect this is your first visit to Government House,' to which he replied, 'No, I was here a year ago to help fix the gas.' Part of Mailey's great charm was that he was never ashamed of his origins.

His first job was pressing trouser seams. It did not last for long because he was soon caught day-dreaming by his boss and given the heave-ho. By then, cricket was already his passion and the only picture in his tiny draughty bedroom was an action photograph of Victor Trumper. In his following days of unemployment he would walk the three miles from his house to the Domain where there always seemed to be some youths playing cricket. Mailey could already bowl a leg break and it was now that one of them taught him how to bowl the googly or the 'bowzie' as it was called in Australia after B.J.T. Bosanquet, the inventor. He practised night and day and, after a few years in the lower grades for Redfern, found himself promoted to the first-grade side. His first game was against Paddington, which was Victor Trumper's club. The great day arrived and Mailey was thrown the ball soon after the Great Man had come in. A well-nigh perfect leg break had been exquisitely driven through the offside for four ('the most beautiful stroke I had ever seen'). Towards the end of his first over, which he felt might be his last, Mailey decided to try the googly. It felt perfect when it left his hand. The spin caused it to drift away from the right-hander and the topspin made it drop late in the flight. After pitching, it spun back between bat and pad narrowly missing the leg stump, but the keeper had the bails off with Trumper two yards out of his crease. As he walked past Mailey, he said, 'It was too good for me.' Mailey famously wrote in his autobiography: 'There was no triumph in me as I watched the receding figure. I felt like a boy who had killed a dove.' It is a story that says as much for the man as it does for his art.

Mailey played in twenty-one Test matches between 1920 and 1926 taking 99 wickets including 9/121 against England at Melbourne in 1920/21. This remains the best analysis by an Australian in a Test match against England. He went on to take all 10 wickets for 66 in Gloucestershire's second innings against the Australians in 1921, figures that he used for the title of his enchanting autobiography. It was at Melbourne in 1924/25, after Hobbs and Sutcliffe had put on 283 in an incomparable display on a 'sticky', that with the first ball the next morning he bowled Hobbs with a full toss that seemed to hang in the air forever. He probably spun the ball as much as Shane

Warne does, but without having the same number of variations. In Mailey's day the art was very much in its infancy. He will, too, have been less inclined to sledge. In 1926/27 he was bowling for New South Wales against Victoria when they made 1,107. Mailey took four wickets for about 350, but complained all his life that the figures did him less than justice because three catches were missed off his bowling – 'two by a man in the pavilion wearing a bowler hat'. When a catch was dropped off his bowling, Mailey was always philosophical and would go over to the fielder and quietly say, 'I'm expecting to take a wicket any day now.'

Mailey's Test career ended when the stuffy Australian authorities kicked him out of the game for writing about it while he was still playing. Clarrie Grimmett was on hand to take over from him in the Australian side and Mailey made a seamless transition from the middle to the press box. He wrote about the game with the same romantic enthusiasm he had brought to his bowling and was always ready to express his latest theory. As well as writing about cricket, he also had a short spell as a general news reporter. His great friend and fellow writer, Denzil Batchelor, tells a lovely story about his crowning experience in that department. Mailey was sent one day by his editor to cover the funeral of an ex-Lord Mayor of Melbourne.

Mailey's story was weighty enough to satisfy the most gloom-laden witness of the sad occasion, but even so his editor sent for him more in anger than in sorrow.

'Do you know how many names you've mentioned?' demanded the editor.

As if he would . . .

'Three hundred and eighteen,' boomed the editor. 'You've got three hundred and seventeen right. The one you've got wrong is the name of the corpse.'

Pausing only to point out that few men can have attained a higher standard of accuracy in their work, Mailey passed resignedly (and the word is chosen with care) out of the office and into the street. He got on a tram which took him to Sydney Airport. A few days later I found him sitting on a Fleet Street doorstep eating an apple.

Mailey loved England and made every excuse to come over whenever he could. He rented a flat in Park Lane while he was in London. When he had finished playing for Australia he loved to captain scratch sides against all and sundry. His two rules were that the other side should always win and that no one should make a duck. When a luckless batsman had just come in and been bamboozled and bowled by that famous googly, Mailey would stand by the umpire and murmur from a face that was as immobile as a ventriloquist's, 'Better say No Ball. Chap hasn't scored yet.' He was generosity and good humour personified and he enjoyed the good life without ever forgetting his origins. It was appropriate that when he was dying he imagined, in his last delirium, he was on board the good ship *Orion* entertaining the captain and officers to a champagne party. One hopes that St Peter had a glass waiting for him.

DON BRADMAN

AN extravagant participant who takes the disciplines and product to new levels occasionally overwhelms every art form. Donald George Bradman played first-class cricket between 1927 and 1949 and while other batsmen have scored more runs, no one, even to this day, has achieved anything approaching his mastery or consistency. He went into bat for the first time in a Sheffield Shield match at the Adelaide Oval in December 1927 and in his first over hit two fours off the great Clarrie Grimmett. His third ball pitched a fraction short and just outside the leg stump. Bradman moved his right foot back and across and the famous leg spinner was staggered to see the ball hit with a flat bat against the spin through midwicket with Bradman rolling his right wrist to keep it down. This stroke was the principal innovation Bradman brought to his art and how appropriate that it should have brought him his first boundary at this level.

As so often happens, his was a genius that appeared from nowhere. He was born in Cootamundra, New South Wales on 27 August 1908, the fifth child of George and Emily Bradman. It is a mystery where the genes came from to create the best and most prolific batsman the world has ever known. George's grandfather, a farm worker, had emigrated from a village on the Suffolk-Cambridgeshire borders. He departed without leaving behind him rows of chastened bowlers going sadly about their business on the edge of the Fens. They settled at Yeo Yeo but years later George was forced to leave a successful farming business because of his wife's poor health and they moved up the road to Bowral where he became a carpenter. He had married a local girl, Emily Whatman, who also came from a farming family, which, as far as anyone could tell, had not left a trail of weeping bowlers in their wake either. It is an extraordinary coincidence that when WG captained Lord Sheffield's side in Australia in 1891/92, they played a match against twenty-four of Bowral. One of the local players was Richard Whatman who was Emily's brother and so there is just the vaguest of connections between the two greatest cricketers of them all.

In Bowral, before and during the Great War, sporting facilities, especially for children, were virtually non-existent. For all that, it was not long before young Don's innate sporting instincts began to shine through. As far as he was concerned the main problem with Bowral was that after he had escaped school at the end of the day, there was no other child in the neighbourhood with whom he could play. Being an innovative young chap, he soon invented for himself a highly effective and satisfying form of DIY cricket. There was a sizeable water tank near their house that had a round brick base. He would throw a golf ball at this base and try and hit the rebound with a small cricket stump. The ball would come back fast, at some pretty exciting angles and it sharpened up his reflexes like nobody's business. With his eye, it was not long before he was hitting pretty well every rebound plumb in the middle of the stump – which will have meant that he will have had a fair amount of fielding practice as well. It undoubtedly taught him an unusual ball sense that will have given him an important start when it came to the real thing.

In those twenty-three years, which include the Second War, Bradman played only 338 innings in all first-class cricket and yet he scored 28,067 runs with 117 hundreds for an average of 95.14. He played no more than fifty-two Test matches for they came round with much less frequency than they do today, and he never played outside Australia or England. One shudders to think what his record might have been if he had been able to take advantage of the limited attacks of the young and emerging Test-playing countries. He probably would have gone to South Africa in 1934/35 if he had been fit, but he had almost died of peritonitis after the tour of England in 1934 and was forced to have more than a year away from the game. As it was, he scored 6,996 runs for Australia with twenty-nine hundreds and an average of 99.94. When he came out to bat in his last Test innings at The Oval in 1948, he needed four more runs to ensure an average of a hundred in Test cricket, but his second ball, from Eric Hollies, was the perfect googly.

Although he was always modest in describing his own fielding, he was outstanding anywhere with a good pair of hands. He had a wonderful throw and loved fielding. 'I enjoyed it,' he said at the time, 'I was never a great catch but had ability in the field. I had confidence in my outcricket and that allowed me to have fun out there ... I have heard of other players being often concerned when the ball came their way. I can't say I felt that way. On the contrary, I loved it.' These were not the words of an arrogant bighead.

Bradman broke the rules of his day by playing across the line, but it was done deliberately and with great security. Nonetheless it raised any number of eyebrows, not to say hackles, for it was not the accepted *modus operandi* of the time. His was a record that would have gone to anyone's head although Bradman managed at all times to keep both his feet pretty firmly on the ground, which says a great deal for his upbringing. His success inevitably caused some of his contemporaries, especially the older ones who had been in the limelight before he burst on the scene, to suffer more than just the odd pang of jealousy. There is no indication though, that, as a young man, he ever tried to throw his weight around in the dressing room. In fact, he listened carefully to everything he was told and if he ever stepped out of line it was only to make too many runs for the good of some of his self-regarding team-mates.

In order fully to appreciate Bradman it is necessary to look in some detail at his career, especially when he was young, and examine the influences that were working against him. It is a compelling story that shows just how remarkable he was and it makes his brilliance even more staggering.

When I first mooted this book, I wondered about Bradman. Of course he had scored a huge number of runs, but had it been all rather too monotonous and repetitious to count as entertainment? A quick look at his record suggests a machine-like automaton. Had he really taken an art form to new frontiers or was it simply mass production masquerading as art? But surely a man who had scored a hundred rather less than every third time he went to the wicket could be nothing less than a genius. He never had a single bad spell in his career, although Douglas Jardine might have liked to think he failed miserably against Bodyline. It is true that he averaged only just over 56 in the four Tests he played then against Larwood and Voce and the others, as opposed to somewhere between 90 and 100 against everyone else. The fact that he averaged as many as 56 against this pernicious form of attack serves to underline his genius. I think these thoughts occurred to me because the one quality that was perhaps missing from Bradman's supremely efficient and clinical batting was romance. In a way, it is paradoxical that two of the game's most romantic batsmen, Ranji and Victor Trumper, should have averaged 44 and 39 respectively in Test cricket as opposed to Bradman's 99.94. His style of batting was superb, but being a short man, he did not possess the flowing elegance that a few extra inches can give a player, although there was something mesmerising about the speed at which he scored his runs and his certainty of stroke. I am one of the ever-diminishing number of people who had the luck to watch Bradman bat. I was taken for my first visit to Lord's on the fourth day of the Second Test against Australia in 1948. Bradman made 89 and I can see him now being caught by Bill Edrich at second slip off Alec Bedser. Unlike almost everyone else in the ground, I remember feeling rather miffed that he didn't get a hundred. He was the most exciting man I had ever seen. I can remember him hitting every no-ball he received for four, and two of them came close to where I was sitting. The baggy green cap was awfully good news, too. How could I even have considered leaving him out?

Bradman was nobody's fool and it will not have taken him long to realise how much better he was at batting than any of his contemporaries or, indeed, any other batsman ever to have played the game, give or take W.G. Grace. He may have been lucky to be given the ability, but he was determined to cash in on it. He revealed this awareness when he said after his first season in the Australian side, against England in 1928/29 when he made 468 runs with average of nearly 67: 'I had no profession. I wasn't a lawyer or an accountant. There wasn't professional cricket, and even if there had been I would not have been one.' He knew full well that if he was going to set himself up for life, he had to turn his genius for batting into as big a financial asset as he could. In that first series in Australia he will simply have been glad to be there, but by the end of it he knew that he had come to stay. Gradually, his mind will have begun to explore the financial possibilities and by the time he set sail for his first tour of England in 1930, he knew, although he was only twenty-one, exactly the path he was going to walk down. When it came to his fellow players, it did not help that he was not naturally gregarious. His colleagues did not regard him as a team man and, in England, began to see him as a money-grabber who was only out for himself. This naturally caused resentment. As far as he was concerned, there was no question of him sharing any of the rewards that came his way with the rest of the side. Because he was so much the best player and such a lot depended on him, he felt that this was his right. Bradman had always been a shy person and as a result he was insensitive to the feelings of others. Maybe, too, he was aware of his lack of inches, always something that can create a self-centred stubbornness. His character became as interesting as his batting the more deeply I tried to look into it.

There is a story about his initial selection for Australia in 1928 that is most revealing. Bradman was playing in Sydney for an

Australian XI against England and living with the Pearces who were family friends. On the third evening of this match, at nine o'clock, the Australians were going to announce their side for the First Test match in Brisbane. When the time came he was sitting by the wireless with the Pearces and they heard the announcer say that the selectors were 'deadlocked'. As there was one day of the current match to go, he got himself ready for bed thinking he would have to wait until the morning to hear the side. The wireless was still on in the next door room and no sooner had he put his head on his pillow when, through the wall, he heard the announcer say: 'At last we can tell you the composition of the Australian Test side to play the MCC at Brisbane on 30 November. The players, in alphabetical order are: D.G. Bradman, J.M. Gregory, C.V. Grimmett . . .' Roland Perry, his biographer, takes up the story: 'Bradman didn't get out of bed to accept congratulations from the Pearces, who were more excited than he was. He simply shut his eyes and went to sleep. To him, it was not a dream. It was the fulfilment of an ambitious goal, nevertheless one he believed he could achieve.'

His First Test match produced one of the few hiccoughs of his career. He managed to score only 18 and 1 in a match that England won by the colossal margin of 675 runs. Bradman was picked in the squad of thirteen for the Second Test in Sydney, but was made twelfth man. This was the only time in his career that he was dropped from the Australian side. Like selectors down the ages, the Australians wanted to stay with the older, more experienced players, but they lost again in Sydney, by 8 wickets, and Bradman was back for the Third Test in Melbourne. He was already a great favourite with the crowds. When Alan Kippax was out for a hundred, the big crowd cheered him back to the pavilion. Then came complete quiet.

'I was in the dressing room with Don,' Ted a'Beckett, one of the Australian side, said after the game. 'There was this eerie drop in the volume as if someone had shut a window suddenly. I wished him luck and he walked out. Then there was a colossal roar that hit us like a tornado in a wind tunnel as Bradman became visible to the spectators. I had heard mighty roars in football games, but nothing like that spontaneous blast. It was absolutely uplifting to every member of our team.'

The country was slipping deeper and deeper into recession, money was desperately tight and unemployment was spiralling. The Australians badly needed a hero on whom they could pin their hopes and Bradman was the answer to their prayers. He gave them something to believe in and to hang on to. More important, he enabled Australia to beat the rest of the world at cricket. In the first innings of that Melbourne Test he made 79 and then, in the second, became the youngest man ever, at twenty years and four months, to score a hundred in a Test match when he made 112. It then deluged with rain and England should have had no chance almost of reaching a hundred, let alone the 332 they needed to win, but the forty-six-year-old Jack Hobbs and Herbert Sutcliffe gave a superlative exhibition of bad-wicket batsmanship, putting on 105 for the first wicket. Sutcliffe went on to reach 135 and England won by 3 wickets. When it came to Bradman's batting there was only one dissenting voice. The somewhat tetchy Percy Fender, the former England all-rounder, who may have been sitting uncomfortably in the press box, reckoned, for some reason, that Bradman owed his success more than anything to huge doses of luck. Even as the evidence to the contrary grew as the series went on, to say nothing of a small matter of 340 not out for New South Wales against Victoria, he refused to budge.

The following season in Australia, Bradman more than consolidated his position. In a trial match for the 1930 tour of England he made a memorable 225 for Bill Woodfull's XI against Jack Ryder's. His most incredible innings of all came when Queensland, who were often victim to Bradman's worst excesses, paid a visit to Sydney. Both sides had been out for just over 200 in the first innings with Bradman making only 3. New South Wales lost 2 early wickets in the second innings when Bradman was joined by his captain, Alan

Kippax, and in the next 145 minutes they put on 272 before Kippax was out for 115. He was angry for he badly wanted to outdo his young partner. It was no secret that Kippax was not a fan of Bradman who was breaking too many records for his liking and taking the limelight away from Kippax and his friends. They found it difficult to stomach the huge publicity that came Bradman's way. It annoyed them, too, that he was such a favourite with the public. A number of those who were playing with Bradman were spiteful and jealous. The fact that he never sought publicity for himself made no difference to them. In addition to that, Bradman had removed business from Kippax's sports store in Sydney in taking his own business to a rival and the public had followed him.

That evening, the second of the match, Bradman was 205 not out. On the Sunday, he made up his mind to go for Bill Ponsford's world record score of 437. It was a record Bradman had decided he would like to have. 'I felt everything was just right,' he said, 'the state of the wicket, the state of the game, the state of my health. Also I was in the mood for runs.'

He set off at a cracking pace on the Monday and reached 300 in 288 minutes, the quickest ever in Shield cricket. After batting for 377 minutes, he became the eighth batsman to score 400 in first-class cricket and he had got there two hours quicker than any of the others. Soon after that, he beat Ponsford's record and at tea when New South Wales had reached 761/8, he was 452 not out. During the interval most of his team-mates came up to congratulate him while he drank his own special mixture of milk, tea and water with his boots off and his feet up. It was getting on towards the end of the interval when Kippax came over to him and said, not in the friendliest of voices, 'I'm declaring.' One or two of the other players were surprised but nothing was said.

'Do I have time for a shower?' Bradman asked.

'No,' Kippax snapped back at him. 'Just because you've beaten a world record doesn't mean you don't have to come out on time with the rest of us.'

Bradman was, of course, chosen to go to England in 1930 and so too was Kippax who must have had an utterly miserable tour, which will have served him right. The agony was not slow in starting because Bradman made 236 not out in the first match at Worcester. From that moment onwards it was nothing less than a triumphal procession around England. In all, he made 2,960 runs, hitting ten centuries for an average of 98.67. His form in the Test matches was even more startling. He began with a modest 131 in the First at Trent Bridge. This was followed by 254 in the Second at Lord's, 334 in the Third at Headingley with 309 coming on the first day, including a century in each session of play, and 232 in the Fifth at The Oval. He scored 974 runs in the five Test matches for an average of 139.14.

Amazingly, Bradman still found some people hard to please and the strangest of all was the writer, Neville Cardus. After his century at Trent Bridge, Cardus wrote about him in a way that suggested he had been dining rather too often with Percy Fender. By the end of the 1930 series, Cardus was doing his best to regain lost ground. 'We have now seen Bradman the brilliant and Bradman the shrewd, playing four-day cricket and cricket that takes no heed of the clock. In these different circumstances he had shown command over the appropriate methods; his versatility is astonishing and he is indeed a great batsman.' That was how he summed up Bradman at the end of the tour, but there were still no signs of the blushes that by rights should have come flooding to his cheeks. Maybe, initially, Cardus had also been disturbed by the absence of romance in Bradman's batting because it was the ingredient he loved and thrived upon the most in his writings.

This tour produced one wonderful vignette concerning the Royal Family. Before the series began, the Australians played a three-day match over a weekend against the University at Cambridge. On the Sunday they drove to West Norfolk to have lunch with Lord Downe at Hillington Hall. After lunch their host decided to take them to meet his neighbour across the fence, who happened to be George V. The neighbouring estate was Sandringham. The King, in a tweed suit, wandered around most informally as he talked to them all. He was obviously in very good fettle. He chatted to Bill Woodfull as if he was an old acquaintance and he sought out Bradman to congratulate him on his run-scoring so far.

Then, turning to the group of players, he said, 'I hope to see you play, probably at Lord's.'

The tall, austere figure of Queen Mary was now seen to be approaching and the King went on: 'Here comes the Queen. Must introduce you boys to her,' and he did.

The Australians were allowed everywhere and they looked at the stables, the gardens, the dairy and the new museum. It was an afternoon none of them ever forgot and during the course of it the players asked the King if they could take some photographs. The monarch, who was very Germanic and never appeared to have much of a lighter side to him, electrified everyone with his answer.

'Fire away,' he said, 'take as many as you like,' which was a little bit like Attila the Hun suddenly slapping his thigh, saying 'Gadzooks' and doing a handstand.

When the photographs had been taken, Queen Mary chipped in with, 'We would love to have some copies.'

Maybe, even in those days, the Royals were a good deal more PR-conscious than anyone gave them credit for, and also nothing like as starched and formal as they were made to seem.

It was during this first tour of England that Bradman's ventures into the commercial side of life got him into trouble with his own Board and also with his fellow players. After he had made that 334 at Headingley, a rich Australian admirer who had settled in England had sent him a present of a thousand pounds which, in those days, was a considerable sum of money. It was also more than double a player's official allowance for the whole tour. Bradman pocketed the money and never considered sharing it with the other members of the side. During the voyage over, and on the tour, he had been putting together with the help of a journalist, *Don Bradman's Book of Cricket*. When it was serialised in a newspaper, the Australian Board fined him £50, which made Bradman furious. His fellow players almost never saw him away from the grounds. His life was a constant stream of appointments and engagements with pound signs never far away. Bradman made no attempt to bridge the ever-widening gap between himself and the other players.

One can only guess at what the likes of Kippax must have thought and said, although they will no doubt have kept it to themselves when he continued to turn in match-winning scores of more than 200 in the Tests. Bradman drank almost nothing, was a non-smoker and was never therefore seen in the bar. He liked his own company and valued his privacy highly so that he became a virtual stranger to many of the party. Being a loner at heart, he may have had an inbuilt suspicion of his fellow human beings. He may also have felt that, as he contributed so much to the side's success when it mattered, it was no one else's business what he did away from the cricket. At the end of the tour the Board appeared to do a *volte-face*. Having refused him permission to stay on in England for commercial purposes, they then agreed that he should be the only player allowed to leave the ship in Adelaide where the side was given a huge welcome when they docked. A motor company took photographs, using them for advertising purposes, and Bradman received a new Chevrolet while the other players got nothing. Bradman then went on to Sydney by train while the others stayed on board ship. This scheme may have been authorised by the Board so that they did not alienate their greatest asset.

Over the next two Australian summers, Bradman cashed in unmercifully upon some poor bowling from first the Indians and then the South Africans. No one had ever batted like this. His lightning fast footwork was the basis of his success for he was never left in the wrong position to play a stroke. He had a full range of strokes, eyesight that enabled him to pick up the length of a ball a fraction of a second earlier than the next man, and an unwavering concentration. This was all backed up by an extraordinarily powerful mind that never let up. His defence was equally impressive. His chief strength was his ability to score runs at such an amazing speed, for it left the bowlers with so much more time in which to dispose of the opposition. Bradman was, more than anything, like Napoleon Bonaparte with pads on, except that he had the sense never to embark upon a cricketing odyssey to Moscow.

The start to his career, which I have gone into at some length, was in many ways as remarkable off the field as it was on it. The country boy dealt so easily with every situation. He never allowed himself to become flustered. He coped with the bullies like Kippax; he handled the Board well enough and he never allowed anything or anyone to stand between him and his inexhaustible supply of runs. By the end of the 1930 tour he had set himself up exactly as he had wanted with the crucial help of Jessie Menzies, a relation of Robert Menzies, a future prime minister of Australia. Jessie had been his childhood sweetheart from Bowral and had joined up with him soon after he had come down to Sydney. She was the single most important influence in a life that, although it reads like a fairy story, had its ups and downs and most particularly so as far as his health was concerned. In 1932 they married and were inseparable until her death a year or two before his own in 2001.

England were rattled by him, although it is a moot point as to whether or not this had anything to do with the choice of Douglas Jardine to captain their side in 1932/33. He had vented his wrath against the Indian and South African bowlers in the two previous Australian seasons. Then came the confrontation with Larwood and co. Bradman was not fit to play in the First Test, but was back for the Second. His homespun method of trying to combat the short-pitched ball coming at the body was to back away to the leg and try to slash through the offside. He met with a fair amount of success and averaged just over 56 in the series. It represented failure by his normal standards, but an average of 56 showed that he had been able to come up with some sort of worthwhile answer. His colleagues were not so successful and England won the series 4–1, but it all left an appalling smell behind it. Probably the only man who might have stopped it was the England manager, Pelham Warner, but he was too weak to stand up to Jardine. Warner liked to be all things to all men and in situations like the one in which he found himself now, he was able to face in many directions at the same time. When he returned home he said he had been a fierce opponent of Jardine's tactics all along. The Australian public were united in their dislike of a man and his side whose intention it had been to cut their hero down to size. Jardine had never forgiven the Australians after Warwick Armstrong had unkindly deprived him of a century against them in the Parks at Oxford in 1921.

Bradman's run-getting powers never deserted him, even when he returned to the fray after the war. He strode through four tours of England never scoring less than 2,000 runs on each tour. There were seven hundreds in 1934, thirteen in 1938 and eleven in 1948 to add to the ten he made in 1930. One of his greatest achievements was surely to come back as he did after the war when he was already thirty-seven. But before he did that he had to survive a number of problems with his health, especially at the end of the tour of England in 1934. He had been in poor health for some time and had missed six matches between the Fourth and Fifth Tests, in which he made 304 and 244, finishing the tour with 1,144 runs from eight innings with an average of 163.

When he returned to London after the Scarborough Festival, he was suffering from severe pains in his stomach. He was diagnosed with appendicitis and the offending organ was promptly removed. The surgeons discovered that peritonitis had already set in and the pain continued after the operation and his temperature took off. Before long they thought he was going to die. Word was sent to Jessie in Australia and she caught a ship as soon as she could. When he received a cable from her telling him that she was coming to London, it proved to be the turning point and when she arrived he was allowed out of hospital. But it had been a close call. It was another strange aspect of Bradman that such a fit athlete should have been so susceptible to illness throughout his career. He and Jessie stayed in England until a week before Christmas and then, in one of those extraordinary coincidences, they met Winston Churchill at Victoria Station. He was there to see his wife off. It was Churchill who saw the photo opportunity.

When England next came to Australia, in 1936/37, it was with the double job of winning back the Ashes and laying to rest the ghost of Bodyline. Gubby Allen, their urbane captain, did the second job with great success. After winning the first two Test matches he should have won the Ashes too, but Bradman, who had failed in the first two, made 270, 212 and 169 in the next three, which Australia won. No wonder he carried the aspirations of so many of his fellow countrymen around in his cricket bag with him.

Bradman's problem now was his own players. The Kippaxes and that lot had retired and their places had largely been taken by a group of Roman Catholics of Irish origin who did not trust Bradman and his staunch Anglican imperialism and there was more than a touch of jealousy too. During that series four of his players, Bill O'Reilly, Chuck Fleetwood Smith, Stan McCabe and Lee O'Brien were summoned to appear before the Board accused of failing to give full support to their new captain which did nothing to help relations. O'Reilly, in particular, was a cussed and most unforgiving bloke who harboured the strongest of prejudices. So too, in many ways, was Jack Fingleton, who was no less opposed to the ways of his captain. Bradman's answer as always was to carry on in his relentless pursuit of runs. In the end he beat Allen's side almost single-handedly, which should have shut up his critics.

Now that Bradman was captain, and firing on all cylinders besides, he effectively ran Australian cricket and there was no one with the temerity to question any personal diversion in the interests of financial gain. He felt that the Board got above themselves during the 1938 tour of England when they insisted that wives could not join the players until the tour was over. The moment he heard the news, Bradman wrote a letter telling them that he was retiring immediately from Test cricket. He was persuaded not to post it, but word will have got back and the next communication from the Board said that wives could join their husbands as and when they pleased.

His other problem on that tour was the England batting in the final Test at The Oval, a match they had to win to draw the series. They won the toss and Len Hutton made 364, beating Bradman's 334 which was the previous highest score in matches between the two countries. At 887/7 Bradman brought himself on to bowl and at once went over on his ankle and broke his tibia. Neither he nor Fingleton, who had pulled a calf muscle, were able to bat and England won by an innings and 579 runs – the biggest margin ever. This result burnt deeply into Bradman's soul and partly accounts for him grinding his heel in Walter Hammond's face when England toured Australia immediately after the war. In the last domestic season before war broke out, Bradman contented himself by start-ing off with six successive centuries, equalling the record that had been set by C.B. Fry in 1901. There was no end to this remarkable process of scoring runs.

When the war ended, not many people thought seriously that they were ever going to see Bradman play again for his country, cer-tainly not Bradman himself. Then the England tour was arranged and suddenly there was a feeling that perhaps the Great Man might have one more try. Bradman eventually agreed to start the 1946/47 season and to see what happened. He made a hundred in Melbourne for an Australian XI against the English and that, together with one or two reasonable performances in the Sheffield Shield, decided him to throw his hat into the ring. He won an important toss in the First Test at Brisbane and soon found himself going out to bat. He immediately had difficulty with Alec Bedser, whom he rated high on the list of seam bowlers he had faced in his career, and he made 7 in the first forty minutes. Gradually, he began to recover some of his timing and placing and he had taken his score to 28 when he faced Bill Voce, who had been Larwood's main partner in the Bodyline series. Voce tried to bowl him an outswinging yorker. The ball was over-pitched and outside the off stump and Bradman tried to chip it wide of the slips. He thought the ball hit the under edge of the bat before going into the ground and that it was therefore a 'bump' ball. It flew to Jack Ikin at second slip who caught the ball at chest height. The England close fielders were all sure that the ball had come from the top edge and that it was a straightforward catch. They appealed, but umpire Borwick agreed with Bradman and gave it not out. At the end of the over, as he walked past Bradman on his way to the other end, Hammond said bitterly, 'A fine way to start a bloody series.' If Bradman had been out for 28 it is more than probable that he would have chucked it all in there and then. As it was, he took the Australian side on to Sydney where he made 234. At the end of the series, which Australia won 3–0, he let it be known that he was prepared to play against the Indians the following season. In his mind he was already thinking of a final valedictory tour of England in 1948.

There were eight centuries the following season, including three in the series against India. There was also a scare when he retired hurt in the last Test match with a torn rib cartilage, but it turned out to be less serious than was at first feared. In April 1948, a somewhat jaunty forty-year-old Bradman stepped on to English soil for the fourth and final time as a player. The next five months were a non-stop lap of honour for him, both on the field and off. He was, by now, as dominant a figure in the world of cricket as WG had been half a century before. Bradman realised this and enjoyed every moment of it. He may not have been quite as mobile as he had been before the war but his form was unstoppable. He made 2,428 runs with eleven hundreds and an average of 89.93. He achieved his last ambition, which was to captain an unbeaten side in England, and he won the series 4–0. Not the least important aspect of the tour was that he used his great experience and his shrewd captaincy to turn this Australian side into perhaps the strongest that ever left Australia.

The only personal disappointment came right at the end. He needed to score those four runs in his final Test innings to ensure that he averaged a hundred in Test cricket. When he came out to bat at The Oval in the Fifth Test, it was a highly charged and emotional moment. Norman Yardley, the England captain, called for three cheers for Don Bradman. Bradman took off his cap in appreciation and when the applause of the crowd had died down, he took guard and faced Eric Hollies, who remembered that Bradman had once had a problem picking his googly. He bowled one with his second ball. It came perfectly out of his hand, drew Bradman forward before spinning back and finding its way between bat and pad and bowling him. Bradman turned swiftly and walked off amid a shocked, eerie silence. In the press box this silence was broken by the loud and hysterical laughter of those two old 'chums' of his, Bill O'Reilly and Jack Fingleton. It only remained for Bradman and his side to be entertained by the King and Queen at Balmoral. O'Reilly and Fingleton would almost certainly have smiled at that too because Bradman was a great royalist and had always got on exceptionally well with the royal family.

On the voyage back to Australia Bradman was tested in another, highly pertinent way. A chap who worked for Payne's Sweets approached him. The company wanted him and some of the other players to appear in some Australian newspaper advertisements. The rep was surprised that Bradman did not ask for more money than the others, for his reputation had preceded him. Soon after Bradman arrived back in Adelaide, the Payne's man came to Adelaide in order that the contract should be signed, and he brought Bradman's money with him. To his great surprise, Bradman told him that he could not go through with the deal although he did not give a reason. He was still offered the money, but he refused to take it and, at his suggestion, it was given to the Spastics Society. It was Ian Johnson who came up with the answer.

'I think he knew he was about to be knighted,' he explained. 'He could hardly appear in a newspaper ad selling sweets.'

More chortles for O'Reilly and Fingleton.

Bradman dutifully obliged with one more hundred, in his testimonial match at Melbourne, before he finally relegated his cricket bag to the attic. Then he was able to turn his full attention to Jessie who had uncomplainingly suffered the years of cricket and all the bouts of ill-health and had always been there when it mattered the most. Her husband was also now able to concentrate his energies on the Adelaide Stock Exchange. That will have been a challenge to which he will have been looking forward. The golf course also saw more of him and will have found him one of its more doughty opponents. His influence over Australian cricket remained enormous and he was never less than interesting and entertaining tucked away in those leather seats at the back of the committee box in the George Giffen Stand at the Adelaide Oval. There will never be another Don Bradman, any more than there will ever be another W.G. Grace.

LEARIE CONSTANTINE

IN many ways Learie Constantine was as significant a figure for
West Indies cricket as W.G. Grace was for England. Statistically,
Constantine didn't amount to much more than a short run when
compared with WG, but it was Constantine who first brought the
innate glamour and spirit of cricket in the Caribbean to the attention of the world. After Constantine, the arrival of Weekes, Worrell,
Walcott, Sobers, Kanhai, Richards, Lloyd and the rest was nothing
more than a logical progression. It was Constantine who first took
West Indies cricket by the scruff of the neck, gave it a huge shake
and prepared the path for those who would follow. He was the first
to show off the true West Indian temperament. In those days –
Constantine's career embraced the years between the two wars –
West Indies cricket was run by the white minority. They captained
all the representative sides, they administered the game and what
they said went, but they must take some credit for it was they who
first gave the game its local status. There had been some exciting
black cricketers, but until Constantine came on the scene there was
no one who captured the imagination in remotely the same way.
Whether batting, bowling or fielding, Constantine brought a
dynamic flare to the game that had never been seen before at this
level. He played eighteen Test matches for the West Indies
between 1928, against England at Lord's, their first ever Test
match, and 1939, against England at The Oval, the last Test played
before the Second War. Just as important for the reputation of
West Indies cricket and for the acceptance in England of the black

man, he played nine seasons between 1929–37 for Nelson in the Lancashire League. His record, in a part of the country where coloured people were a rarity, was phenomenal and in those years Nelson were the champions seven times and runners-up twice. In Lancashire, Constantine's progress was both a cricketing and a social triumph.

Constantine was considerably more than just a cricketer. It was through his astonishing feats on the field of play that he acquired the status to wage a war against the subjugation of the black man. He began his crusade on the 1928 tour of England by the West Indies, continued it in his years in the Lancashire League and beyond. The British first awarded him an MBE for his work in the West Indian community during the war, before he graduated to Sir Learie Constantine and ended up, two years before his death in 1971, in the House of Lords as Baron Constantine of Maraval, the now well-to-do suburb of Port of Spain where he had spent part of his childhood.

Constantine, the son of L.N. Constantine and nephew of Victor Pascall, both highly able but self-taught players, was imbued with cricket from his birth. He later wrote: 'When I was five years old, I used to get a piece of barrel-stave and with an orange in the other hand begged passers-by to bowl to me.' He and his friends were soon playing every day of the season. 'After a day's work, my father [who scored the first West Indies hundred made in England, stumped off WG for 113, at no less a place than Lord's] used to join us and began giving instructions according to his own ideas. Batting was essentially the individual's choice and in his style. So long as he was comfortable in his stance and lifted the bat freely, he was left alone. For bowling, he told us of the cart-wheel action . . . what an off break was and how it differed from the leg break . . . But fielding, yes fielding, he took into his own hands, and what a martinet he was! "Concentrate," he would say. "To mis-field or drop a catch is sheer carelessness." This was an unforgivable sin. All kinds of tricks were devised to catch us out.'

Just as important, the Constantines were a good family and his father, old Cons, was an overseer on an estate, usually a white man's preserve. C.L.R. James takes up the story: 'His father was the most loved and most famous cricketer in Trinidad, and Pascall, a slow left-hander, a most charming person and a great popular favourite with all classes. We cannot overestimate the influence of all this on young Constantine. He was born to the purple, and in cricket circles never saw himself as inferior to or dependant for anything on anyone.'

He played for Trinidad in the inter-colonial tournament and in 1923 was selected to play for a West Indies side in England. He learned much in all three departments of the game, but it was not until he went back to England in 1928 that he was seen as the Constantine who set West Indies cricket on the map. It was then he showed himself as a forerunner of all those famous West Indians who were to come over the next three-quarters of a century – and in all three disciplines. On that tour, Constantine took 107 first-class wickets at 22.95 each and made 1,381 runs at an average of 34.52. In addition to this, he had brought a new dimension to the art of fielding and nothing like it had ever been seen in England. No one else had been so dominant in this aspect of the game. This was an all-round performance with more than just a hint of Sobers about it, not only the figures, but also the way in which they had been achieved. They came at the moment when, to call upon C.L.R. James once again: 'Constantine, the heir-apparent, the happy warrior, the darling of the crowd, prize pupil of the captain of the West Indies, had revolted against the revolting contrast between his first-class status as cricketer and his third-class status as a man. The restraints imposed upon him by social conditions in the West Indies had become intolerable and he decided to stand them no longer.'

His most compelling cricket on that tour was played in the West Indies match against Middlesex at Lord's that will forever be known as 'Constantine's match'. Ian Peebles, in his first season for Middlesex, took part and recalled the match in his autobiography.

The West Indies made a pedestrian start and were 79/5 [in reply to 352/6 declared] when Learie came in to bat. We were immediately caught in the eye of the hurricane. One of his many spectacular strokes was a square cut off Gubby Allen that went for six into the balcony of the grandstand, but he attacked every bowler with a fine impartiality. In less than an hour he had got to 87 and I was bowling to him with some trepidation. I still bowled basically medium pace, but, in desperation, I let go a slow googly. He went to give it such a clip that I could hear the swish of the bat at our end of the pitch, but it dipped in and he hit outside it. To his manifest disgust it hit the middle stump.

By the end of the day we were nearly 250 ahead with seven wickets in hand, so seemingly well on top. But the third morning Learie, who had bowled a pretty sharp pace throughout the match, suddenly took off as one possessed and, from the pavilion end, he bowled at an awe-inspiring pace. No one looked like coping with the tempest, and the morning's haul brought him six wickets for eleven runs . . . The West Indies finally needed 259 to win and five went for 121. Learie started again exactly where he had left off. J.W. Hearne, a most courageous man, sought to catch him off his own bowling and suffered such damage to his hand that he played no more that season. The ball in this case went smack into the bottom pavilion step whence it rebounded almost to the bowler's feet. Runs came at a roaring pace and in under an hour Learie had reached his hundred and his side were all but home. This was the greatest all-round performance I was to see in my career – and possibly my life.

In recent times, spectators have been able to gorge themselves on the fielding of the two South Africans, Colin Bland and Jonty Rhodes. There have also been such superb exponents of the art as Norman O'Neill, Neil Harvey, Paul Sheahan, Derek Randall, Clive Lloyd, Gus Logie, Clive Lloyd and the others. Great fielding has become an accepted art form, brought to the height of its fever by the demands of one-day cricket. Constantine was the first of all, not just in the covers, but anywhere in the field. His exploits were legendary. People turned up to see him, knowing they only had to wait a short time before they would be able to see for themselves the levels to which he had taken his art. The stories of Constantine in the field are manifold. One will be enough. When England went to the West Indies in 1930, Constantine's ability to create catches was never better illustrated. George Gunn's footwork repeatedly took him down the wicket to get to the pitch of the ball. Constantine was fielding at second slip when Gunn again set off down the pitch. The Trinidadian moved fast and was effectively walking side by side with the batsman. Gunn did not completely control the stroke and the ball went sideways to Constantine who did not bother to use two hands. There were many other similar instances.

These were the talents that Constantine took to Nelson. In his seven years he acquired almost godlike status in those parts. At the same time as looking after the prosperity of Nelson both on the field and off, for his success earned the club much money, it was all the most wonderful single-handed public relations exercise for the West Indies. The writer C.L.R. James joined him in Nelson and together they developed their arguments for West Indian self-government, making frequent speeches and spreading the gospel. This was the first time the West Indies had found that they had a political voice in England. Together they were advocates.

Constantine occasionally left Nelson in those seven summers to help the West Indies. Then, in 1939, when he had finished there, he took part in the full West Indies tour that was carried out to music orchestrated by Adolf Hitler. Bowling slow and at medium pace with a few googlies thrown in, Constantine took 103 wickets for an average of 17.7. Appropriately enough, he kept one of his most remarkable innings to the very end. In his last innings in Test cricket, at The Oval in 1939, he made 70 out of 103 runs in ninety-two balls, hitting the ball with what may have seemed an exhibition of spontaneous gaiety but was really an audacious selection of serious strokes systematically and deliberately thought out. The sheer daring, impudence and audacity of the strokeplay over the years gave a false impression of light-hearted intent.

The Second World War ended Constantine's serious cricket and gave him more time to attend to his political ambitions and ideals. He was also a regular contributor to one of Fleet Street's tabloids and was always the friendliest of faces and the most cheerful of companions in the press boxes throughout England. In 1969 he became a life peer for the last two years of his life. He made enemies as well as friends, as he was bound to do with what will at the time have seemed to be his extreme political views, as he fought for the equality of black people everywhere. He attacked this problem with the gusto he brought to his cricket and it is hard to think of a man, let alone a cricketer, who was more entertaining than Learie Constantine and to whom the West Indies population owes a much greater debt.

PART THREE

1946–1966

As the Second World War ended, cricket began to change to keep pace with the new order that the post-war society threw up. In Australia, which had been virtually unscathed in comparison to Europe, it was business as usual on good pitches and in sunny conditions with vibrant newcomers, including Keith Miller, Ray Lindwall, Arthur Morris and all the others, ready to burst through. A somewhat reluctant Bradman, who had suffered health problems in the war, again decided to take the helm. In England it was different. A nation that had just emerged blinking from the air-raid shelters was not immediately attuned to the demands of Test cricket against an exuberant Australia. Nonetheless, Len Hutton, Cyril Washbrook, Bill Edrich and Denis Compton were not a bad first four in the order and, with Bedser and Godfrey Evans also in the side, all was not lost. Sadly for England, this was not enough for them to be able to compete on an even basis with Australia. It was now that the West Indies emerged as a real force in world cricket, which was another problem for England.

The West Indies were the front-runners of the developing nations. Before the war, New Zealand and India in addition to the West Indies had dipped their toes into the waters of Test cricket without making too much of a splash. During the next twenty years, cricket gathered considerable strength in these parts of the world. This was excellent for a game that had until now relied upon England, Australia and South Africa. As the years were now to go by, the concept of Empire and colonialism was to be increasingly criticised and attacked, not to say abhorred. It can safely be said, however, that if it had not been for the British Empire, cricket might have advanced about as far as *boules* has done across the Channel in France. These developing countries were to play a big part in the worldwide advancement of the game during the rest of the twentieth century.

Cricket's law-makers and administrators have not always been known for their judgment and foresight and over the years some pretty ludicrous decisions have emerged from those hallowed portals at Lord's. Now, during the war, when perhaps they had nothing better to do, they came up with a beauty. An MCC Select Committee had at some stage had an idea that the game would be improved if the new ball was more readily available, suggesting one should be on offer to the fielding side every fifty-five overs. It strains credibility that in 1946 the powers-that-were at Lord's decided they were on to a good thing and this was adopted. I suppose one has to give it to them that they had not yet seen or read about Australia's likely post-war Test side, although the Victory Tests between the two countries in 1945, when admittedly neither was at full strength, should have given them a clue. Miller and Lindwall could hardly have believed their ears when they heard the news. What, too, did this futuristic piece of legislation do for the art of spin bowling? It meant that spinners became virtually superfluous. With careful preservation, enough shine would remain to make it reasonable to bowl the quicker bowlers until the next new ball was at hand. An inconvenient partnership or a badly prepared pitch might induce a captain to throw the ball to a spinner, but that was about all. It was an alteration that will have served only to slow the game down, although over rates after the war were still in the region of twenty an hour. If the authorities were today to arrange for a new ball to be available every fifty-five overs, the game would stagnate almost completely. It is now for each country to decide when the new ball should be available when it hosts Test series, but it cannot be taken until a minimum of seventy-five overs have been bowled.

The effects of this tortured decision were far-reaching. After the immediate post-war euphoria had died down, the bowlers directed their attention to the leg stump by means of inswing. Fast medium bowlers operating like this were seldom expensive and sometimes remarkably successful. Groundsmen who consistently produced grassy pitches, often with a loose surface, helped these bowlers, and inswing became all the vogue. Their appearance also produced a generation of brilliant short leg fieldsmen and wicket keepers to match. The art of bowling had taken a step forward to try to counter a bad piece of legislation and to prevent batsmen cutting loose outside the off stump. Now their options were severely restricted and of course the excitement and appeal of the game suffered. When batsmen encountered a pitch that turned, they found the ball was being consistently spun into them by off spinners and the problems remained.

These types of bowlers held sway for a decade and as a result batting became a much less glamorous art. Only those tinged with something really special could make their way as they will have liked. The game at all levels became slower and the sense of adventure grew less. Even Denis Compton found that his progress was checked. The reverse side of the coin was also disappointing because bowlers had easy pickings at their disposal and outstanding figures obtained this way and in these conditions did not guarantee success in Test cricket.

Fortunately, during the fifties three young men burst upon the scene, all of whom were high-quality fast bowlers, Fred Trueman, Brian Statham and Frank Tyson. Peter May and later Colin Cowdrey, their batting equivalents, also appeared to help Hutton and Compton and Co. It was a combination of these players that enabled England to win back the Ashes in 1953 and hold on to them in 1954/55 and 1956. In the last series, the off spin of Jim Laker also played a huge part, especially with his 19/90 at Old Trafford.

While all this was going on out on the field, the finances of the English game became under increasing pressure. All sorts of outside income had to be found and the counties inevitably put greater dependence on their annual handout from the MCC. This came from the profits the MCC made from the Test matches and all their attendant income. Then the sixties dawned and cricket, like the rest of society, became increasingly restless in its desire for change. The number of amateurs had decreased markedly for many could not afford to play the game at their own expense. A few found sponsorship and some became county secretaries, but amateurs had by now become a threatened species. This obviously had an effect on a game that needed as many independent spirits as could be found. In the winter of 1962/63 the authorities took the final step and abolished the distinction between amateurs and professionals.

It was in 1963 that the first one-day competition, the Gillette Cup, came into existence. It immediately caught the public imagination and was a help to the game's finances. It was during the sixties, too, that the counties were allowed to employ overseas players in an attempt to lift their standards and to raise the popularity of the game. The residual downside of this is that it leaves fewer opportunities for players who are qualified for England. By the mid-sixties, the post-war euphoria, which had produced big gates and plenty of excitement, seemed a long while ago. In twenty years the face of English cricket had changed almost beyond recognition.

The characters I have written about in the following section were all desperately needed to lift England out of obscurity and to inject some fun and inspiration into both county and Test cricket at a difficult time. Colin Ingleby-Mackenzie may not have been the batsman that Denis Compton was, or a bowler to compare with Keith Miller or Garry Sobers, but he was the last of the old fashioned English amateurs.

One of the universal blemishes on the game at this time was the impurity of several important bowling actions round the world. The West Indies had Griffith. The problem came to a head in Australia during England's tour in 1958/59 when Ian Meckiff, Jim Burke and Keith Slater were all thought to throw. In the same series, Gordon Rorke dragged his back foot such a long way that when he released the ball he was well down the pitch. England had had trouble with left-arm spinner Tony Lock and fast bowler Peter Loader. The Australians had coped swiftly and decisively with the issue, but other countries dragged their feet. To solve the problem of dragging, the MCC, the custodians of the Laws, changed the no-ball rule so that the front foot now had to be in contact with the front or popping crease at the moment of delivery. The old rule required the back foot to be in contact with the return or bowling crease. This had the desired effect as far as draggers were concerned, although it made the job of the umpire harder for now he could only call the no-ball much later. This hardly gave him time to look up and adjudicate if there was then an appeal against the batsman at the other end. It is a problem that remains to this day and is not made any easier by so-called electronic expertise, which surely must be seen to be foolproof before it can be fully embraced.

COLIN INGLEBY-MACKENZIE

ENGLISH cricket is always badly in need of fiercely independent spirits like Colin Ingleby-Mackenzie. It was his sparkling character, his enormous charm, his up-boys-and-at-'em approach to the game together with his gambling instincts and his ability to make opposing captains see the game through his eyes, especially when it came to making declarations, that enabled Hampshire to win the County Championship for the first time in 1962. No challenge was too great for him, no set of odds too forbidding and no situation however desperate was without its funny side.

Hampshire have been extremely lucky to have had two such uninhibited captains. As we have already seen, Lionel Tennyson was in charge after the Great War. He masterminded his campaigns largely from the bar in White's at the top of St James's Street where 150 years earlier the Duke of Richmond and his chums had plotted the path that the game was going to follow. Full of vintage port, they then staggered down the hill to the Star and Garter in Pall Mall where they dished out some more to the lads before unsheathing their pens, thumping the table, and writing down the Laws of the game. Tennyson and Ingleby-Mackenzie would have been in the vanguard of that lot. As it was, Ingleby-Mackenzie probably decided on some of his field placings with the help of the salt, pepper and mustard pots in the coffee room at White's. If Ingleby-Mackenzie had lived earlier and had played his cricket at a time when the amateur ethic reigned supreme and not when it was merely an amusing throw back to a wicked past, he, like Tennyson, would surely have been given the chance to lead England out of trouble – and the side would have been the better for it.

Ingleby-Mackenzie had the undying respect of all his players, with the exception of his leading batsman, Roy Marshall. The Bajan batted as if he had been born with pints of the amateur ethic coursing through his bloodstream, but when he took off his pads he put away frivolous things and turned into one of those Victorian matrons who were forever trying to pull their skirts down even lower to hide a recalcitrant ankle. Ingleby-Mackenzie, who had bounced his way uproariously through five years at Eton, was a decent enough left-handed batsman. In county cricket he saw it beholden upon him to swashbuckle with the result that there were more low scores than there should have been, but when the big ones came along, it was worth crossing a continent at least in order to be there. He batted with the chuckle that was permanently around his lips and was, and still is, the most engaging of men. Ingleby-Mackenzie's statistics were the least important part about him. The MCC and Lord's is a better place for his two years at the helm as president of MCC in 1997/98.

His great confidant while he was captain of Hampshire was his wicket keeper, Leo Harrison. They travelled round the country in the same car, staying as often as not with one of the captain's friends. Ingleby-Mackenzie's permanent instruction to Harrison was, 'Bring your dinner jacket with you in case we get lucky.' It was probably the understatement of the millennium when Harrison said: 'Ingleby was not a cricket disciplinarian. Whenever we finished at places like Leicester, Nottingham or Derby that were within reach of London, he was off to the metropolis the moment the game was over with a wave and a cheery, "See you at Southampton (or wherever) in the morning."' Off he would tootle – almost certainly to the bar in White's to work out some more subtle field placings for Derek Shackleton. The next morning he would be there, the same as ever, ready to get to work to brainwash another captain into making another indiscreet declaration. He defined his leadership skills and his rigid insistence on law and order within his side when, after a stirring victory over Kent at Canterbury in which he had made a hundred, he was approached by a journalist. He was asked what he put his success down to. 'Wine, women and song,' came the immediate reply followed by the usual chuckle. The next question was: 'What time do you like to see your players in bed?' 'I think it's a good thing if they try and get in before breakfast,' he answered.

Ingleby-Mackenzie swelled the subscription list of *Sporting Life* from the age of fourteen at Eton and never looked back. There was one occasion when Hampshire had finished a county match on Tuesday, which also happened to be the first day of Royal Ascot, and the players had driven on to Leicester for the following day's game. A group of them were having breakfast together the next morning when Henry Horton looked up from his newspaper and said, 'Leicester did well yesterday.' Ingleby-Mackenzie's immediate reply was, 'Yes, a hat trick. He's not a bad performer.' Horton was bemused, but most of the others realised that their captain was thinking of Lester, as in Piggott, and not Leicester, as in county. The stories about Ingleby-Mackenzie are legion and they all show him up in the best possible light.

While captaining Hampshire, Ingleby-Mackenzie was always prepared to take chances no one else would have considered and he mostly got away with it. Although he was not the greatest of fielders, he was a better batsman than his record shows and his players adored him and always pulled hard for him. It was his attitude and charisma that enabled him to get something extra out of them. The final word comes from Harrison. 'Ingleby was a great man. There is no question about that.' What would both Hampshire and England give for an Ingleby-Mackenzie today?

MARTIN DONNELLY

ARTIN DONNELLY was one of only two batsmen to have
made hundreds at Lord's for his country in a Test match, for
the Gentlemen against the Players, and in the University match, a
feat also achieved by Percy Chapman. These facts are remarkable
enough and yet they tell only part of the story. Donnelly, a left-
hander, used his bat as if it was an extension of his character. He
was the most charming of men who was full of that delightful,
unostentatious old world courtesy. He never projected himself.
There was the same unhurried elegance about him at the crease.
His strokes were never rude to the bowler; the ball was despatched
with grace and timing and almost a note of apology, unless it was
with the hook. He had the sort of clean, uncomplicated good looks
every girl's mother longs for and it would have been no surprise if
he had been caught beating a track to the Ealing Studios to play an
awfully nice major in a war film.

The night after he made 142 for Oxford against Cambridge, generally considered to have been as good an innings as anyone could
remember being played in that match, he took part in a light-
hearted broadcast back to New Zealand with Denzil Batchelor, at
that time C.B. Fry's Man Friday. Just before they went on the air,
Donnelly asked Batchelor not to speak too effusively of his innings,
even though his last 113 runs had come in an hour and three-quarters. He was modest to a fault.

The ball flowed effortlessly from his bat. His two most beautiful
strokes were the straight drive and the late cut. The on drive, the

most difficult stroke of all, the leg hit and the hook, although there was an element of earthiness about the latter because he hit the ball with ferocious power, were not far behind. His entertainment value did not end there, either, because he was one of the great cover points who lured many batsmen to their destruction as they set off in search of a seemingly safe single. Donnelly was something of a shooting star, not only because of the way in which he scored his runs, but also because of the short time he was on the stage. Most of his 219 first-class innings were played in England, although he was born a New Zealander and played his Test cricket for the country of his birth; he did play one rugger international for England. After one first-class match he was chosen for New Zealand's tour of England in 1937 where, as a nineteen-year-old, he made his mark. There was one ball on that tour that he particularly remembered. He made a pair of spectacles in the last game before the Lord's Test and he made a duck in the first innings of that match. Another failure and he would have been out of the side. His first ball in the second innings, bowled by Alf Gover, was a bouncer, which he hooked with a thunderous ferocity for four.

In the war he fought in North Africa and Italy with the New Zealand Division. When it was over he came back to England and in 1945, playing for the Dominions against England, he put together the first of all his remarkable innings at Lord's where, in the first innings, he made 133 out of a total of 307. Walter Hammond made two centuries in the match and Keith Miller 185 in the second innings. The Dominions won, by 45 runs, with eight minutes of the third day remaining and no wonder *Wisden* described it as 'one of the finest games ever seen'.

The following year came that 142 in the University match. The year after that, 1947, he put the bowling of the Players to the sword. It was in C.B. Fry's box that Batchelor heard *The Times* correspondent give it as his view that 'The best bat in England is Martin Donnelly. The second best bat in England is Walter Hammond.' In this same inner sanctum, CB, when asked which of the left-handers of his day he would rate superior to Donnelly, replied unhesitatingly, 'Not one.' When forced, he admitted that Clem Hill and Frank Woolley 'were also rather good'. Donnelly's 206 for New Zealand against England in the Lord's Test of 1949 was more the cement around which the innings was built rather than a knock studded with remarkable and imaginative strokeplay.

That was his last year as a competitive cricketer. He was offered a job in Australia where he settled in the Western Suburbs of Sydney. He and his wife, Elizabeth, became the kindest and most generous of hosts to all of us visiting Australia for one form of cricketing duty or another.

WG Grace, the father of the game as we know it, with the magical KS Ranjitsinhji outside Ranji's house at Shillinglee Park in 1908. Rain had stopped play.

Alfred Mynn, a fast bowling all-rounder, was perhaps the most formidable of all the early players.

Charles Fry – a classical scholar at Oxford and a classical performer on the cricket field. Fry was in the frame to become king of Albania.

The hardest hitter of them all, Gilbert Jessop's 104 in an hour and a quarter against Australia at The Oval in 1902 was his *tour de force*.

Victor Trumper's genius, like his personality, was irresistible. The strokes flowed, he cared not a jot for figures and his generosity was legendary.

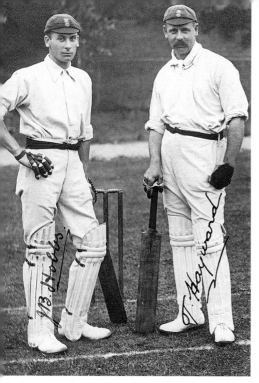

A young and serene Jack Hobbs, who was such a pivotal figure, with his guide and counsellor Tom Hayward, who was also born and reared in Cambridge.

A playful WG at Shillinglee Park with other guests of Ranji's. WG would have fancied himself as a Maharajah or even as a Jam Sahib.

The England party to tour Australia in 1911–12, photographed in a delightfully dated and most impressive display of hats. They won the series 4–1.

Left: Arthur Mailey's ink drawing of an avuncular looking Warwick Armstrong. On the right we have inimitable self-caricature.

Below: The Hon. Lionel Tennyson, at his most aristocratic, saunters out to have a look at the pitch before The Oval Test in 1921.

The youthful and capless Don Bradman at Headingley in 1930 on his highly composed way to a small matter of 334.

It's almost all over. Don Bradman enjoying his testimonial game in Melbourne in December 1948 when he contented himself with 123.

The young, hopeful and good-looking Denis Compton in his first season at Lord's, with that wise old owl Patsy Hendren in his thirtieth.

Martin Donnelly from New Zealand, one of only two players to have made hundreds at Lord's in the University Match, the Gentlemen v. Players and a Test match.

Denis Compton sweeps backward of square in his last game for Middlesex, against Worcestershire at Lord's. He made 143.

Learie Constantine *in excelsis* against Middlesex at Lord's in 1928. In between making 86 and 103, he picked up seven wickets for 57.

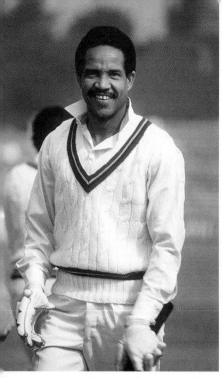

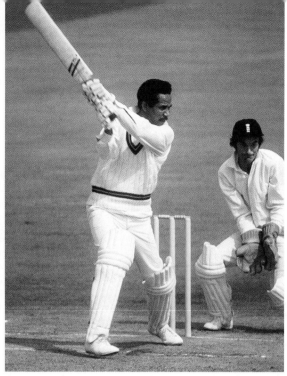

No one enjoyed his cricket more than Garry Sobers, surely the game's greatest ever all-rounder. Here he is in his last Test at Lord's, in 1973.

Garry Sobers means business through backward point, watched by the delightfully impish Alan Knott.

The irresistible and flamboyant Keith Miller, smiling even in mid-stroke at Arundel in 1956, is watched over by Billy Griffith, later to be secretary of the MCC.

Colin Ingleby-Mackenzie's humorous devil-may-care approach to cricket has done wonders for the game. He is watching Jim Swanton's Arabs with Simon Parker-Bowles.

A genius cut down in his prime. The Nawab of Pataudi lost an eye in a car accident while at Oxford, but still went on to make a double century against England.

Colin Milburn gets to work on that fearsome West Indian fast bowler Wes Hall. This photograph describes perfectly the essence of both men.

DENIS COMPTON

D ENIS COMPTON was as truly innovative as Ranjitsinhji. While Ranji invented the leg glance, Compton's trademark was the paddle sweep to fine leg, which had never been played in that way before, although Gilbert Jessop thought about it. If this stroke was Compton's contribution to the coaching book, it was by no means the only way in which he brought joy and wonderment, not to say bewilderment, to those who watched him. In some ways he stood accepted technique on its head as he darted hither and thither, taken there by feet that danced for him like some Rudolf Nureyev, and seldom left him out of position. If they did, his extraordinary ability to improvise took over. At the end of 1947, his *annus mirabilis* with 3,816 runs and eighteen centuries, a record that is unlikely ever to be beaten, he played for the Champion County, Middlesex, against the Rest at The Oval. During his innings of 210, which he felt was the best he ever played, he came down the wicket to Tom Goddard, the Gloucestershire off spinner. He managed to spike one boot with the other, and he fell on his chest like an uncoordinated sack of potatoes. As he fell, instinct took over and somehow he managed to unwind a sweep that sent the ball out of the middle of the bat to the square-leg boundary. Even when he found himself in this predicament, he managed to conjure up a split-second balance that enabled him to play an authentic stroke.

Although he often appeared to defy the basic technical require-ments, his game was based on a perfect understanding of them. It was from this plinth that he was able to improvise as he did. The icing on the cake was an incomparable sense of natural timing that took the visual bite out of even the most violent of strokes – even though fielders everywhere were left ruefully wringing their hands. In the immediate post-war years heroes were badly needed. Compton was as big a sporting hero as England can ever have had. His filmstar good looks, together with the charm, the slightly nervous smile and the black hair glistening with much-advertised Brylcreem, shone down on the public from myriad hoardings. He was every schoolboy's hero, except perhaps for the cussed Yorkshire lot who preferred Len Hutton. His enduring popularity was underlined when, in January 2003, nearly six years after his death, he was voted the winner of the Greatest Sporting Briton contest in the *Daily Telegraph*, two places ahead of Ian Botham. Compton, like his great friend and spiritual brother, Keith Miller, was a colossal hit with the ladies, although in this aspect of his life Compton may have lost concentration sooner than his Australian rival.

Although his parents gave him every encouragement to play cricket and football, there was no family history of brilliance at either, although his brother Leslie was a most competent wicket keeper for Middlesex and a shrewd and solid centre-half for Arsenal. It was in terms of character that Denis was a genetic freak. There was a delightful happy-go-lucky insouciance combined with a distinguished and unfailing absent-mindedness. He joined the Lord's groundstaff in 1933 and two years later he was given a chance to play for MCC against Suffolk at Felixstowe. The side went down by train and, on arriving, Denis discovered that he had left his cricket bag behind at Lord's. He sent an urgent wire for them to forward it and the reply was not long in coming: 'Bag on the way. You'll leave your head behind one day.' Denis was five foot eight in his stockinged feet and for the first day's play he was forced to borrow gear from his good friend, George Brown, the old Hampshire player. He was fitted out with size twelve boots and trousers that were four inches too long. Back in his own stuff the next day, he made a hundred.

He was, too, spectacularly absent-minded when it came to running between the wickets. I use the words absent-minded deliberately because if such a talented batsman had been prepared to put his mind to the problem he must surely have solved it. John Warr, one of his Middlesex captains, said that an initial call from Denis never ought to be regarded as anything more than an opening bid. Ian Peebles, a Middlesex colleague before the war, wrote benevolently about his running. 'There was a rather endearing quality about the whole performance. Whereas the methodical runner is like a traveller who consults weather, routes and timetables, Denis was more akin to the lover of nature who, seeing a glimpse of sunshine, snatches up his hat and sets out just for the joy of life.' Denis's views probably coincided with those of Robert Louis Stevenson who wrote: 'To travel hopefully is a better thing than to arrive . . .' He even ran out his brother Leslie for a duck in his benefit match.

Failure to remember his kit was a recurring theme. In 1955 England played the Third Test against South Africa at Old Trafford. Denis had forgotten to turn up when England practised the day before the match. As a result Peter May, England's captain, and Gubby Allen, the chairman of selectors, decided to drop him from the side. When they arrived in the dressing room the following morning with their minds made up they were mildly disconcerted to find that the only England player to have arrived was Denis who was all ready for a net. They relented. What they did not know was that he had left his bat in London. When the other players arrived, he asked his Middlesex colleague Fred Titmus, who was twelfth man, to lend him a bat. A not very distinguished and fairly elderly blade that looked as if it might just have been a family heirloom was hastily produced. Denis waved it around, pronounced it OK and proceeded to go out and score 158 and 71 with it. Neil Adcock, the South African fast bowler, who was one of his opponents in that match, said he had never seen batting like it.

Compton improvised like some cricketing James Bond and, like

007, he gave the impression of making it all up as he went along. Behind this slightly hazardous exterior there was an organisation of sublime thoroughness based on instinct. Compton feared no bowler, just as Bond feared no gangster however sophisticated. But Compton was free-range while Bond was scripted. In 1950/51 in Australia, England's batsmen including Compton himself were somewhat bemused by the unorthodox spin bowling of Jack Iverson. They were playing Victoria and Compton was batting with David Sheppard, the future Bishop of Liverpool. Runs were coming too slowly and, between overs, Sheppard came down the pitch and sought Compton's advice. It was: 'You go on just as you are. I'll attend to the antics.' 007 might have had an identical exchange with one of his more nubile assistants with Ernst Stavro Blofeld just round the corner.

While cricket was Compton's main occupation, football kept him busy most winters until his knee brought an end to all that in 1950. The trouble had begun in 1938 when, playing for Arsenal, he had collided with the Charlton Athletic goalkeeper, Sid Hobbins. Seventeen years later, after Compton had had to have his knee-cap removed, he received a letter: 'Dear Mr Compton, I am terribly sorry for the trouble I have caused you over all these years.' It was signed by Sid Hobbins. The knee forced him out of football in 1950 but not until he had played an important role in Arsenal's FA Cup victory that year over Liverpool. He had a poor first half and was somewhat dejected at half-time. The Arsenal manager, Tom Whittaker, had a word with him. 'Denis, you are giving up football. You have just forty-five minutes of your career left. Now, I want you to go out there and give every ounce you've got.' The trainer endorsed these comments with a good strong whisky – a half-time incentive that has possibly gone out of fashion. That was all the encouragement he needed and, with his right knee bandaged up as it had been all season, he went out, had a marvellous second half and helped Arsenal win the Cup. Of course, it affected his mobility on the cricket field too, and from now on was a recurring factor in a career that would have gone on for longer and been even more successful but for this wretched joint. It is an awful thought, but one can only wonder what the humourless present-day coaches would have made of a player with such a suspect knee.

Compton played some extraordinary innings for England. In 1946/47 at the Adelaide Oval he made a hundred in each innings against Australia. In the second, he was involved in an interminable rearguard action with Godfrey Evans, who batted for more than a hundred minutes before he scored his first run. During that innings, Compton sat firmly on his easy-going nature and had the better of two conversational bouts with no less an opponent than Don Bradman. It was his job to protect Evans and for over after over he refused to take a single to the deep-set field until the sixth or seventh ball of the over. Bradman thought he would be able to pull rank over Compton. He walked over to him looking annoyed.

'Denis,' he said sharply, 'this is not cricket. Do you realise that all these people are here to see cricket and what you are doing is not the way cricket should be played.'

'All right, Don,' Denis answered, 'perhaps you are right . . . but if you bring your fielders in and set a normal field, we can put things right, can't we?'

He set a normal field and Compton hit the first ball for four. Bradman came over again.

'I am not going to give you runs,' he said.

'Then we go back to the same procedure,' Compton answered.

He was using his feet to the spinners and, as he was wearing spikes, he naturally made a few marks on the pitch. It was fair enough. It was not long before Bradman began another conversation.

'Denis,' he said, 'look at this wicket. We've got to bat next . . . look at your spike marks.'

'That's the way I play, Don,' Compton answered, 'you know that. You can't blame me for those marks. I am terribly sorry.'

'Ah, but we have to bat on this.'

'Well, Don,' Compton answered, 'I am terribly sorry . . . but I'm playing for our side.'

Bradman did not like to be thwarted, but Compton was in no mood to be intimidated and, happily for England, was prepared to rattle his sabre every bit as much as the Don.

In 1948, in the First Test against Australia at Trent Bridge, England began their second innings 344 runs behind and lost 2 early wickets. With all too little support at the other end, Compton battled for almost seven hours while making 184 before he slipped while hooking at Miller and fell on his stumps. At Old Trafford in the Third, England soon lost 2 wickets in their first innings and Compton took up the fight. Before long Lindwall bowled him a bouncer at which he played a powerful hook and was hit a nasty blow on the forehead. He was helped off the field and had several stitches inserted in the wound. He then announced he was ready to return to the fray, but the medics managed to keep him in the pavilion until the score was 119/5. Compton was still not out at the end of the day when the score was 231/7. The next day he received great support from Alec Bedser and they put on 121 for the eighth wicket until Compton ran his partner out. He called him for a quick single to Sam Loxton, one of the best of cover points. When the innings ended he had batted for four hours and twenty minutes while making 145 not out.

The following winter he toured South Africa with England. In a game against Northern Transvaal at Benoni, he made 300 in 181 minutes in a remarkable exhibition of strokeplay. The first hundred took him sixty-six minutes, the second seventy-eight and the third thirty-seven. Then, in 1954, at Trent Bridge, always a favourite ground, he played an extraordinary innings of 278 in the Second Test against the first Pakistan side to tour England. *Wisden*, never given to going over the top, was moved to report that he made his runs: 'with a torrent of strokes, orthodox and improvised, crashing and delicate, against which Kardar [Pakistan's captain] could not set a field, and the bowlers knew not where to pitch.' When

Compton was asked about the innings, he replied, trying to keep a straight face, that once he had reached a hundred all he was aiming to do was to get himself out.

Perhaps his most remarkable innings of all came right at the end. In 1956, after he had had that knee-cap removed, he inched his way back to county cricket in the second half of the season. He was chosen to play in the Fifth Test at The Oval after England had won the Ashes. He made 94 in what Don Bradman described as the best innings of the series before Alan Davidson held a pretty good one at leg slip. He retired the following year, scoring a hundred against Worcestershire in his last county match. After that, he played an occasional first-class match for a year or two. In 1959 he turned out for MCC against Cambridge University at Lord's and made 71 runs that prompted Neville Cardus to write that this innings 'was virtually a restoration, not to say a resurrection, of his genius, brilliant, original, happy'. 'Happy', that is the operative word in a description of Denis. It was an innings I had the luck to watch, mostly from mid on and third man.

Then there was a small matter of 613 wickets, 25 of them in Test matches, with a joyful mixture of left-handed chinamen and googlies. At Headingley in 1948 when Australia scored a record 404/3 to win in the fourth innings, it was only poor captaincy by Norman Yardley and even poorer fielding and wicket keeping that prevented Compton from bowling England to victory. His bowling, like his batting and fielding, always seemed to be accompanied by the tinkle of laughter. No wonder people flocked to the grounds to see him. All of this and he was totally and utterly without side. There can never have been a more likeable cricketer.

There are so many definitive stories of Compton and maybe this last reflects the man and his ability as well as any. Soon after the war, probably in 1947, Walter Robins said to him during a tea interval, 'It's a funny thing a strong chap like you can't drive the ball straight. We never see you hit it over the bowler's head.'

'Yes, it is funny,' Compton replied. 'Look out for the third ball after tea.'

A few minutes later the third ball bowled came rocketing into the members' seats in front of the pavilion. As the umpire signalled six, Compton waved his bat cheerfully to his colleagues on the Middlesex boundary. Few cricketers have used what the gods gave them to such wonderful effect, and yet then came the knee. Those whom the gods love . . .

KEITH MILLER

KEITH MILLER'S natural habitat should have been Hollywood. If he had surveyed the Pacific Ocean from Malibu rather than Sydney, it is easy to imagine him in the thick of it with David Niven and the others as they scaled those cliffs on the way to silencing the guns of Navarone. He may have been Australian to the core, but heart-throbs are international currency. Miller was tall and loose-limbed with filmstar good looks, an unanswerable charm the ladies could not resist, outrageously uncontrollable floppy dark hair, an instinct to make friends and an indefinable and incalculable athletic ability. As luck would have it, he settled for cricket after tumbling around the skies of northern Europe in the Second War as a sergeant pilot at the controls of a Mosquito. He was one of those few who showed a form of bravery it is hard for those of us who were not involved to understand and appreciate. In a sense, the war provided Miller with the perfect platform from which to launch his compelling character. After three and a half years of fighting for his life and for the civilised world, cricket could never be anything other than a game for him, a matter of fun, and he never let anyone forget it. Life for him was always fun and an amusing challenge. In 1944 Miller crash-landed his Mosquito near King's Lynn. Within an hour he was playing in a nearby soccer match. He found it difficult to sympathise with modern cricketers when they complain of the pressure they are under. His answer to that was that when you were flying a Mosquito and saw two Messerschmitts through your rear-view mirror, that was pressure.

It was appropriate that he should have been christened Keith Ross Miller after those two intrepid aviators, Sir Keith and Sir Ross Smith, who made the first-ever flight from England to Australia. That was a challenge Miller would have relished – with or without the Messerschmitts.

There was a charming turbulence about Miller's cricketing career, just as there was about his life. Miller played under three long-term Australian captains and two of them, Don Bradman and Ian Johnson, both of whom were too straitlaced for his taste, he will at times have driven mad. The third, Lindsay Hassett, had a wonderfully impish sense of humour and would have found Miller much more his cup of tea and would have been able to shrug his shoulders and laugh at his more reckless antics, and to humour him if things became tense. At Southend, in 1948, the Australians made 721 in the day against Essex. Miller went in to bat in the middle of a carnage that he found mildly sickening and allowed Trevor Bailey to bowl him first ball. Bradman, who was at the other end, was not amused and let his feelings be known. He had never been worried by cheap runs and was not going to allow them to upset him right at the end of his career. The Don was nothing if not relentless and made an inevitable century.

Another of Miller's colleagues that day was Ian Johnson, who was to take over the captaincy from Hassett. He was prim and proper with an unrelaxed sense of humour. Probably in order to keep up appearances, he strenuously denied that Miller had given Bailey his wicket and insisted that the ball was a fast yorker. When Johnson was made captain of Australia there were many who felt the job should have been given to Miller. It was a sign of the times that the authorities felt that Miller was too hot to handle. In writing about Miller in Denzil Batchelor's anthology *Great Cricketers*, Johnson makes slightly patronising allowances for some of Miller's excesses and, in places, tends to damn with faint praise. In reading the piece it is possible to feel the tension that existed between them. It will almost certainly have been made worse by the fact that Miller will not have given a damn about Johnson or his views and have made no secret of this. If Miller had been in charge and not Johnson, one can only wonder if the Australian tour of England in 1956 would have been such a disaster for Australia. Miller would surely have created a more combative frame of mind with which to deal with the off spin of Jim Laker (19/90 and all that at Old Trafford). Johnson did have enough of a sense of humour to tell one excellent story about Miller, even if there may have been just a smidgeon of underlying distaste.

Miller was playing golf one day in South Africa with a colleague, Alan Walker, who went on to play for Nottinghamshire. It was at a time when there was much talk about the deadly South African snake, the black mamba. Walker had hit his ball into the bushes and went to look for it. Johnson takes up the story.

> Miller waited for Walker ahead of a ladies' four-ball but suddenly there was a scream from the undergrowth and Walker emerged holding the leg of his trousers, yelling, 'Keith, Keith, a snake's up my leg and he's bitten me. I've got hold of it. What'll I do now?'
>
> Keith, startled, looked back at the ladies, who were now quite close, and suggested that all Alan could do was take off his trousers and shake the snake out while he himself waited with a golf club. Keith helped the trembling Walker undo his pants, then stood back ready to deal the deathblow. Walker took off his trousers, shook them . . . and out fell a lizard, six inches long. Miller solemnly presented both lizard and trousers to the lady golfers.

Miller seldom did anything by halves. At the age of sixteen, when he was very short, his ambition was to become a jockey, which was appropriate enough as racing was always his second love in life. In the next twelve months he grew at least a foot and he was only seventeen when he made his debut for Victoria against Tasmania, and made 181 in his first innings. He played on and off for Victoria in the next three and a half years before he was called to the colours. Then came those death-defying episodes in the Mosquitoes from his base at an aerodrome in Norfolk where stories of his exploits are still told in the local pubs.

He first made his mark as a cricketer in England when, in 1944, playing in a one-day Bank Holiday match at Lord's between England and Australia, he made 85 out of the Australian total of 193. In the following year he played for the Australian Services team in the five Victory Test Matches and his average of 63.28 was the highest on either side. In those days he was a batsman pure and simple, although he picked up 10 wickets when he was used as a stopgap bowler. His supreme innings that summer, which is still remembered although by increasingly few people, was his 185 that enabled the Dominions to beat England at Lord's. He was 61 not out on the second evening and scored another 124 in ninety minutes before lunch on the last morning. At one stage he helped Learie Constantine put on 117 in forty-five minutes. The ubiquitous Sir Pelham Warner said of Miller's innings, which produced seven sixes, 'In an experience of first-class cricket of nearly sixty years I have never seen such hitting.' One straight drive off Eric Hollies glanced off the roof of the broadcasting box above the England dressing room. If it had not been for the box, the ball would have cleared the pavilion and enabled Miller to match Albert Trott's massive blow in 1899.

Miller himself wrote about the Victory Tests and in doing so summed up to perfection the man that he is.

> When all is said and done it boils down to the attitude in which the game of cricket is played. The best cricket I ever played in was during the 1945 Victory Test series in England and I think we just about had cricket in its right perspective. Cricket was a game and not a war. We all knew only too well what war really was. The matter of life and death was behind us. After six years we were back to normal, we were into something the result did not mean anything more than a pat on the back for the winner and a drink together in the bar. What a pity it is that cricket is not played in that way today. The importance attached to winning and losing becomes hopelessly distorted.

The summer of 1945 was the beginning of a cricketing metamorphosis in Miller who, until then, had been only a batsman. It was now that his bowling began to come into the reckoning. In March 1946, he played for Australia under Bill Brown in the single Test match they played against New Zealand in Wellington. Miller did not bowl in the first innings and had taken 2/6 in the second when his back went. This back injury, the legacy of crash landing in the war, was to haunt the rest of his career. He was fit again for the start of the series later that year against Walter Hammond's England side. It was then that he joined forces with Ray Lindwall and they shared the new ball. On his first outing in Brisbane, Miller took 7/60 and his career as one of the most dangerous fast bowlers in the game was under way. In fact, from then until the end of his career in 1956, he was more destructive as a bowler than he was as a batsman.

Miller was at his best when his side was in crisis. It was then that he played his most commanding innings. If there was nothing in the situation or runs were two-a-penny, his mind soon switched to other things. His threshold of boredom could be exceedingly low. In 1950/51, England were having great trouble reading Jack Iverson's unorthodox spin. 'Why don't you chaps get into Jack and beat the hell out of him?' Miller asked Neville Cardus. 'New South Wales are playing Victoria next week. Come along and I'll show you.' Cardus went along and watched Miller destroy Iverson with considerable relish. It was often the same with his bowling. In Sydney in January 1951, England, who were two matches down, had won the toss and looked like making full use of an excellent pitch. Len Hutton and Reg Simpson had taken them to 128/1 when, shortly before the tea interval, Lindsay Hassett threw the ball to Miller, as much as anything to give the other bowlers a rest. At a deceptive medium pace he now got rid of Hutton and Denis Compton in the same over and removed Simpson immediately after tea. In twenty-eight balls he had taken 3 for 5 and effectively won the match and the series for Australia. The England opener, Cyril Washbrook, once said, 'If Keith had never gone in for batting, he would have been the most dangerous fast bowler ever.' It was at Melbourne in December 1954 with England and Australia at one-all, that he told his captain, Ian Johnson, the night before that because of his knee he would not be able to bowl the next day. After some loosening up exercises in the pavilion the next morning he revised that opinion. He bowled for ninety minutes before lunch and again took 3/5, this time in nine overs.

In the very next Test match, at Adelaide, England needed 94 to win the match and the Ashes. Miller grabbed the new ball and in no time England were 18/3, prompting Hutton, in the pavilion, to exclaim, 'They've done us – the buggers,' or words to that effect, to which Denis Compton, the next man in, was quick to offer the alternative point of view. Peter May went soon afterwards when Miller held a brilliant diving catch in the covers and it was left to Compton to see England home.

Miller thrived on lost causes. His last hundred was made in 1959 for Nottinghamshire against Cambridge University and, needless to say, this was not in a lost cause. He reached his hundred by kind permission of the author of this book who, to almost universal delight, dropped an easy catch at deep midwicket when Miller was in the sixties.

The last word on Miller comes from the Australian cricket writer Ray Robinson. 'Long before Keith Miller gets near the wicket you can tell that something extraordinary is going to happen. The erect set of his capless head on his square shoulders, the loose swing of his long legs, the half-smile on his handsome face and his ease of manner all signify that no ordinary cricketer approaches.' His tally of 2,958 runs at an average of 36.97 and 170 wickets at 22.97 tell nothing either of the way they came or the man who produced them. Keith Miller was so much more than just a cricketer.

ROY MARSHALL

O PENING batsmen can be a perverse lot. Anyone who batted as magnificently and extravagantly as Roy Marshall should have been nothing if not a happy-go-lucky extrovert, just as anyone who batted with such yawning boredom as Australia's Bill Lawry should, logically, have been as animated as a Centurion tank with engine failure and not the life and soul of the party. Marshall was an introspective gloomy guts and yet he batted like a tidal wave on a good day. While he was perhaps the one discordant note in Colin Ingleby-Mackenzie's dressing room when he took Hampshire to their first ever County Championship title in 1962, no one will have played a greater part in taking them to the title. In his career, which ended in 1972, he scored more than 35,000 runs with an average of only 35. It should have been higher and was evidence of the devil-may-care attitude he brought to his batting, but which did not spill over into his everyday life.

There can never have been a more exciting opening batsman. Marshall came out to bat as if it was his avowed intention to hit all six balls of the first over to the boundary or even over it. John Woodcock, the famous cricket correspondent of *The Times*, told me that he thought that if Marshall had stayed on to play with the West Indies, he would have been as good as the three Ws, Frank Worrell, Everton Weekes and Clyde Walcott. Leo Harrison, who kept wicket for Hampshire and played for many years with Marshall, thought that this was a little over the top. Nonetheless, the fact that serious argument should have been entered into shows how good Marshall must have been.

Behind his apparently amiable rimless glasses, there lurked an extraordinary mind. Here was a man who was determined to make the cricket ball and the bowler suffer as much as he could. If you arrived twenty minutes late for a Hampshire match and they were batting, Marshall might have scored at least 30 runs. His driving, square cutting and hooking were his most memorable strokes and they were played with an unforgettable West Indian exuberance. The fact that he was prepared to trot them all out in the first over of the day made them seem even more memorable. His advantage to the side was that he scored his runs so fast that he gave his bowlers more time to bowl the opposition out twice. His huge advantage to spectators was that he made all but the most partisan supporters of Hampshire's opponents feel that the county game was after all worth watching.

It was inexplicable that Marshall and his wonderfully imaginative and flamboyant captain, Ingleby-Mackenzie, the swashbuckling Old Etonian, should have found the dressing room almost too small to hold them both. The batting of Marshall should have been exactly in step with the character of his captain. Without Ingleby-Mackenzie's flare and willingness to take what the kind would describe as a calculated risk, Hampshire would never have won the title in 1962. Without Marshall's ability to destroy an attack at the start of an innings, Ingleby-Mackenzie would never have been in the position to take those extraordinary gambles. On one occasion against Gloucestershire, at Portsmouth, Ingleby-Mackenzie declared Hampshire's second innings when Marshall was 96 not out. If they had scored any more runs, the final equation would never have enticed the opposition. In the dressing room when the players had left the field after the declaration, Marshall threw his bat at his captain. Another paradox was that Marshall, in Ingleby-Mackenzie's words, 'was in the first eleven as a serious cocktailer and used his elbow to its fullest extent.' Here, one would have thought, was surely a meeting point for Hampshire's captain and his best batsman.

Roy Marshall was born in Barbados for whom he made his first-class debut just before his sixteenth birthday, and he played four Test matches for the West Indies. He toured England with John Goddard's side in 1950 when Sonny Ramadhin and Alf Valentine spun the West Indies to victory, but he did not play in any of the Tests. Then, in 1953, he decided to come to England and qualified for Hampshire two years later. He was an extraordinary paradox. On the one hand he batted against all-comers, going in first, with supreme confidence and scoring his runs more quickly than any of his contemporaries. Yet he was always very nervous and while he was a splendid ground fielder, he was one of the worst catchers in the first-class game. He was never an easy man in the pavilion and, if he had been, he would almost certainly have been a regular member of the West Indies side and would never therefore have come to England to play county cricket. When John Woodcock asked him why he did not score at least 4,000 runs a year, he answered unemotionally saying, 'It was not for me.' When playing for Hampshire he could be almost guaranteed to score runs against the best bowlers he came across. When he found he was up against someone who was roundly considered to be not much more than a net bowler, he would often get out straight away. There was no doubt that for many years Marshall was the most dramatic batsman in England. If one were within a hundred miles of where Hampshire were playing a game, it would have been folly not to have taken the chance to watch him. There was no batsman in the country who was consistently better value for money – and spectators did not have to cope with him in the dressing room. The irony was that when Ingleby-Mackenzie gave up the Hampshire captaincy, he was succeeded by Marshall. Although he had a wonderful cricketing brain and a great tactical awareness, he could hardly have orchestrated a dressing room with a more different atmosphere in his five years in charge.

GARRY SOBERS

GARRY SOBERS was the complete all-rounder and there has never been another to compare with him in the entire history of the game. In 93 Test matches for the West Indies he scored 8,032 runs with twenty-six hundreds at an average of 57.78. As if this wasn't enough, he also took 235 Test wickets at just over 34, bowling in three different styles and, just to rub it in, hung on to 109 catches, most of them close to the wicket. These are all-round figures that are never likely to be equalled, let alone beaten. He played cricket in a manner that made it look as if original sin had never been invented. C.L.R. James in that wonderful book, *Beyond a Boundary*, touched the spot in summing up the supreme performer in cricket's own Magic Circle. Sobers captained the West Indies for the first time, having succeeded his guide and mentor, Frank Worrell, at Sabina Park, Kingston in the First Test against Australia in 1964/65. James wrote of Sobers in that match: 'To see in the course of one day Sobers despatch the ball to all parts of the field with his bat, then open the bowling, fielding at slip to Hall or Griffith, change to Gibbs and place himself at short leg, then go on to bowl slows, meanwhile placing his men and changing them with certainty and ease, this is one of the sights of the modern cricket field. I cannot visualise anything in the past that corresponds to it . . .'

Sobers was the personification a generation later of all the brilliant and exciting West Indian ways of tackling cricket that had been unleashed upon the world in a much more raw form by Learie Constantine. Constantine was a good vintage, drunk in its infancy, out of the barrel; Sobers represented what it had become fifteen years later: smooth, controlled, the right blend between instinct and technique with a deliciously long finish. In Constantine there was all the precocious enthusiasm of a discovery first made. He was hectic, exciting, dramatic and wholly unexpected. Whether batting, bowling or fielding, he was the newest wonder of the world – the Empire State Building way above the skyline on a first visit to New York. Sobers came after Headley, Weekes, Worrell and Walcott, all of whom had in their own ways taken the raw material that Constantine had handed down a stage further.

When Sobers drove a fast bowler on the up through the covers it was breathtaking, incredible, beautiful and yet not unexpected. When he punched the ball through the covers off the back foot or played that searing square cut or hooked – all strokes of artistic beauty – the same emotions came into play, not only because of the art gallery effect, but because they were all played, and with such frequency, by the same person. Not content with that, he now turned his hand to swinging the new ball from left arm over the wicket. Then, lo and behold, he turned either to orthodox left-arm spin or to a mixture of chinamen and googlies out of the back of the hand. After this, he stationed himself in the slips or at short leg and caught swallows. All of it was lithe and artistic, and almost everything was done with a smile on his face. It was a glorious outrage, not to say sublimely unfair, that one man should have been blessed with such powers. It was a personalised form of supremely elegant atomic warfare on the cricket pitch and one could not get enough of these particular nuclear warheads. He was an incomparable athlete and the first thing one noticed about Sobers, which gave off a wealth of advanced publicity about all that was to come, was his walk. From the moment he appeared on the pavilion steps with that light, angular, lissom walk one knew that one was in the presence of a remarkable sportsman. He glided to the wicket and this approach heightened the anticipation of what was to follow.

Some batsmen shuffle, some walk like mechanical man, some stride and some just appear in the middle without giving anyone the faintest idea of how they got there, and often bat in the same way, but Sobers' approach made everyone sit up.

Perhaps his captaincy did not quite live up to James's hopes and expectations because, having won eight of his first twelve matches as captain, he was only once more victorious in his remaining twenty-seven. This in part reflected the passage of time. The wonderful side that Worrell had captained and then handed down to Sobers was getting too long in the tooth. Reflexes were not quite as they once had been and *anno domini* had dimmed enthusiasm for the fight, especially when things were no longer progressing with the invincibility of old. The passing years also began to take a toll of Sobers himself who, on occasions, could still produce his old magic. One such instance was his innings of 150 in his last Test match at Lord's, in 1973, by which time he had passed on the captaincy to another considerable contemporary, Rohan Kanhai. For all that he had lost some of the sharp cutting edge that had set him apart when he was in his twenties, it was not unlike watching a great conductor in his seventies whose arthritic fingers had unreasonable trouble in flicking over the pages of the score. One was only too well aware that it had soon to come to an end. Sobers in his mid-thirties, with joints that were beginning to creak complainingly, was yet another cruel example of Peter Pan being cut down to size.

One of the most fascinating and incomprehensible aspects of nature is the way in which genes come together without apparent rhyme or reason to produce an athlete or sportsman who is severely tinged with genius. There is no easy explanation of the fact that the fifth child of Mr and Mrs Shamont Sobers, born in a small wooden house in Walcott Avenue, Bay Land in the parish of St Michael in Barbados, should have grown up to become the greatest all-round cricketer the game has known. It is no less inexplicable why the eighth child of Dr and Mrs Henry Grace born in

1848 at Downend in Gloucestershire should have shown more than just a passing aptitude for the game. The sports master at the Bay Street Boys' School soon told Sobers, 'You're going to have a big future in cricket.' He was only twelve when he was asked to bowl at the Test batsman Denis Atkinson in the nets at the Wanderers Club ground in Bridgetown. He commanded respect. A year or two later he met Captain Wilfred Farmer, a police inspector who captained the Police cricket team. A week after Sobers had hit Captain Farmer's stumps in the nets with a beauty, he was asked if he would like the chance to play first XI cricket. 'I could get you into the Police Band and that would qualify you to play for the team,' said Captain Farmer. The young Sobers leapt at the chance and was drafted into the Police Band as a bugler. In his first match for the Police he was struck in the mouth trying to hook, which put bugle-blowing on hold for a while. The bandmaster decided that enough was enough and found a replacement and – who knows? – a great musical career was still-born. Nonetheless, the captain was determined to keep Sobers and arranged for him to join the Police Boys' Club and so all was well. He soon scored his first hundred in senior cricket, 113 against Wanderers, and within a season was in the Barbados side, principally as a slow left-arm bowler. It was something of a royal progress.

It was typical of the West Indies that when, in March 1954, the seventeen-year-old Sobers was picked as a replacement for the Fifth Test against England in Kingston, he should have been playing cricket in the street outside the family's small house in Walcott Avenue when the message arrived from the secretary of the Barbados Cricket Association. He made a gentle beginning, batting at number nine and scoring 14 not out and 26, although he took 4/75 off 28.5 overs. Jim Swanton wrote: 'Sobers made an excellent impression. He is a slim young man who runs lightly up to the wicket and the arm almost touches the ear as it comes over. On what might serve as a model action for a slow left-hand bowler, he builds changes of flight and spin in the classical manner. It will be surprising if we do not come to know his name well in the years ahead.' I doubt if even such a shrewd prophet as Swanton had any idea when he wrote those words of how right he would be.

Sobers made a quiet start to his Test career. He picked up some wickets and made useful contributions with the bat, but he did not take Test cricket by storm. There was one innings, however, against Australia in Barbados in 1954/55 that made an emphatic statement. Keith Miller, who was bowling that day, had no doubts: 'He didn't show us anything out of the ordinary that would indicate what brilliance was yet to come . . . until Sobers was sent in to open the West Indies innings. There, for an hour, cricket hell broke loose. This little-known Sobers kept hammering fours at Ray and myself until we were punch-drunk. That one innings set Sobers alight as a batting wizard.' When he came back to Sabina Park in 1958 for the Third Test against Pakistan it was his seventeenth match for the West Indies and his highest score had been 80, scored in the previous Test against Pakistan. He was to put that right with a vengeance. Still only twenty-one, he batted for ten hours and fourteen minutes while making 365 not out, the highest score ever made in Test cricket, beating Hutton's 364 against Australia at The Oval in 1938. Before this, Sobers had made six scores of more than 50 and his problem had been to keep his concentration going. He realised this and set himself to put the record straight at Kingston against a Pakistan attack suffering badly from injuries. Sobers' driving and square cutting, which brought him most of his thirty-eight fours, was exceptional, but in this innings there was a relentlessness that had not been evident before. It made his batting no less entertaining, simply rather more permanent. In the Fourth Test he made a hundred in each innings and he followed this up with three more in the series against India in 1958/59 and another three a year later against England. The one problem that was holding Sobers back had been well and truly put in its place and he had taken over from the three Ws as the main draw-card of the West Indies side. He was able to show the world that more cricketing skills had come home to roost in one man than ever before.

In 1960/61 the West Indies went to Australia where, for the first time, a black man, Frank Worrell, captained them. This was something that was long overdue. Learie Constantine, for one, had often said that the West Indies would never play their best cricket until a black man was in charge. They were as fortunate that such an outstanding person with the astutest of cricket brains should have been the first black incumbent as South Africa were that Nelson Mandela should have been their first black president. In neither instance were there recriminations for the past, but a steady determination to face the future and go forward. Worrell had already marked Sobers as his natural successor and had taken him under his wing.

When the tour began no one gave the West Indies much of a chance. They were well beaten by New South Wales and Sobers himself was in all kinds of confusion when it came to trying to read Richie Benaud's wristy variations. Shortly afterwards they arrived in Brisbane for the First Test, which ended in Test cricket's first-ever tie. Worrell won the toss and before long the West Indies were 65/3 when Sobers and his captain came together. He left in the pavilion any doubts that Benaud may have instilled in him and proceeded to score 132 in 123 minutes. He reached 50 in fifty-seven minutes and went on to complete an innings Worrell later said was the best he had ever seen him play. The hundred partnership with Worrell took ninety minutes and Sobers unleashed a withering display of strokes. Benaud, who did not take a a wicket in the innings, was made to suffer along with the rest. Runs came so fast that the second new ball, which was available then after only 200 runs, was taken at twenty minutes past two on the first day of the match, in spite of all the fielders Benaud had placed in the deep.

The former Australian opening batsman Jack Fingleton, always a stern critic, wrote in *Fingleton on Cricket*: 'It is not easy to decide which innings is the greatest one has seen. In the circumstances, one would give the accolade to McCabe's in 1932 [McCabe made 187 not out in the First Test of the infamous Bodyline series] yet I consider myself fortunate to have seen this one by Sobers.' Don Bradman also watched the match and afterwards said to Sobers, a trifle sardonically, 'Thank you very much, son, I knew you wouldn't let me down, and it's a good thing you can't pick Richie, or you would have murdered him!' Sobers made another hundred, 168, in the Third Test in Sydney, took 15 wickets in the series and hung on to twelve catches. During that first hundred in Brisbane he passed 3,000 runs in Test cricket and he was still only twenty-four.

It was Bradman who made sure that Sobers joined South Australia for the following three seasons. The first was relatively uneventful, but in the second he became the first player ever to achieve the double in the Australian first-class season. In South Australia's ten Sheffield Shield matches he made 1,000 runs and took 50 wickets and, just for good measure, he did it again the following year. The last game in that second season was against the all-powerful New South Wales in Adelaide. Alan Davidson bowled South Australia out for 190 in the first innings. Sobers then took 9 wickets in the match in addition to making 251 in South Australia's second innings. This enabled South Australia to inflict the first defeat of the season on the Sheffield Shield champions. There was a great moment of conflict in the second innings. When Sobers had reached 150, Davidson took the second new ball. His first ball was a beamer, which came straight at Sobers' head. He just managed to get his bat up in time and snicked the ball off the back of the bat through the slips for four. Davidson rushed forwards apologising and saying that the ball had slipped from his hand. Two overs later he bowled Sobers a bouncer. He got into position early and smashed it with a flat bat from outside the off stump. The Adelaide Oval has short square boundaries and enormously long straight ones. The ball flew on and on down the ground, went over the boundary and the sightscreen and must have carried 150 yards. Sobers reckons that he never hit a ball further. The interesting postscript came from Col Egar who was umpiring the match. He said to Sobers a year later, 'You know, Garry, I don't believe that Davo's beamer slipped. When he passed me on his way back to his mark, he said, "I'll show him a thing or two."'

On reflection, Sobers thought that his best innings for the West Indies was his 163 not out that saved the Second Test at Lord's in 1966. They were 86 behind on the first innings and 95/5 in their second when his cousin, David Holford, joined Sobers. They put on a record unbroken 274 for the sixth wicket and Holford finished with 105 not out. Once more, Sobers' innings was a magnificent blend of concentration and breathtaking strokeplay. Lord's always brought out the best in him, but never more so than it did then. The other innings that must stand comparison with this one at Lord's was the 254 he made for the Rest of the World against Australia in Melbourne in 1970/71. Dennis Lillee's bouncers had been causing him trouble and he had been caught off his first ball in the first innings. When Australia batted, Sobers retaliated in kind when Lillee came in. He rattled him with his first ball, a bouncer, and got him out with his second. Lillee was furious. The score was 146/3 when Sobers came out to face Lillee in the second innings. This time, as a form of double bluff, he pitched the first ball up to the bat and Sobers straight drove him for four and took 29 off his first three overs. He unwound stroke after stroke on both sides of the wicket to the amazement of the bowlers and the delight of the crowd, reaching a hundred off only 129 balls. He himself said of this innings: 'It was probably as near to perfection as I ever came with the bat.' Only Sobers can decide where that puts it in relation to the 163 not out at Lord's. Bradman himself was in no doubt: 'I believe Garry Sobers' innings was probably the best ever seen in Australia. The people who saw Sobers have enjoyed one of the historic events of cricket. They were privileged to have such an experience.' Perhaps Sobers himself felt that more was at stake in a Test match between two countries.

By then, Sobers was in the middle of a seven-year spell with Nottinghamshire in the English County Championship. The Test and County Cricket Board had decided that counties should be allowed to employ overseas players to try to revive the flagging popularity of the competition. Sobers' years with Nottinghamshire boosted their cricket but never took them to the trophies they were hoping for – they had to wait for Clive Rice and Richard Hadlee for that to happen. By the end of Sobers' sojourn at Trent Bridge, the constant repetitiveness of county cricket had begun to blunt even his enthusiasm. His first season, 1968, will never be forgotten for their match against Glamorgan at the St Helen's ground in Swansea. With Nottinghamshire past 300 for the loss of 5 wickets, Sobers, the batsman and captain, was in search of runs for a declaration. Malcolm Nash was bowling steady left-arm spin from the pavilion end. The first three balls were despatched over mid on, midwicket and mid off. The fourth disappeared over the square-leg boundary. He hit the fifth too high on the bat and was caught on the midwicket boundary. Sobers began to walk off, but was called back by the umpire for the fielder had carried the ball over the boundary. The last ball of the over was a seamer, but Nash pitched it too short and it was last seen disappearing in the general direction of the Swansea town hall. Peter Walker, who had begun the over at slip, said of the final blow: 'It wasn't a six. It was a twelve!' Ravi Shastri later repeated this feat in a game in Bombay.

Sobers' one cricketing blind spot was the job of captaincy. One of the problems was his own essentially easy-going approach to both life and cricket. Cricket was never a matter of life and death to him. He loved the game and wanted nothing more than to have a good sporting game of cricket. At Test level there were unfortunately other issues that were sometimes at stake. In the West Indies, victory in the Test arena was seen as a great boost for nationalism. After all, cricket was one of the very few aspects of life in which the West Indies stood at least on level terms with the rest of the world. This was dramatically underlined in 1967/68 in the West Indies when Sobers captained them against Colin Cowdrey's England side. England had been unlucky not to win both the first two Test matches and when they came to Port of Spain for the Fourth, it was still 0–0 in the series. The West Indies made 526/7 declared and gained a first-innings lead of 122 when England replied with 404. At that stage it looked a certain draw. Everton Weekes was the West Indies team manager for that series and apparently, sitting next to Sobers in the pavilion, he had said, 'It only needs ten balls to win the match.' Sobers, a gambling man if ever there was one, will have understood exactly what Weekes was saying. Suddenly, when the West Indies score was 92/2 and their lead 214, Sobers jumped to his feet clapped his hands and waved his batsmen in. England had been left to score 215 to win in 165 minutes – a generous target. By all accounts, Cowdrey was initially reluctant to go for it. With less than three hours to bat against a depleted West Indies attack that was without Charlie Griffith, who had pulled a thigh muscle, it would not have been that difficult to play out for a draw if things had begun to go wrong. It took the combined efforts of John Edrich and Ken Barrington to persuade him otherwise and excellent batting by Cowdrey himself and Geoffrey Boycott saw England home by 7 wickets. Locally, Sobers was in disgrace for having played with West Indian nationalism, such as it was. When the teams arrived in Georgetown, Guyana the next day for the Fifth Test, Sobers had to be given a police guard. Innings of 152 and 95 not out in the last Test helped deflect some of the criticism, but there are those who, to this day, still hold that result against Sobers.

There has never been the smallest piece of arrogance, conceit or side in Sobers. Cricket to him was never anything other than a game that was to be played hard and enjoyed. He was brought up in Bay Street all those years ago, to 'walk' if he knew that he had hit the ball. He never forgot this and always did his best to make life easier for the umpires if he could. He realised that this was something that had to be a personal decision and he did not try to force his views on his colleagues, but Sobers himself was the most honest of cricketers. He was also the most exciting and not for one moment in a first-class career that began in 1954 and ended in 1974 was he anything other than an entertainer par excellence. With that reservoir of talent, even in cricketing old age one never knew for certain what might turn up next. It will be a long, long time before the game again sees the like of Garry Sobers.

COLIN BLAND

IN South Africa the argument will rage forever as to whether Colin Bland or Jonty Rhodes was the better fielder. What is beyond argument is that fielding at the level to which these two have taken it is as entrancing as any other aspect of the game played at its best. For me, the palm goes by a whisker to Bland. He was more clinical, less obviously ebullient than Rhodes, the killer instinct seemed sharper, and there was perhaps a greater precision with Bland. He did not sprawl about on his knees as much as Rhodes, thereby giving his launderer less of a headache; he lurked like a predator whose anticipatory antennae never sent out the wrong signals; and he moved in for the final kill with the deadliest throw the game has known. He was an exciting strokemaker too, but it was as a fielder he will always be remembered.

He produced his definitive exhibition of fielding, appropriately enough, in front of a big crowd during the Second Test match at Lord's in 1965. England had bowled out South Africa for 280 and had reached 240/4 themselves with Ken Barrington 91 not out and playing an innings that was as typically reassuring as most that he played. He was at the Pavilion end and played the ball towards a gap at mid on. He called his partner, Mike Smith, for what seemed a straightforward enough run. Twice before he had pushed into the same gap and completed the single easily enough. Bland, who was at forward square leg, was the nearest fielder and on each of the earlier occasions he had allowed Barrington the run without exerting himself. Now he had anticipated the stroke. He sprinted ten yards to his left, picked the ball up in his left hand, transferred it in a flash to his right and in a blur of movement threw down the stumps at the Nursery end with Barrington short of his crease.

Later on in the same innings Bland was fielding at midwicket when the ball was turned to square leg. Jim Parks had started for a run from the non-striker's end, only for his partner to send him back. Bland picked the ball up, twisted his body at least ninety degrees and catapulted the ball at the bowler's stumps. It went like a guided missile between Parks' legs and crashed into the middle stump with Parks well out. They were two astonishing pieces of fielding and they changed the course of a match that England had seemed to be winning and yet in the end they came close to losing. When the last ball had been bowled they needed 46 to win with 2 wickets to fall. Just to underline his worth, Bland made 39 in the first innings and the highest score of 70 in the second. Nobody who saw those 2 wickets fall, as I was lucky enough to do, will ever forget them. Fielding has never attained a higher peak than this.

The secret of Bland's amazing fielding was simple. No one, not even Rhodes, can have worked harder at perfecting the art. During this tour of England he gave one or two exhibitions of swooping on the ball and throwing down a single stump from the cover point/midwicket distance. There was one such at Canterbury that was remarkable for his accuracy and consistency in hitting the stump. His catching was almost as astonishing. The one he took that accounted for the New Zealand captain, John Reid, at deep cover at the Wanderers in Johannesburg in 1961/62 is still talked about. Diving at full stretch he caught a full-blooded drive in his fingertips. No wonder crowds would flock to see him wherever he played. No athlete was ever finer tuned.

THE NAWAB OF
PATAUDI

'TIGER' Pataudi inherited his cricketing genes and his aristocratic features from his father, with a liberal dose of charm, humour and worldliness thrown in together with an instinct to go for his strokes. Whether he would ever have been able to bat for just over five hours for 102, as his father did in his first Test match for England against Australia in Sydney in the Bodyline series of 1932/33, is a moot point. Tiger was in the Winchester XI for four years in which he scored 2,036 runs, the highest aggregate by any Wykehamist. In his last year he made 52 for Sussex against Yorkshire, the county champions. He had a prodigious talent. His first year at Oxford was notable for a century in the University match, but the following year when he needed 92 more to beat his father's record of 1,307 in a season for Oxford, he was involved in a car accident in Brighton which cost him most of the sight of his right eye. This was a grievous handicap, but Tiger's character, determination and courage did not allow it to be terminal as far as his cricket was concerned.

In spite of this appalling injury, he went on to play in forty-six Test matches for India and in twenty-two of them he captained his country. A total of 2,793 runs for an average of 34.91 was good enough for a man with two eyes, let alone for one with fractionally more than one. His highest score of 203 not out came against England in Delhi in 1963/64. His batting consistently impressed the Australians, but never more than in Australia in 1967/68 when, in the Second Test match in Melbourne, batting with a torn hamstring, he made 75 and 85.

Considering his handicap, Tiger's record told of an extraordinary ability, but it hardly hinted at the character of the man or, in a sense, his talent, which was seen at its unspoiled best for such a short time. I was lucky enough to play in the Eton/Winchester match in 1956 when Pataudi made his first appearance at the age of fifteen. Eton batted first and soon after the start the heavens opened and when play began again the ball behaved as if it was a 'sticky' at the Gabba in Brisbane. Eton failed to reach a hundred and it was no easier when Winchester began their innings. Tiger batted in the middle of the order and began to play in impossible conditions as if it was just about the easiest thing in the world. When he had got into the twenties one ball behaved even too extravagantly for his extraordinary talent, but by then all those watching knew they had seen something very special.

When natural cricketing instinct is handed down in this measure, it is as unmatchable and as incomparable as a 1961 Chateau Latour. It is a gift of the gods that cannot be rivalled by human endeavour, however committed, persistent and single-minded. A friend of mine, who was up at Oxford at the same time as Tiger, will never forget the innings he played against Gloucestershire in the Parks in 1962. When he arrived at the crease at the fall of the second wicket, his partner, Duncan Worsley, had already made 92 and yet Pataudi, who still had both his eyes, beat him to his hundred. David Allen, whom Garry Sobers regarded as the best off spinner he ever faced, was in the Gloucestershire side that day and it was not long before he was bowling with both a long on and a long off. Within moments, Pataudi's footwork had taken him down the pitch and he had driven the ball between the two into the pavilion. Soon afterwards he came down the pitch again as if to repeat the stroke. He was committed to it when he had a sudden change of mind, went down on one knee and, with his bat parallel to the ground, drove the ball square past cover point for four before the fielder could move. This was batting in the class of Denis Compton. The following year it was thanks to some brilliant batting by Pataudi that Oxford gave the West Indies a good run for their money. The other aspect of his cricket that is still talked about in the Parks and everywhere else he played was his superb fielding.

As a man, Pataudi has a delightfully sardonic, almost patrician sense of humour that came with a poker face tinged with mischief. He was never better or funnier than when dealing with Jim Swanton, who invariably picked Pataudi for his private tours to foreign parts. He had every possible qualification Swanton could have wished for and, as a result, was allowed to pull his leg unmercifully. There was one occasion when 'the Noob', as he was affectionately known, was congratulated by Gubby Allen for scoring a Test hundred against England soon after he had lost one eye.

Allen asked him: 'Tell me, when did you think you might still be able to make runs despite having only one eye?'

'When I saw the English bowling,' came back as quick as a flash.

PART FOUR

1967–1987

FINANCING cricket was still a problem no one had managed to solve in the seventies. The game has always been the poor relation among major sports, lacking, as it does, any television appeal in the United States. One-day cricket, inspired by the healthy example of the Gillette Cup, began to proliferate. Two more one-day competitions sprang up in England: the John Player Sunday League, a forty-over competition, began in 1969, permitted by a general relaxation of the rigid principles espoused by the Lord's Day Observance Society. Three years later, in 1972, another cigarette company jumped on to one-day cricket's bandwagon and the Benson & Hedges Cup came into being. The limited-overs game was soon seen to be having a bad effect on two-innings cricket. Batsmen, in the helter-skelter pursuit of runs, dangerously adapted their techniques, while bowlers, interested only in containment, began to forget about the importance of taking wickets which is, of course, the best way of winning a two-innings match.

The number of overseas players counties were allowed to employ increased; there were signs of a homespun transfer system between the counties coming into play, and behaviour in the middle deteriorated sharply. Because winning had now become so much more financially important, players were doing their utmost to bend the rules where they could. For a number of years the first innings in a County Championship match was restricted to 100 overs, thereby effectively turning the three-day game into two one-day matches. It was all done to try to raise public interest and therefore to generate more money. It has taken a long time for those in power to realise that the best way of increasing the game's popularity is to produce a national side that makes a habit of winning. Generations of England's administrators have nibbled away at the edges of the problem without ever having the courage to attack its main body, which is essentially a top-heavy and ineffectual County Championship. This is a situation that is still with us. The only real gain from this paranoid lurch towards one-day cricket was a dramatic improvement in the overall standard of fielding and, of course, rather more money, although not enough.

Other countries introduced their own one-day competitions, but they did not flood their market place in the same way as England where the tail was beginning to wag the dog. In fact, the standards in what were once considered to be the lesser Test-playing countries continued to improve. The renaissance of the West Indies under Frank Worrell, who passed the captaincy on to Sobers, continued until 1966 when they came back to England and again won 3–1. Old age then took over and, while new players were found, blooded and given experience, they fell away before re-emerging about ten years later. India won a series in England for the first time in 1971 when, wonderful to relate, their main reason for victory was the skill of their four spinners, Bishen Bedi, Bhagwat Chandrasekhar, Srini Venkatraghavan and Erapalli Prasanna. New Zealand won a Test match against England for the first time, in Wellington in 1977/78. In 1983 they won their first in England and they were victorious in the next two series, in New Zealand in 1983/84 and in England in 1986. Pakistan were also nipping away at England's heels, although they had to wait until 1983/84 before they beat England in Pakistan. This was excellent for the world-wide strength and appeal of cricket, even if it did not help England much with their problems.

One has then to set against this the outlawing and excommunication of South Africa whose government continued to persist with the abhorrent policies of apartheid. Their last series was in 1969/70 when Ali Bacher's formidable side won all four Tests against Australia. Even then they continued to cause problems because, masterminded by Bacher, a number of rebel tours found their way to the Cape. This inevitably caused great unease among the coloured countries and, in time, caused the cancellation of scheduled tours and also of individual matches because of the lurking presence of players who had been on one of these jollies to South Africa.

Then, towards the end of this period, the game suddenly found itself submerged by the greatest single crisis of its history to date. In 1977 Kerry Packer, frustrated in his wish to buy exclusive rights in Australia to show international cricket on his Channel Nine network, set up his own professional breakaway troupe of Test cricketers. In the Establishment game, the best cricketers were not being paid much and the authorities were always pleading poverty. The mere fact that the Australian Board was able in the first place to turn its back on such a munificent fairy godfather as Packer showed how dyed-in-the-wool they were. This went for other countries' administrators, too. To be successful, this revolution almost certainly had to be unpleasant, and it was.

With all this turmoil affecting world cricket, it was just as well that these two decades should have produced cricketers who were as brilliantly compelling and entertaining as any to have graced the game, even if they were not players who fundamentally changed its form. Nonetheless, they took their own arts to new and exciting levels. Graham Gooch, Ian Botham and David Gower came into the England team in the second half of the seventies and it is not often that the same side is blessed with three such brilliant strokemakers. They were all fiercely independent people. Botham and Gower were more relaxed than Gooch and it was their different approaches to life that made them so fascinating. All three went on to captain England and here it was the more disciplined Gooch who was the most successful, even if his methods were at times more sullenly bureaucratic than those of the other two.

Imran Khan led Pakistan like a member of the warrior race from which he was descended, while Kapil Dev, tall and rather stately, would unanimously have been made President of India at any time he chose. The other two who lit up this period, often did so while having the most exciting battles between themselves. In the seventies, Dennis Lillee was the fast bowler who dominated world cricket until he himself, as the seventies turned into the eighties, was dominated by Viv Richards. Their contests, won initially by Lillee, provided the real red meat that makes cricket such an absorbing game. Cricket owes an awful lot to all these characters for it was they who kept the game on the road throughout this tricky period.

COLIN MILBURN

COLIN MILBURN was in the same league as P.G. Wodehouse's Right Hon. friend who looked as if he had been poured into his clothes and had forgotten to say 'When!' Fat men are often naturally humorous and Milburn always seemed to be the ideal chap to audition for the job of Stan Laurel's partner if ever another had been needed. History does not reveal what he clocked in at when he was first weighed, but it is probable that he gave both his mother and the scales a nasty shock. He first put in an appearance at Burnopfield in County Durham on 23 October 1941 and it was in the north-east that he played his early cricket. He was blessed with a Falstaffian figure and happily he batted as one would have imagined that Falstaff would have batted. A half volley was a half volley and a long hop a long hop, whether it was in the first over of the day or the last. He came as a breath of fresh air for English cricket and it was cruel that after playing in only nine Test matches for England, in which he averaged 46.71 in sixteen innings, he was involved in a car crash that cost him the use of one eye and damaged the other. For a time he tried bravely to overcome this enormous handicap, but it was too much for him and his career ended just when he should have been tearing into bowling attacks all round the world.

Olly, as he was known, was larger than life in every sense. From the moment he picked up a bat his only intention was to hit the cover off the ball. He batted with a wide-eyed, boyish, almost humpty-dumpty freshness that was infinitely attractive. At a time when county cricket was rather in the doldrums and was being injected for the first time with overseas players, Milburn became one of three or four Englishmen whom people would come a long way to see. There were never any pretensions about Milburn, just a good down-to-earth realism.

'I've always been a slogger,' he said, 'and my father was a slogger before me.'

Of course, he underestimated himself because he was far from being just a slogger. He was instead one of those splendid batsmen who realised the ball was there to be hit. He played orthodox strokes all round the wicket, he played them more frequently than most and he hit the ball a great deal harder. He was in his village team at thirteen and, four years later, in 1959, was playing for Chester-le-Street in the Durham Senior League. After making a couple of hundreds for them he was chosen to play for Durham against the Indian touring side. He made a quickish hundred. Within days of this innings Northamptonshire had signed him up, which meant that a week after leaving school he was playing cricket for his living.

Milburn's figure will have raised a few eyebrows at the county ground in Northampton. He takes up the story. 'When I first came down to Northampton they got me on these training runs, but I'm just not built to run a long way. I'm all right on a short sprint, but after about half a mile the others left me behind, so I thumbed a lift on a milk float. We sailed past the rest of the boys a bit further up the road.'

On another occasion, Keith Andrew, his county captain, suggested that he should try and do something about his weight and also get some more hundreds. The weight was the problem.

'Why don't you drink halves instead of pints?' Andrew asked. Milburn made 150 that day and it was only about halfway through the afternoon.

'What are you going to drink then, Colin?' Andrew asked him.

'Two halves, please, Guv.'

It is fair to say that his strokeplay made as big an impression at Northampton as his weight. He was forced to spend a year qualifying for his new county and then he began at number six in the order but worked his way up to open. 'I don't like sitting around,' was his view of it. 'I like to get on with it.' He began 1966 in tremendous form and with five hundreds beneath his belt he was the first to 1,000 runs and was selected to play against the West Indies in the First Test at Old Trafford. After being run out for a duck in the first innings, he was soon hooking Wes Hall for six in the second and was out eventually, bowled by Lance Gibbs for 94. He was never entirely happy against off spin. He only had to wait one more game for that hundred, for he made 126 not out in England's second innings in the following match at Lord's. Milburn was a fine catcher, too, and holds the record for the number held other than by a wicket keeper in a season for Northamptonshire. He held on to anything close to the bat, but when playing for England he was usually stationed in the outfield, which meant that, with his figure, he came in for quite a bit of ribald comment.

He was in and out of the England side but this never bothered him or prevented him from enjoying county cricket. There was no more popular player on the circuit and there are a great many stories told about him. He had a strong baritone voice, which I remember came into its own on a few occasions during the successful England tour of the Caribbean in 1967/68 when he did not play in any of the Tests. Just before the last Test, the Mighty Sparrow, who at the time was the greatest of the Calypsonians, came to Georgetown to give a concert or two. At one of them, Milburn provided the warm-up act when he sang, 'The Green Green Grass of Home'. He brought the house down. Although he was never likely to win a place in the side, his cheerfulness throughout that tour was remarkable and he can only have been a splendid influence in the dressing room, unlike some members of the 'second eleven'.

It was after that tour that an agent got hold of Milburn and proposed that he should give cabaret performances wherever Northamptonshire were playing. Ken Turner, the county's charming but mildly idiosyncratic secretary who saved the club from bankruptcy, called Milburn to his office. He asked him what the hell he thought he was doing even considering the offer. Here he was, an England player, and he would continually be going to bed at four in the morning. Milburn thought for a moment.

'Well, it would only make one hour's difference because I'm never in bed before three o'clock anyway.'

In 1968, he played a fearless attacking innings of 83 against Graham McKenzie and the Australians on a hostile pitch at Lord's, but he was injured during the summer and, although he returned for the last Test, he was not selected for England's tour of Pakistan. His way of playing was still meat that was too strong for some of those blinkered nincompoops that have made such a habit of trying to run England's cricket. That winter he went to Perth and played for Western Australia in the Sheffield Shield. It was there that he played perhaps his most famous innings of all when he struck 243 against Queensland of which 181 came in the two hours between lunch and tea. His form was so good that when England needed a replacement for the Third Test in Pakistan, Milburn was the obvious choice. He made a joyful 139 in what was to be his last innings for England. The following May, on the evening after Northamptonshire had beaten the West Indies for the second tour in succession, Milburn was involved in a car accident that effectively finished him. He did all he could to come back but after thirty-five innings his top score was 57 and he packed it in.

Even after this dreadful accident his humour never left him, even if his sense of direction, not surprisingly, may have done. He was playing against Derbyshire with only one eye and was bowling. As he ran in to deliver one ball, he suddenly stopped and shouted that his eye had fallen out. Everyone searched around the crease and the umpire found it. Milburn took out his handkerchief, gave the glass eye a rub, shoved it back in and, after a good chortle, finished the over. Without cricket he was a lost soul. He was used on several occasions by the BBC on *Test Match Special* and made some telling contributions but he will probably be best remembered for an unfortunate gaffe during a Test at Headingley. He was asked to be in the commentary box at about eight o'clock one morning to do the early breakfast-time programmes. When the time came, they were unable to raise him at the ground and so checked at the hotel. Sure enough, he had overslept but was told it would be fine and he could do the programme on the telephone from his room, making it sound as if he was at the ground. The interview started promisingly, but halfway through the interviewer suddenly asked him what the weather was like.

'I don't know, I haven't opened the curtains yet,' was the reply he got.

Olly died on 28 February 1990 at the age of forty-nine, a life cruelly unfulfilled. All of us who were lucky enough to know him and to watch him play miss him still. So should all those millions of cricket-lovers who were deprived of the many exciting innings he was on the threshold of playing.

ALAN KNOTT

WICKET keepers are the clowns in cricket's pack. They are adventurers on the grand scale, entrepreneurs in spirit, a perpetual irritation to batsmen who tend to find them as cuddly and sonorous as a covey of mosquitoes dive-bombing from just above the pillow in the small hours. Immediately after the Second World War, Godfrey Evans, with those irresistible gloves, faced with red ping-pong-bat rubber, was supreme – standing up to the wicket to Alec Bedser and that quick leg spinner, Doug Wright, defied the laws of gravity. However, after plenty of soul-searching, for it had been Evans who had been the reason for my own metamorphosis into a wicket keeper, I came to the conclusion that the best value of them all was Alan Knott. In a lifetime spent watching cricket, there has been no more inspiring sight than Knott standing up to Derek Underwood on a drying pitch, both for Kent and England. Underwood was at least a generous medium pace and yet, however much the ball may have turned or bounced unexpectedly, Knott was as unhurried as he was unflurried. His reflexes and his anticipation were phenomenal and he had a gymnast's ability to cover the ground. His hands followed the ball as if they had been attracted by a magnet. Standing back he held the improbable, not to say impossible, goalkeeping catches that Evans had grasped amid a blur of tumbling red and white before ejaculating an appeal that sounded more like a thunder clap. Knott's appeal was also decisive if less of a declaration of war.

Knott never seemed to miss while Evans put a few down in his time, although he covered up the fact with amazing speed and dexterity. Illogically, it was Knott's batting that made me plump for him. Evans might be a bit peeved here, too, because in 1952 against India at Lord's he came within a run or two of scoring a hundred before lunch. While Evans swashbuckled according to character, Knott fizzed, fizzled and twinkled as his footwork took him all over the place and his wrists enabled him to perform similar deeds with his bat. He made five vastly entertaining Test hundreds and thirty fifties besides in his ninety-five Test matches, which would have been more if he had not embraced Kerry Packer's World Series Cricket. Bob Taylor, who had been the permanent bridesmaid to Knott, took over and did a pretty good job too, although as the lesser among equals. It was John Thicknesse who summed up Knott to perfection:

> Small, perky, alert as a cat, he was unmistakable from the furthest corner of the ground, whether crouching low beside the stumps or poised wide-eyed in front of them, as alive to the possibilities of misadventure as a boy playing French cricket on a bumpy lawn. His fanaticism for health and fitness, manifest on the day by innumerable exercises during breaks of play, and off it by faddiness in what he ate, stemmed from fear of losing his agility – someone had once told him his knee-joints had too little play in them. There was never any need to ask if Alan Knott had eaten: the pile of banana skins, flanked by a milky glass or two, told all.

Knott was a perfectionist in everything that he did and as little as possible was left to chance. Yet whatever he was doing, from the moment he appeared at the top of the pavilion steps, his huge enjoyment was always as obvious as his spring-heeled bounce and, for all his intensity, a smile was never far from his lips. His athleticism was deceptive. Many wicket keepers feel the need to throw themselves this way or that at the slightest opportunity, but Knott remained upright if he possibly could and indulged in goalkeeping exploits only if there was no alternative. The wicket keeper is the hub of the fielding side and the whole business of fielding revolves around the keeper. In this aspect Knott was supreme, as Evans had been before him. If things were going badly for England or Kent, Knott did his utmost to make them look better. He was on his toes from the first ball of the day until the last. At the end of the hottest of days in the tropics Knott would race out from behind the stumps to take a poor throw on the full and so make it look smarter than it was. He was an inspiration to his bowlers and his fielders, as well as being a great help to his captain, for nothing would go unnoticed by Knott. He was quick at detecting what he thought was a weakness in the batsman, he would let captain and bowler know at once if he felt the field could be changed to advantage, and all the time his keeping was faultless. It was always worth spending a bit of time looking only at Knott. It was like watching a piece of quicksilver in mid-season form. He was never still, whether keeping or batting. If he was not doing his best to unsettle the opposing batsmen, he was doing his best to make the life of the bowlers as difficult as possible – and all the time he looked as if he was Mr Punch on a jolly.

Knott was the most unassuming and modest of men and seldom spoke of his achievements. He had time for anyone who spoke to him and in all the years I watched him play or travelled with him on tours, I never remember a single instance of his being surly, stand-offish or uncommunicative. I have no doubt that the captains he played under and the bowlers he kept to would never have wanted anyone else in his position behind the stumps. When the batting was in trouble and Knott emerged from the pavilion with that jaunty quick-stepping walk of his, you felt that help was at hand. When the odds were stacked against him, Knott was at his best. He relished the challenge with both relentless determination and good humour. It is impossible to know what is said between players in the middle, but Knott was certainly not one of the most talkative and sledging would have been foreign to his nature. When he was sledged, it will probably have amused him, but he won't have let it upset him and I daresay that talkative opponents found that it was not worth the trouble. Knott became a devoted Christian in 1974 and from then it has played a most important part in his life. Some batsmen may have felt that he didn't have a Christian bone in his body, but he always had religious leanings.

> Prayer had come into my life when I was a young lad. I used to have dreadful nightmares, which caused me problems in getting to sleep. At one school Christmas service there were prayers ending: 'Through Jesus Christ our Lord, Amen.' I can remember lying in bed one night praying that I would not have those nightmares. They stopped and I prayed every night from then on, ending with the words I had learned from that Christmas service.

Come to think of it, there was something of a saintly aspect to Knott. That bony chin and those piercing eyes would not have been out of place in a monk's habit, even if he might have found the solemnity of a monastery a little irksome.

His autobiography, *It's Knott Cricket*, is a masterpiece of unemotional understatement. He shrugged off the brilliance of his keeping to Underwood. Perhaps his best-ever catch for England was the one that sent back the Australian captain, Bill Lawry, at Lord's in 1968. He describes it thus: 'Lawry got an inside edge off David Brown, bowling with the new ball, and I dived wide to my right and managed to catch it, my hand skidding along the ground.' Nothing too boastful about that. His wicket keeping, like his batting, is glossed over and he hardly seems aware of his own extraordinary ability.

> The summer of 1969 . . . saw me reach my peak as a wicket keeper. It came during the Third Test against the West Indies and continued during the three Tests against New Zealand. My best seven years as a wicket keeper were between 1966 and 1972. In 1969 I was named Man of the Series against the West Indies and *Wisden* honoured me as one of their Five Cricketers of the Year. Then just before the final Test in Australia on the 1970/71 tour, Bill O'Reilly, the former Aussie Test cricketer, wrote the most favourable article I have ever read about myself.

That was it. Not a word of what O'Reilly had said or even an example or two of a catch or a stumping in 1969.

He did speak of his approach and attitude to the business of playing cricket.

> I trained my mind to accept pressure and even demand it. When the pressure wasn't on I only got average scores and I wasn't at my best behind the stumps. You have to approach the game in the most realistic way possible. If I was facing Dennis Lillee for example I'd be telling myself that my judgement had to be just right to cope with the one that moves away or nips back. I wouldn't be taking the negative view and praying he didn't bowl a great ball, which I'd nick to the slips. That never came into my thinking. They call it visualization these days but I was lucky that I could do it instinctively. I didn't need any outside help. I've heard stories of Olympic teams being made to train while the noise of the crowd in the stadium is played to them at full blast. I used to do something similar but without sound effects. I'd dream I was in the cricket stadium in Calcutta or Melbourne in front of 100,000 people. Then I'd wake up and feel I was actually there. I could smell the atmosphere. It was *real*. I recreated it just by dozing off in a chair. There can't be any better way of preparing yourself mentally for what's to come. All those things affect you – sights, sounds, smells. You have to think that way. Others were relieved when Lillee or Thomson couldn't play. I was disappointed. Nothing better than taking the sting out of a fast bowler. The best way of demoralising him wasn't to blast him around the ground but defend soundly. Let him roar in and throw everything at you then watch you kill the ball stone dead with soft hands. That's the most demoralising thing of all.

There were two innings of Knott's it is impossible to forget. In 1967/68 in the West Indies, England came to Georgetown, Guyana for the Fifth Test match, one game up in the series after Garry Sobers had left them a charitable target in the final innings of the Fourth Test in Port of Spain. In those days, if the series had not been decided before the final Test was played, an extra day was added and so this game, at Bourda, became a six-day match. As it happened, England were left to bat out the last day for the draw, which would give them the series. It could hardly have gone worse for them and they were 46/5 when Knott came out to join his captain, Colin Cowdrey, towards the end of the morning session. Cowdrey was out seventy minutes before the close of play and then, with the ball turning and bouncing, John Snow, Tony Lock and Pat Pocock all perished. Knott and the last man, Jeff Jones from Glamorgan, had to survive the last six minutes. By what turned out to be an error of judgment, Jones faced the last over, bowled by off spinner, Lance Gibbs. Knott takes up the story:

> When Jones came in I said to him: 'Good luck! If we can stick this out there'll be a welcome in the hillsides for you tonight.' I reckoned there would still be time for another over (after Gibbs's) and when Jones arrived in the middle we agreed that we wouldn't change ends because it would mean him facing Sobers's chinamen and googlies. The fifth ball of the over hit Jones in the chest as he played forward extraordinarily low and we could have run a leg-bye, but we turned it down because we thought that there would be another over. After Gibbs had bowled the sixth ball I was about to mark my crease and prepare to combat Sobers when umpire Kippins said, 'That's time.'

Knott was 73 not out at the end of his most valuable innings for England.

He played the other innings at Trent Bridge against Australia in 1977, which was the Test match in which Geoff Boycott chose to make his return to the England side after three years of self-imposed exile, missing thirty matches, a curious episode even in his career. After running out Derek Randall, much to the dismay of the Nottinghamshire crowd, Boycott was becalmed. He sheltered behind that well-nigh impregnable defence and became completely bogged down. It was only the arrival of Knott, when England were 82/5, that brought him back to life and got him going again. Knott was at his cheekiest as he swept and then lay back and cut wristily behind square before using his feet to dance down the pitch to the spinners or to make room to play the fast bowlers through the off side. He had a mischievous habit of seeming to laugh at the bowlers. It was a wonderful innings to watch. He outscored Boycott and was the driving force in their partnership of 215 that took England to a winning position.

Knott was a genuine all-rounder and his and Tony Greig's presence gave the side great balance and length. Knott was a wraith-like phenomenon the like of whom we are unlikely to see again for some time. Jack Russell showed the sort of form and style that hinted at a blood relationship but, alas for England, one that was just too distant to produce the goods in the same way. Knott was a true Jack-in-a-box of a cricketer and his impish way brought a delight to the world's main cricket grounds that is not often seen.

BARRY RICHARDS

IN all the years I have spent watching cricket I have never seen anyone make the art of batting look simpler than Barry Richards. I was lucky enough to see the four Test matches he played for South Africa against Australia in 1969/70 when Australia were demolished 4–0. Richards scored 508 runs in that series for an average of 72.57 with two hundreds. He contributed handsomely to one of the great sessions in the history of Test cricket. After lunch on the first day of the Second Test in Durban, he was joined by Graeme Pollock and, although their third-wicket stand of 103 may not have been unusually large, it provided one of the rare instances of two great players batting at their best at the same time. Admittedly, Australia's attack was not the most formidable they have ever put into the field, but Graham McKenzie and Allan Connolly were not the worst pair of opening bowlers, taking 246 and 102 Test wickets respectively. Then there was John Gleeson, one of those mystery spinners Australia produce from time to time, who took a bit of reading. One has to say, too, that the Australians had just emerged from the other side of the Indian Ocean after a long and debilitating tour of India that had taken a considerable toll. Nonetheless, Richards could hardly have taken his chance at the highest level of the game with much greater conviction. Little did he realise at the time that it was to be his last chance.

Just after tea on the third day of the Fourth Test against Australia in 1970, I drove at Laurie Mayne, Australia's opening bowler, with the carefree approach of a twenty-four-year-old bursting with exhilaration at a three-figure total under his name on the St George's Park scoreboard at Port Elizabeth. I felt no pang of disappointment when Ian Chappell threw the ball up in triumph as he clung onto the catch proffered by the recklessness of the stroke. Why should I? In my first Test series I had played my part in what was to become the greatest triumph in the history of South African cricket, a clean sweep in four matches against Australia. I had scaled the heights of my ambition, and from the top I enjoyed the atmosphere. As I acknowledged the applause from the packed audience at St George's Park I could have known no greater contentment. Yet, when I walked out at the end of that innings, I walked out on a career as a Test batsman. Or to be more accurate Test cricket walked out on me and a number of other equally ambitious South Africans.

It is interesting, if unrewarding, to consider the likely course of events if England's selectors had not been so obtusely pusillanimous and had picked Basil D'Oliveira for the proposed tour of South Africa in 1968/69. As it was, the day after the Fifth Test against Australia at The Oval when he had scored a small matter of 158, their considered opinion was that he was not one of the best seventeen cricketers in England. Then, when Tom Cartwright, the bowler, became unavailable through injury, these same far-seeing selectors replaced him with D'Oliveira, the batsman. They thereby gave the South African government all the ammunition they needed to call off the tour on the basis that D'Oliveira's was a political selection. These sad events are worth regurgitating to pour even more shame on the heads of those who were party to D'Oliveira's non-selection and selection. If he had been picked in the first place, South Africa would have found it difficult to refuse him. If that had happened, who knows how events in the Republic would have subsequently unfolded. The sporting isolation might never have happened and Barry Richards might have been the batsman to have come closest to Don Bradman.

After having a look at the rigours of county cricket with Gloucestershire in 1965, Richards joined Hampshire in 1968 and it was abundantly clear from the first time that he took guard for them that here was an extraordinary player. In his career he made 26,956 first-class runs at 56.27 with seventy-nine hundreds: figures that were hardly in Bradman's orbit, but perhaps they were not a true reflection of his ability. No one was hurt more by the effects of the sporting isolation that gripped South African cricket from 1970 to 1991. No one was more conscious of how he had been robbed of the chance to reach his true place in batting's pantheon of excellence. Small wonder if the feeling of despair that this caused him from time to time made him shrug his shoulders and not always worry if he did not perform at his best for Hampshire on the county circuit or, indeed, for Natal in the Currie Cup, although his average against all the other state sides comfortably exceeded 50. The evidence of that one series against Australia was that he was not going to have any trouble in raising his game for the big occasion. I do not think it fanciful to suggest that if he had had a full Test career, his average might have been in the seventies or eighties.

Of course, it will be said by the most churlish that he never proved himself consistently at the top level of the game and that therefore this is at best speculation and that he should not be allowed to shake a stick at those who have the figures in the record books. But figures, on their own, can never talk fluently of class. They can never distinguish between class and determination. In four Test matches, Richards averaged 72.57; in 108 Test matches, Geoffrey Boycott made 8,114 runs for an average of 47.72. These figures present a comparison of a sort, but certainly not of entertainment value.

Here is Richards' take on Boycott, when Richards later played for South Australia:

We provided the opposition for the MCC's opening first-class match of the tour. My single memory of the first day is Geoff Boycott. I arrived at the ground before the start of play and Geoff had already been in the nets for half an hour. He then batted all day for 173 not out before going back for another session of practice after stumps. The second day began the same way: another long net. But in the first or second over he gently guided an easy-paced delivery down the leg side into the keeper's gloves: 173 out. Somehow it seemed hilarious, such a tame departure after all that preparation.

Those few sentences say a lot about both of them.

It has been said, too, that Richards was not happy against the swiftest of fast bowling. This again can only be conjecture. When he played for Hampshire, what was the point of getting injured? If he had been playing for South Africa, I daresay he would have decided that there was every point. The meat could hardly have been redder if Barry Richards had been able to bat against Dennis Lillee and Jeff Thomson in a Test match, to say nothing of Andy Roberts and Michael Holding. Sadly, these battles never happened, but if they had, I believe that the Richards I remember so well would not have come second. That was not in his nature and he had the technique and ability to match, to say nothing of a passionate determination.

Hampshire may not be the most glamorous of the cricketing counties in England, but how lucky their supporters were to have been able since the 1950s to feast upon Roy Marshall, Barry Richards and Gordon Greenidge. Like Richards, Marshall only played four Test matches before he decided to make Hampshire his home. Unlike Richards, he averaged only 20.42 in those few games. Greenidge, like Boycott, played 108 Test matches and scored 7,558 runs at 44.72. There is no question that Richards was the better batsman. It would be impossible to play the ball much later than Richards did. It is because of this that his feet appeared hardly to move at all when, in fact, they made quicksilver seem relatively sedentary and invariably took him to the right place unless it was one of his more absent-minded days. Bowling at Richards was not a particularly enjoyable occupation. Once, about thirty years ago, I watched Essex at Chelmsford on a Saturday, the first day of a Championship game, before going down to Southampton to watch a Sunday League match between Hampshire and Essex the next day. As I was driving out of the ground at Chelmsford, I stopped to talk to David Acfield, who was preparing to make the same journey. I asked how he viewed the prospect of Richards and he laughed. 'It's got to the stage,' he told me, 'that when I come on to bowl to him, he blocks the bad balls and only hits the good ones. It seems to amuse him more.'

Richards, tallish and strong with a ready smile, sauntered out to bat with his long hair flowing out from the back of his cap. He took guard quickly and despatched the first two half volleys through the covers with imperious strokes, but as soon as the ball left his bat he gave the impression his mind was already on other things. There was always a certain world-weariness about him at the crease. A short one came along and was either pulled or square cut for another four and he would fidget around in the crease giving the impression that he wasn't really sure why he was out there in the first place. A beautifully timed straight drive in the next over was made to seem just about the easiest thing in the world. There was never the slightest air of satisfaction, let alone triumphalism, about Richards at the crease. He was doing his job in the only way that he knew how to do it. If Richards had been the third trombonist to end all third trombonists, there would have been as little emotion in his performance as there was with his batting. When he reached 50 the applause was vibrant because everyone will have felt that they had seen something breathtaking and phenomenal. Richards acknowledged the applause perfunctorily, knowing it was the done thing but without giving the impression that he was seething with inner satisfaction. It was the same when he got out in that there was again no visible emotion and he sauntered off as he had come on, without giving the impression that he was about to conduct a lengthy post-mortem about the way in which he was dismissed. Nor, quite obviously, was he going to throw his bat through the dressing-room door. It was, of course, a moment of great sadness for those of us watching. The sun had gone out of the day and the rest of the menu could only be an anticlimax. Even if Gordon Greenidge still remained, there was not the same majesty in his strokes, although he was a more than adequate second best.

All innings played by Richards were to some extent the same, whether he was out for 8 or 158. The same slightly disdainful sense of ennui prevailed, although of course it was a false impression. No one whose instinct for his art was as sure as his can have failed to work at it, even if it was with this overwhelming air of indifference. The innings he played in that Test series against Australia will always remain as abiding memories, as indeed must any sizeable innings from him. For those who saw it, the 356 he made for South Australia against Western Australia in Perth in 1970/71 must remain as the best they have ever seen. Richards made 325 on the first day against an attack that included, among others, the young Dennis Lillee and the ageing Tony Lock and Graham McKenzie. Rod Marsh was keeping wicket and the day benefited from his humour, although it is Richards who tells the story.

> McKenzie ran in, in that wonderfully coordinated style, and bowled the first ball of the match, a gentle outswinger which I felt for and missed. As Rod tossed the ball back round the field he turned to John Inverarity, the first slip, and said: 'Geez, I thought this bloke was supposed to be able to play a bit.' That evening when Lillee bowled the last ball of the day, I simply walked down the wicket, drove the ball back past him to the sightscreen for four and without breaking strike continued towards the pavilion: 325 not out. Inverarity turned to Marsh and with remarkably quick recall considering the hours in the field, commented cryptically: 'I suppose he can play a bit.' Recalling that innings now is like a dream. Somehow I managed to sustain for a complete day the sort of form that usually materialises only in short, glorious moments.

He had a wonderfully successful season with South Australia. 'In first-class matches I could hardly have been more pleased with my final total of 1,538 runs at an average of 109.86. I fell short of Don Bradman's record of 1,690 runs for New South Wales in 1928/29, but it was an honour to come that close to the great man . . .'

Perhaps that first comparison of mine may not have been so far wide of the mark. Frustratingly and unhappily, it is a question that will for all time remain filed in the folder headed 'might have beens'.

DENNIS LILLEE

DENNIS LILLEE caused an amazing buzz of anticipation around the ground when he grasped the new ball. When the umpire called 'play' and he started his run in, the whole ground seemed to catch its breath – especially if it was in Australia. Anything was possible. Lillee, all tousled hair and moustache, a wide and colourful sweatband around his head, a deep-throated scowl and a challenging, hairy torso with three shirt buttons undone, flowed in to the bowling crease with all the smoothness of a long rolling wave. Then, as it rose towards its climax, came that glorious action from close to the stumps that propelled the ball at fierce pace towards the batsman before curving away late in its flight towards the slips. This was followed by the prancing follow through, which took him to within whispering distance of the batsman. He was a fearsome sight and, during his career, he will have frightened batsmen into submission. He was in charge and didn't he let the batsman know it!

His partner, Jeff Thomson, ran in at the other end like a primeval caveman giving his all, come hell or high water, but there was something much more Machiavellian about Lillee. His dislike of the batsman was a more personal matter and it was more obvious. He was starkly sinister and, when he thought he had trapped the batsman lbw or had had him caught at the wicket, downright terrifying. As he yelled his appeal he would turn round to face the umpires squatting on his haunches with both hands raised and his pointing index fingers already anticipating the decision. There was always a dramatic sense of theatre about Lillee as well as a vibrant air of confrontation, especially when he came up against highly critical journalists whom he considered to be self-important, pompous, living in the past and beyond the pale. His was an appeal that may have prompted a number of inexperienced umpires to answer it in the affirmative whereas, upon cool reflection, they may have decided a quiet shake of the head would have been the better answer. Lillee was a hard man to deny. To appreciate him fully, it is necessary to look briefly at the story of his early career to see what he had to overcome in the way of injury. This makes his subsequent achievements even more remarkable and only added to his popularity in Australia and the respect he gained everywhere else.

He did nothing by halves. At the bottom of all the prima donna-ishness he is a man of good humour, but as a fast bowler he set himself a part to play and played it exceedingly well. But long before he entered the world of histrionics he had understood the need for unrelenting hard work to take him to the pinnacle of his profession. Not only that, but he also had to conquer serious injury that would have brought the career of a less dedicated man to an early close. Like most fast bowlers, he burst upon the scene as a young tearaway. In his first full series, in England in 1972, after starting the season with back trouble, he took 31 wickets in the five Tests matches. Then, after three matches against Pakistan in Australia, he was off to the West Indies but, after playing in the First Test in Kingston, he broke down with what was diagnosed as three stress fractures in his back. He did not play again on that tour and ruled himself out of all state and Test cricket the following season in Australia. It was now that he showed what he was made of as he gritted his teeth and embarked on a long and frustrating struggle to get himself back to the bowling crease. He played Pennant cricket in Perth, mainly as a batsman, although about halfway through the season he could not resist the temptation to turn his arm over. He did not dare attempt to reach his full pace but at a lesser speed he learned a lot about control and he began to do more with the ball. Ironically, his enforced lay off turned him into a better and more complete bowler. It says a great deal for his character, too, that he was prepared to submit himself to the fierce and painful rehabilitation exercises and schedules that the medical profession gave him.

The following Australian season, England were the visitors, which provided Lillee with a succulent goal at which to aim. All went well in training during the previous winter and, as luck would have it, Western Australia's first Shield match in 1974/75 was in Adelaide against South Australia a couple of days after the England side had arrived in Adelaide at the start of their tour. Without hinting at what was to come, he coped with a press conference and took 7 wickets in that match. He then came through the other Shield games before the First Test and found himself back in the Australian side. His partner in arms was Jeff Thomson, who had played one Test against Pakistan in 1972/73 without taking a wicket. He had subsequently moved from New South Wales to Queensland where he had been bowling fast and with considerable success. It is a matter of history that the unknown Thomson and the supposedly convalescent Lillee destroyed the England side in a series Australia won, 4–1. They became one of the great fast bowling combinations in the history of the game. Lillee's progress was a triumph with 25 wickets in the six Tests, although he was able to bowl only six overs in the Sixth before he suffered a bruised right foot. Some convalescent!

Lillee was never as fast as Thomson, but he was more cunning. He had a great variety at his disposal, moving the ball in the air and off the pitch, and also had a most deceptive slower ball. His bouncer was a fearsome weapon, too, and he had the habit of bowling it in that awkward spot where the batsman found that he had to play it. The short ball often followed the batsman as he was trying to take evasive action by pulling inside the line. All these attributes combined with the frightening ferociousness of his run-up and action put him at the top of the pile of the many fast bowlers I have been lucky enough to see. His behaviour could be infuriating, but never for a single second was he boring, whether bowling, giving a press conference or going about his everyday life.

Lillee was a particularly fearsome prospect in Australia because the crowds were behind him to a man. When he ran in to bowl, it was to the background of huge crowds chanting, 'Lillee, Lillee, Lillee'. It was a sound that undoubtedly inspired him and of course there is nothing more that Australian crowds love to see than the Poms being beaten. As Lillee was the principal means to that end, there was no end to the hero-worship. Good as he was on that tour by England in 1974/75 and the following summer when the West Indies were beaten 5–1, he reserved his best for the Centenary Test match at Melbourne in 1977. Australia won an excellent game by 45 runs, which had been the exact margin of their victory in the first-ever Test match at Melbourne in 1877. In England's first innings, when they were bowled out for 95, Lillee took 6/26 in the defining spell of his life, and in the second he finished with 5/139. There was something compelling and irresistible about the way in which Lillee ran in to bowl during that match and also about the way his late outswing destroyed the England batting.

There was in Lillee a strong streak of arrogant obstinacy that led to one or two bizarre instances during his Test career. John Woodcock, as always, put his finger on all the particular spots when he wrote: 'Lillee had the resolutely independent streak of many fast bowlers, only more so. If he was requested not to practise in short trousers at Lord's, the chances were that he would wear them. He was a magnificent bowler, an irrepressible exhibitionist, an impenitent bully and a great student of the theory and practice of bowling, which enabled him to be wonderfully effective to the day he retired from Test cricket at the age of thirty-four.' His deserved reward was 355 Test wickets, which at the time was more than any other Australian.

When Lillee kicked over the traces, he did so in the grand manner. The Australian crowds loved him for it. They have always warmed to anyone who has been prepared to cock a snook at authority and Lillee's own form of larrikinism was much to their liking. I was present at three memorable incidents, all of which will have added to the value for money he regularly gave. All three took place in Australia, which may not have been entirely a coincidence. The first occurred in March 1977 on the last day of the Centenary Test match in Melbourne, which was by some way the best organised and the greatest success of all the anniversary matches I have been to. At tea on the last day, when the match was poised for a dramatic finish, the occasion was graced by the presence of the Queen. Over to Lillee himself:

> Her attendance at the game complemented the occasion beautifully. Well, I decided to capitalise on the situation. In for a penny, in for a pound . . . I would ask her for her autograph. I asked the twelfth man during lunch to make sure to put my autograph book and a pen in my blazer pocket, so I could have it at the ready at the line-up later. As the Queen met the player next to me, I reached into my pocket and brought the equipment out. Then Greg Chappell introduced me to Her Majesty. I bowed most respectfully and then from behind my back I produced the book and the pen and stuttered out, 'Would you mind autographing this for me?' She was obviously taken aback. She smiled embarrassedly, paused and said, 'Not now.' With no disrespect, I wondered, 'If it can't be now, when will I ever get it . . . you surely won't be coming in for a drink after play.' But as it turned out, that was by no means the end of the matter. It was followed up by a cricket official, who got in touch with her aide and she signed a photograph taken of the incident. It is now one of my most prized possessions.

Two years later, Kerry Packer's World Series Cricket and the establishment had come together, although in reality it was more than anything a capitulation by the establishment. Australia played two three-match series against England and the West Indies in 1979/80 and a plethora of one-day games besides. At this time, Lillee was promoting an aluminium bat, which was much cheaper than the normal willow cricket bat. He had used it in a state game without comment being made, perhaps because he had made a brief duck, against the West Indies in Brisbane. He brought it out again for the First Test against England in Perth. After driving Tony Greig through extra cover for three, he was approached by Mike Brearley, the captain, who told him the aluminium bat was damaging the ball. Brearley complained to the umpires and they told Lillee to change it and Rodney Hogg, Australia's twelfth man, brought out a willow blade. Lillee again takes up the story:

> I wanted to get the position clarified, so I left the field. As I walked towards the dressing room I saw a W.A. Cricket Association official in the crowd and asked him what was my position. He told me I was within my rights to use the bat. I went on to the dressing room and was about to change the bat when Rod Marsh asked me what I was doing. I replied, 'I'm going to change my bat.' He said he thought I was within my rights continuing to use it. 'Damn it,' I thought, 'he's right.' I grabbed the aluminium bat again and walked back out with it. I went straight to the crease at the non-striker's end and waited for the game to continue. However the umpires told me I couldn't continue until I'd changed the bat. I said, 'Look, I'm ready to continue.'
>
> The reply came firmly, 'No, no, you can't continue unless you have a willow bat – and if you don't get one we'll retire your innings.' Then I saw Greg Chappell coming out with a selection of bats and I thought, 'Well, obviously I'm not going to win out here . . . and if I'm retired I'll harm the team.' That's when I became so emotionally upset, and knowing that what I was doing was within the Laws of cricket and feeling that I was being 'got at'. So I flung the bat away.

It was a petulant and childish act and if it had not been for this throw, which propelled the bat some twenty yards towards the pavilion, perhaps it would not have seemed such a reprehensible business. It was all to do with publicity, and being the man he is, Lillee had wrung every last drop out of the incident. He could be an awkward customer if he wanted to. But I daresay the Western Australians who were at the game that day will remember it longer for Lillee and his aluminium bat than for any of the cricket, which,

I suppose, meant that he had been extremely successful. The afore-mentioned bat, meanwhile, lives in peace at his home, signed by all the members of both sides. In the end, I can't believe it will have helped the sale of the wretched things.

While Lillee has been a pretty accurate witness to what went on in both these two events, his description of the third, when the Pakistani batsman Javed Miandad collided with him in mid-pitch when he was completing an easy single to mid on at no more than walking pace, has been accompanied by a good deal of poetic licence. It was by far the worst of the incidents, even allowing for the fact that Miandad's nature was nothing if not contentious. From the boundary it looked more as if Lillee had deliberately blocked Miandad than that the batsman had first attempted to strike Lillee with his bat from two paces distance, which is the fast bowler's version. Lillee then aimed a nasty kick at Miandad as he went past and it ended with Miandad holding his bat two-handed above Lillee's head as if he had decided that summary execution was called for. The fearless umpire, Tony Crafter, deserved a size-able medal for stepping between the two and showing a greater firmness of purpose than any United Nations peace-keeping force. Although the Australian Board's disciplinary arm was usually as pusillanimous as a wet dishcloth when it came to dealing with their own players, this time they at least suspended Lillee for a couple of one-day games.

Love him or hate him, Dennis Lillee was always very much his own man. He bowled like a god and perhaps if he had not had all those other sides to him, he would not have been the fiery and effective performer he was with the ball in his hand. Perhaps, too, he would not have had the determination to overcome those stress fractures of the vertebrae. He was at his peak in the mid-seventies, but as he slowed down his cunning increased. He developed a splendid leg cutter, which served him famously well in the last years of his career. He was always a good friend and very loyal to those he liked, and he has gone on to do a lot for the game and for modern players. He has been a successful fast-bowling coach, especially in India where he has run coaching clinics and the young hopefuls could not possibly look for a better role model.

Nonetheless, he was full of the traditional irascibility of fast bowlers – the best have seldom been angels. It is the measure of his brilliance as a fast bowler that in his admirable book, *One Hundred Greatest Cricketers*, John Woodcock has put him three places above Ray Lindwall and thirteen ahead of Fred Spofforth whose fire and fury had repeatedly impaired WG's technique and whom Lillee came closest to imitating. There was also a distinct physical likeness between the two. Lillee was a great fast bowler and a redoubtable character.

IMRAN KHAN

IMRAN KHAN does not fit easily under any one heading. He was a brilliant fast bowler and a good enough batsman to average 37.69 in 126 innings in Test cricket; his 362 wickets cost 22.81 each. These are staggering figures with both averages better than Ian Botham or Kapil Dev could manage, even if there was not quite the same weight of runs or wickets. For all that, one was often left with the impression that Imran could have scored many more runs if he had put his mind to it. Maybe if he had, his bowling figures would have suffered. He had plenty on his shoulders, too, because he was probably the best captain that Pakistan has ever had. He has subsequently become a considerable politician within his own country, although whether he will ever be tough enough or be prepared to do what it takes to become a potent political force remains to be seen. He emanates from the upper echelons of society in Pakistan and is also a formidable ornament of manhood who, if he has not exactly set the social scene alight in the West, has had at his beck and call just about any of the fashionable beauties he may have fancied. He has ended up by marrying Jemima Goldsmith, the daughter of the financier, Jimmy Goldsmith – and that is an achievement that perhaps calls for a book on its own.

Urbane and charming, rational and reasonable, Imran was a fierce and immensely able competitor, the most determined of men, the shrewdest of captains and the smoothest of deb's delights who, after a spell as a polished lothario, has become the happiest of married men. He is a man who has been equally at home in the royal enclosure at Ascot and at Annabel's nightclub in Berkeley Square as he is up the road at Lord's. He is comfortable on Jemima's arm at a fashion show in Paris, or in local dress at a downtown bazaar or coffee shop in Lahore where Urdu and not English is the order of the day. He would be as much an asset at any Government House or Embassy get-together in whatever part of the world cricket, politics or his social calendar should take him. He is truly a man for all seasons and with a gun under his arm in the shooting season no bird or animal is safe, be it pheasant or partridge in England or wild boar or shakoor back home in Pakistan. His one blind spot has been that he is an obsessive man. In the end, this was to cost him his cricket career when he apparently put the need to raise money for his beloved cancer hospital above the requirements of his players who had helped him to an extraordinary victory in the 1992 World Cup in Australia and New Zealand.

Anyone who does not know Imran and who reads this last paragraph may think of him as too much of a social butterfly that flits from one subject to the next as the mood takes him. This is not true, for Imran takes himself and his life pretty seriously. He leaves as little to chance as possible; he works out his position carefully on everything and it is difficult to deflect him from his course. He expresses himself in that deep resonant voice, which, I daresay, speaks to the innermost depths of those beautiful women he has taken out over the years. His political position has been as carefully considered, if not more so, as any other, and his arguments have been well thought out and are expressed with great feeling. He talks carefully and deliberately and his style might not be ideally suited to the noisy cut and thrust of a debating chamber. For all that, he has been pretty good in the atmosphere of the dressing room, which at times must resemble a barrack room. He also did uncommonly well in the High Court when defending a libel action brought against him by Ian Botham and Allan Lamb. Imran had made some disparaging remarks about the two of them in a paper in Pakistan. He had the luck to have George Carman fighting his corner, although Imran's eventual victory came as a surprise even to that skilful and experienced advocate. The judge, Christopher French, summed up heavily in favour of Lamb and Botham, but the jury found for Imran – I was in court. Imran thinks quickly on his feet in the middle of a cricket match, too, and has always given the impression of taking the trouble to understand his fellow Pakistan players better than any of his immediate predecessors or successors. This may be because Imran has always been certain of his own position, both from within the team and as far as the administrators on the outside were concerned. He has always commanded respect through apprehension if not fear, something underlined by the support he received from the President of his own country, General Zia-ul-Haq. Unlike most other captains of Pakistan, he never felt the need to look over his shoulder.

He was an inspirational captain who led by example and was always the man in charge. In the field, Imran could never have been mistaken for anyone other than the captain for he was an authoritative figure with a walk and a manner to match. It was difficult to misinterpret his instructions. He had a great knowledge of cricket and the highways and the byways through which the game runs. He is someone who knows his own mind and there was always a shrewd logic about him as a captain – a job that he obviously enjoyed. His finest hour in charge came during that 1992 World Cup in Australia and New Zealand. But first came the agony that was both collective and personal. Pakistan made a dreadful start to the competition, winning only one of their first five matches. Imran himself hurt his right shoulder a couple of days before their first game, against the West Indies, and was unable to play. He could not bear to watch from the sidelines and so, without batting or bowling, he played against Zimbabwe whom they beat in their next match. He made his shoulder injury worse while practising and doctors told him that the more he played the worse it would get. Eventually, a gadget was found that sent magnetic currents into his shoulder. This enabled him to take the field but results did not improve. Nonetheless, Imran still believed Pakistan could win the competition and spoke to his players accordingly.

A score of 220/9 surprisingly proved to be too much for Australia and after that they coped with Sri Lanka's total of 212/6. They then had to go to Auckland and beat New Zealand who had yet to lose a match. Imran put New Zealand in and after Wasim Akram and Mushtaq Ahmed had destroyed the opposing batting, Pakistan won by 7 wickets. New Zealand were again their opponents in the semi-final. This time they made 262/7. Although he was in such pain he could hardly lift a cup of tea, Imran bowled ten relatively expensive overs and then made 44 going in third. It was left to the young Inzamam-ul-Haq, who scored a massively powerful 60 off thirty-seven balls, to see Pakistan into the final. They now beat England more convincingly than the margin of 22 runs suggests with Imran himself contributing a most resourceful 72. It was an amazing triumph and it was only afterwards that Imran let himself down.

For some time his obsession in life had been raising funds on a worldwide basis to build a cancer hospital in Lahore in memory of his mother who had died from the disease. There is no doubt that he used cricket to promote this eminently worthy cause. He was now carried away by the moment. After being presented with the World Cup he made a speech of acceptance that turned him from hero to villain in the eyes of some of his team. 'I would just like to say I want to give my commiserations to the English team. But I want them to know that by winning this World Cup, personally it means that one of my great obsessions in life, which is to build a cancer hospital . . . I'm sure that this World Cup will go a long way towards completion of this obsession. I would also like to say that I feel very proud. At the twilight of my career, finally, I have managed to win the World Cup. Thank you.' His players did not feel that they were being given enough credit for what they had achieved or recompense for the harsh treatment they had often suffered during the competition at the hands of their captain.

The expectations of victorious Pakistani cricketers are huge. They have always been paid a pittance to play for their country, and the government rewarded them for winning. They felt strongly that Imran should not have used the World Cup victory as a vehicle to raise funds for his hospital rather than his players who made the victory possible. They had an excellent point – no, his speech afterwards was not a direct appeal for cash, and he did not divert the cash awarded for victory, but it showed how his mind was working. It might all have been viewed differently in the west, but in Pakistan, Imran was wrong. Of course, Imran himself did not see it like this and disillusionment coupled with the pain he still suffered from that injured shoulder persuaded him to go back on his original promise to be available for Pakistan's tour of England in 1992.

Both Imran's parents came from Pathan landowning families and they are a fiercely proud and independent people and in this respect Imran has been true to his inheritance. He is not a man who has ever been dominated on the cricket field or off it. He tells a revealing story about himself as a thirteen-year-old. 'Once, when I was thirteen, I was stopped by the police while driving my father's car. I knew I was driving without a licence, so I bribed the policeman and got away with it. The chauffeur reported the incident to my mother. She was furious. She felt stooping to bribery was a real loss of dignity, and that I should have gone to jail instead. I tried to defend myself by saying that other boys of my age had done the same in similar situations. Her answer was brief: "You are a Pathan." In her eyes that was synonymous with pride and honesty.'

He also came from a family that had a remarkable tradition of cricket, especially on his mother's side. His mother and her two sisters all produced sons who went on to captain Pakistan, Imran, Javed Burki and Majid Khan. Eight of Imran's cousins have also played first-class cricket, the result of the coaching they received on their own ground at Zaman Park where the family lived in Lahore.

Imran played his first game of first-class cricket when he was sixteen and was still at Aitchison College. He did not lack in self-confidence or precociousness. 'I made my first-class debut for Lahore against Sargodha. The chairman of selectors was my uncle, while the captain of the Lahore side and the senior player were my cousins. Some called this nepotism. I, of course, preferred to regard it as pure coincidence. I then behaved as if I was doing everyone a favour by gracing the occasion. I was to be the opening batsman and the opening bowler, and I was still only sixteen. It rained before the match, and rather than hang around the ground I went back to where I was staying and went to sleep. After a long rest, I returned to find that the game had started and that someone else had gone in to open the innings instead of me. Needless to say, I got hell from the captain, Hammayun Zaman, while the team thought me spoilt and unworthy of being given a chance.' These two stories give a good idea of the cool customer that Imran has always been.

Although he played, with limited success, against England in 1971 and 1974, it was not until 1976/77 in Australia that Imran became a regular member of the Pakistan Test side. In the Third Test in Sydney he took 6 wickets in each innings, taking Pakistan to their first Test victory in Australia, by 8 wickets, and to a draw in the series. He was the most compelling of cricketers. He had a lovely fluent run up to the wicket and a giant leap preceded the delivery. It took him a while to perfect his art and he was continually bedevilled by injury. With remarkable persistence he coped with stress fractures to his back and then in 1983 he found that the continual pounding of his left foot into the crease during the delivery stride had fractured the ankle. After the World Cup in 1983, he unwisely continued to play for Sussex and was then asked to captain Pakistan in Australia in 1983/84. He was able to play in the last two Tests only, and then just as a batsman, although at Melbourne he reckoned his 83 was as good an innings as he ever played. Pakistan were easily beaten and it was a tour that gave plenty of fuel to Imran's many detractors in Pakistan, where he received a dreadful press.

There were many people who were idiotically jealous of Imran, and his position was undermined from within the team by that brilliant batsman, Zaheer Abbas, who should have known better. When the tour was over, Imran soon returned to London where his leg was put in a cast for the six most trying months of his life. He had been told after an x-ray that his career was at an end. His friends kept him going and in October 1984 another x-ray showed that his leg had completely healed. After playing for New South Wales in 1984/85, he was back in the thick of it for Pakistan the following year. He had the satisfaction of taking Pakistan to victory over India in the final of a competition in Sharjah when he himself took 6/14.

The story of this ankle injury is worth telling for it shows what a tough streak there was running through Imran and it makes his performance as a player seem even more remarkable. The fact that he never gave up is in itself admirable, but more than that, whenever he returned to the fray he was turning in match-winning performances in no time at all. His bowling took pride of place but every now and then he produced an innings like that 83 in Melbourne that showed what might have happened had he put his batting first. I was lucky enough to see perhaps his best innings of all, against Australia at the Adelaide Oval in 1989/90. He made 136, his highest Test score and his sixth hundred. He and Wasim Akram joined forces when Pakistan were 90/5 and losing the match fast. They put on 191 for the sixth wicket and enabled Pakistan to draw. Both played innings of the highest quality. Imran batted for 485 minutes and showed off his impeccable technique. His innings of 82 not out in the Third Test at Sydney, which was washed out, was not far behind.

In whatever he chooses to do, Imran will remain the most engaging of men. His opinions will always be worth listening to from whichever pulpit he preaches them. One of his cricketing achievements, of which he is most proud, was his determination to see to it that neutral umpires supervised Test cricket. He was the moving force behind the decision to use Indian umpires when the West

Indies visited Pakistan in 1986/87. This first experiment was a great success. He has never been afraid to be critical of the game's authorities, especially those in their ivory towers at Lord's. It was the intransigence of the traditional authorities that made it necessary for a Kerry Packer-like figure to come on the scene. Imran, a Packer supporter and participant, was as passionate about his feelings then as he is today about the illegality of the Second Gulf War and what he considers to be the shameful pusillanimity of the Blair government in England in its failure to take any sort of lead when it comes to Mugabe's Zimbabwe. The soap box may have become his platform now that he is past fifty, but I have no doubt that his ability to entertain will continue unabated just as he will remain the most charming and convivial of companions.

VIVIAN RICHARDS

FOR almost two decades the world's leading bowlers were in thrall to Vivian Richards. Only a handful of batsmen in the history of the game have dominated as he was able to. Richards was talked about with bated breath from an early age in his home of Antigua. He was in his mid-teens when he first took his place at the Recreation Ground in the side that represented the Leeward Islands against the touring side. His father was a warder in the prison just across the road and Richards always remained proud to have achieved what he had coming from such humble origins. I first saw him play against the New Zealanders in 1971/72 when he was on the verge of his twentieth birthday. He emerged from the pavilion, young, brimming with enthusiasm, and there was about him an extraordinary self-confidence, but not yet that tinge of world-weariness that was increasingly to affect his stroll about the ground as the years went by. He was known by everyone as Viv and the expectation was enormous. I was in the commentary box for that match with, among others, Lester Bird who was later to succeed his father, Vere, as Prime Minister of Antigua, and Tim Hector, a rebellious trade unionist at the opposite end of the political spectrum. On the air, Hector unleashed a raucous, half-shouting voice that was stretched to the limit that day when Richards lent into the first peerless cover drive for public consumption. Lester and Tim agreed not to disagree on air, but there was one person about whom they would never have disagreed. I don't think anyone who left the ground after that match had any doubt that a prince had been born on an island where cricket and religion were both vibrant forces. One of the highlights of that match, too, was Richards' fielding in the covers where, as he was to do throughout his career, he swooped like a swallow in mid-season form and threw to the top of the stumps as if he was using a bow and arrow. Who will ever forget the direct hits from Richards that ran out three Australians in the first World Cup final, at Lord's in 1975?

Just over two years later he was taken to India by the West Indies and in his second Test match he batted for five hours and made 192 not out and most of the rest is well-documented history. He had a mildly unhappy time in Australia in 1975/76 where, like many others before him, he took time to work out the steeper bounce on the Australian pitches, and until he had done so Lillee and Thomson were a problem. In the New Year, the West Indies visited Tasmania for a couple of games and it was there that the West Indian management came up with the brilliant idea of putting Richards in first. In Hobart, he scored a hundred in both innings. He then made another in the Fifth Test and scores of 50 and 98 in the Sixth. Suddenly, the confidence that he had been lacking came flooding back and those three innings were the prototype of so many he was to play in the Test arena. They were terrific value to watch, full of all the trademark Richards strokes, and he will have returned home in much better spirits than many of his colleagues, for Australia won the series 5–1. When he took guard for the West Indies the following month against India in the Caribbean, he was batting at number three and if any doubts remained about Richards they were now comprehensively dispelled. He hit three hundreds in the series and made 556 runs in all. The next year in England, he played in only four Test matches and made 829 in a series that had been given a somewhat obtuse start by England's captain, Tony Greig.

Although born of Scottish parents, Greig's home and upbringing had been in apartheid South Africa. When, before the start of this series, Greig had publicly said, 'We will make them [the West Indies] grovel,' it was, to say the least, not the most tactful of remarks, especially coming from one who was a white South African. No one was more upset than Viv Richards. He said afterwards, 'I felt it was not too brilliant a thing for a South African to say about West Indian players and it made me more determined to do well,' – the master of the understatement. When he went out to bat in the First Test at Trent Bridge, he will have thought of his bat more as a weapon of war than an implement for playing a game. He took root for seven-and-a-half hours, hitting four sixes and thirty-one fours with even greater ferocity than usual while making 232. As one writer put it: 'The graduation of Vivian Richards from student of the highest potential to master of the batting art, stuffed Tony Greig's battle cry down his throat.' He put on 303 with Alvin Kallicharran for the third wicket. Then, after driving Derek Underwood over long on for one last six, he holed out to long off. Michael Melford takes up the story in the *Daily Telegraph*: 'The catcher, Tony Greig, was promptly mobbed by a crowd of small boys, not unnaturally excited because they'd all been a lot younger when England had last taken a wicket.' It had been Richards at his pluperfect best, even though England managed to draw that match and the next at Lord's.

Even so, he kept his best until the end, at The Oval. Driving, cutting and pulling almost at will, he cut the England attack to ribbons and at the end of the first day's play was 200 not out. The West Indies always receive plenty of support at The Oval and their supporters had the best day of their lives. After heavy celebrations on the first evening, which the England players will have wished had been even heavier, he scored another 91 on the second day with the same verve and excitement, although it was obvious that he was growing tired. Before he was out, driving carelessly at Greig, there were West Indian hopes that he might go on to better Garry Sobers' 365, but Richards kept his mind free from such considerations.

You can't play an innings in that way, going after a record. Every ball has to be played on its merits and concentration is important throughout. And thinking about how many runs you want to make, or about some batting record set by someone else could disturb your concentration. I was out there to bat and stay as long as I could. I never let myself think of making 365.

It was in *Wisden* that John Woodcock wrote:

> . . . the presence of Richards, the world's greatest player, was an inspiration to the side. There seldom seemed much reason for him not to make a large and entertaining score and his runs came so fast that he could be given by way of a rest, a lower place in the order and still have time to make a telling contribution. It would be hard to overpraise Richards, either for the brilliance with which he bats or the spirit in which he plays the game.

Richards was the most exciting batsman I have ever seen. When he was in the mood to destroy it did not matter where you bowled to him. His lightning reflexes enabled him to find an attacking stroke for every ball, provided it was within his reach. One wonders if any other batsman in the history of the game has had the same ability to obliterate an attack. He was mesmerising to watch from the moment his cap came into view as he walked down the steps of the pavilion past the members. There was something pantheresque about the way in which he prowled to the wicket; there was just the touch of a swagger and a hint of wry humour, too, as if he was already saying to the bowlers, 'Now we'll see how good you are.' Of course, it did not always come off, but the fun of it was that one knew that something dramatic was going to happen, even if it was the loss of his own wicket. While there was a punitive ferocity in both the conception and the power of his strokes, there was also an impeccable technique underpinned by brilliant footwork. So often there seemed to be no reason why he should ever get out. The fact that he did was often the result of him having a cheeky and well-nigh impossible dart in an attempt perhaps to send the bowler to the one part of the ground he had so far missed. When he was at his pulverising best, he took risks that no one else would have attempted and sometimes they did not come off. Then there were the occasions when a good ball soon after he had come in would make him look as mortal as the next batsman. Just occasionally, he had a bad day at the office, which left us all scratching our heads. It was said in Barbados of all places that when he played there for the Leeward Islands, or the Combined Islands before that, he was not always at his most dominant against an attack that invariably contained at least a couple of formidable fast bowlers, one of whom was Malcolm Marshall.

He played orthodox strokes with a withering power and certainty. There were touches of improvisation and what made it all even more fun was that he usually gave the impression that a smile was not too far away, although it may have been more of self-satisfaction than humour. But, more than anything, he left the impression of overwhelming power. If Richards himself was deadly serious, then it was his bat that was smiling – and from ear to ear. A big innings by Richards was a medley of all those wonderful strokes that had flowed down the years from the bats of Headley, Weekes, Walcott, Sobers and those other exciting West Indians. Richards was supercharged West Indian from his toe nails upwards and he had a formidably strong character. Being the genius he was, he inevitably carried around the world almost the full weight of West Indian hopes and aspirations upon his shoulders. A four or a six by Richards was yet another crack for freedom in a world that had become increasingly racial.

These not inconsiderable burdens did not always, and perhaps understandably, sit lightly upon Richards' shoulders. He paid Greig back handsomely for his 'grovel' remarks at the same time as giving the West Indian communities around the world, and most particularly in England, pride in being West Indian and greater confidence in their own ability to stand up and face the world on their doorsteps with a greater sense of self-respect. Richards knew what was expected of him in this sense, but he never allowed it to deflect him from his course. He did not allow himself to become a more introspective, defensive batsman who was hell-bent only on survi-

192

val and producing enormous figures at the end of the day, no matter how long it took. He stood up, as always, and belted the hell out of the opposition. He did it the grand way with a broad sweep of the brush and provided cricketing entertainment as few have been able to do.

In his many triumphs he was never obviously vindictive and nor did he gloat, apart from that swagger as he strode back and forth to the pavilion that was open to interpretation. When he batted he laid his intentions down plainly for all to see and, stepping back, allowed the world to come to their own conclusions. Richards has a sharp mind and he knew exactly what he was doing, and he achieved his ends in the best possible way. His fellow West Indians owe him a huge debt. Peter Roebuck, who played with him for Somerset and knew him well, writes: 'Viv rarely gives vent to his strong views; his innermost beliefs remain hidden from all but his small circle of friends. Consequently his anger at injustice and prejudice surprises those who know only his ready smile. He has the presence, the personality and the discretion to emerge as an impressive and weighty ambassador for his colour and country.'

Richards was enabled to play cricket for Somerset because of a bookmaker from Bath who was also a Somerset County Cricket Club committee member. Early in 1974, Len Creed visited Antigua with a touring side called the Mendip Acorns, but his main concern was to have a look at Richards with Colin Cowdrey's words of praise for the young man ringing in his ears. Richards had still not played for the West Indies. Creed, who had a reputation for spotting the player who would save Somerset about once every ten days, failed to convince Colin Atkinson, the chairman of the club, of the need to sign him post haste. Creed suggested, therefore, that he would himself bring Richards to England and put him up in Bath so that he could play for the Lansdowne Club and Somerset could take it from there. Richards made a solid if not brilliant start for Lansdowne and owed his elevation to the Somerset side to the fearful ear-bashing Creed gave to fellow committee members and anyone else who would listen. Richards was taken on to the Somerset staff and it was only then that they began to realise at Taunton just how lucky they had been. He was soon scoring hundreds for Somerset and won his county cap in that same season, in 1974.

He returned to Antigua at the end of this first season with Somerset an improved and more versatile player, having learned to cope with English conditions. Soon, and to his great surprise, he found himself selected for the West Indies tour of India. When Richards began to play for the West Indies, Clive Lloyd was his captain, and he was later to write this of the young Richards: 'Earlier in his career Viv suffered from a little bit of nervousness and did not make as big an impression as he thought he was capable of. Despite all the critics, I knew in my own heart that it was only a matter of time before this acorn grew into a big tree.' Lloyd himself helped that process when he promoted him to open the innings on the tour of Australia the following year.

Richards played for Somerset for thirteen seasons between 1974 and 1986. Ian Botham's first season was also 1974 and, with so much in common, it was hardly surprising that he and Richards should have become the closest of friends and almost inseparable. The West Indian fast bowler Joel Garner joined them at Taunton in 1977 and these three were the main reason for the county's best years ever in the various domestic competitions. At this time they won the Gillette Cup and the NatWest Trophy, as this competition was to become in 1981. They also won the Benson & Hedges Cup twice and the Sunday League once, although the County Championship remained tantalisingly just beyond their reach. Richards' prodigious batting feats had much to do with this success. His secret was that he scored his runs so quickly, making sure that the bowlers had the time they wanted to bowl the other side out twice. For years Richards delighted a generation of Englishmen with his dramatic and incredible run-scoring feats as Somerset travelled the country season after season. He provided many cricket-lovers with first-hand entertainment that might otherwise have been reserved for the Test grounds in England and therefore would not perhaps have been so well or so widely appreciated.

It was sad that his terrific efforts on that loveliest of county grounds at Taunton should have been somewhat soured by the way in which he, Botham and Garner were all kicked into touch by Somerset in 1986. The arguments as to the rights and wrongs of this will rage on for ever and, as with so many of these affairs, one is left with the inescapable feeling that things might have been organised better. But if it had not been for those years of Richards' at Taunton, present-day county cricketers would not have inherited quite such a rich legacy. The county felt they had outlived their usefulness and it was time to move on.

Surprisingly, the only bowler with whom Richards openly admitted he had a score to settle was Bob Willis, who did not normally provoke that sort of reaction in batsmen. Richards had never forgotten a rather unfriendly encounter with Willis in 1973/74 when England visited Antigua for their game against the Leeward Islands. He felt that Willis had given him a hard time bowling bouncers that consistently whistled past his head. He was eventually caught in the deep trying to hook Willis and the memory rankled. He itched to get his own back and when, on the 1980 tour of England, Willis spoke of having a plan up his sleeve to get rid of him, Richards felt that it was time to act. England were bowled out on the first day of the Third Test at Old Trafford for 150 and the West Indies then lost Gordon Greenidge for a duck. It was now that Richards had his revenge. In as ferocious an exhibition of strokeplay as one could wish to see, Richards drove Willis through the covers, straight drove him back over his head and pulled him with withering power to the legside boundary. He made 53 of his 65 runs off Willis whose fourteen overs cost 99 runs. The flailing bat of Richards continued to haunt Willis at Old Trafford. In 1984 in the first of the three one-day internationals, England were beaten almost single-handedly by Richards in probably the most remarkable innings ever to have been played in the shorter game. The West Indies batted first and made 272/9 in their fifty-five overs and no less than 189 of these were made by Richards, who was not out at the end.

Richards himself reckons that innings was the best he ever played. It may have been that Willis's presence in the England side in what turned out to be his last season was the spur the Antiguan needed. The statistics alone were bewildering. He faced 170 balls and hit five sixes and twenty-one fours in an innings of astonishing power and authority. With extras contributing 10 to the total, the batsmen at the other end made 73 runs between them. Richards played all the strokes on both sides of the wicket that day. But most bewildering of all was the way in which he kept coming down the pitch to Willis and driving him far over extra cover into the crowd at the Stretford End. In the final fourteen overs of the innings, Richards and Michael Holding put on 106 at more than 7 runs an over with Holding making 12 of them to Richards' 90.

This innings was one of the great virtuoso performances in the history of the game. It was an innings that encapsulated the full God-given genius of Richards – the glorious technique, the full range of strokes, the extraordinary footwork, that amazing *je ne sais quoi* he brought to his art that has to go down under the heading of flare. It was all topped off by this scintillating desire to attack, something that was always uppermost in his mind, no matter what the situation or how desperate the plight of his own side. Small wonder that the people of the West Indies felt that their hopes of a better world lay with Richards. That day at Old Trafford those sixes and fours blazed a trail for West Indian equality. Each searing hit had a message written all over it.

While it was his ability to hit a cricket ball that placed him on a pedestal, it was all made to seem so much more impressive by his apparently impassive nature. Whatever his inner feelings, which were formidably strong and manifested themselves in a loose attachment to the Rastafarian cause and a strong belief in the sanctity of Emperor Haile Selassie of Ethiopia, he managed for the most part to keep them under control. He was sure that he had to use his ability as one of the best batsmen in the world to publicise the plight of West Indians in general and to do his utmost to help advance their cause so that they were given an equal opportunity with everyone, both at home and in the wider world. He hoped, more than anything, that his own high profile would popularise the causes he was fighting for, which combined black awareness, black pride and black dignity.

No one could have been more opposed to going to South Africa while the old apartheid regime was in power, although he always added the rider that it was up to the individual concerned. He himself adamantly refused a number of extremely well-heeled offers to go. The one occasion on which he was never passive was when confronted by racist taunts. His anger when these were shouted at him across cricket grounds was frightening, but on the whole he let his bat do the talking. In everything that he did on the cricket field he was irresistible, and when one considers the pressures that he felt rested upon him his record becomes even more amazing. It will be a long time before we see his like again. Richards put the West Indians in the mood for Brian Lara, but he has not come to the party in the same way. It was highly appropriate that he became Sir Vivian Richards, the latest in an increasingly long line of West Indian cricketing knights, following on behind Sir Learie (later Lord) Constantine, Sir Frank Worrell, Sir Clyde Walcott, Sir Everton Weekes and Sir Garfield Sobers.

GRAHAM GOOCH

IF Regimental Sergeant-Major Britten, the raucous doyen of RSMs in the sixties, had ever been transformed into an opening batsman, he would have been the spitting image of Graham Gooch – before the advertisers persuaded Gooch to shave off his moustache. The crack of the Gooch cover drive had something of the barked commands of the RSM about it. When it came to voice production though, the two of them would have had to go their separate ways. Britten spat out his commands in the fruity *basso profundo* RSMs are expected to produce on the parade ground, while Gooch was blessed with an altogether higher, less penetrative and commanding tone of voice that would have been hard pressed to make its mark on military matters. Having said that, no one other than Gooch has hit a cricket ball more precisely, as the RSM would have done had he been blessed with the skills of batsmanship. Every attacking stroke was the cricketing equivalent of a strident, no-nonsense command from behind a flourishing black moustache that quivered a good deal at the moment of impact.

Nevertheless, Gooch was a contradiction. For such a wonderfully forthright strokemaker who hit a cricket ball as if he had just caught it with its hand in the till and was giving it a thorough ticking off, he should have been a man of complete certainty and conviction. As it was, he allowed things to worry him and was, at times, dreadfully insecure. His first Test match, at Edgbaston against Australia in 1975, can hardly have helped. Max Walker and Jeff Thomson disposed of him for an unconvincing nought in each innings. After one more unsuccessful Test, at Lord's, he was returned post haste to county cricket and had to wait until 1979 for another chance to pull on his England cap. For all that, no one batted more regally or entertainingly for England in the last two decades of the twentieth century.

He played many of his strokes as if he was a latter day Ted Dexter. The cracking strokeplay and the slight swagger that accompanied it seemed to tell of a public-school education and three years at Oxbridge after that. This was an illusion made more remarkable and splendid by the fact that he came from a working-class family in the East End of London. He was not much more than a drive and a three-iron from being a Cockney. No man could have been luckier in his parents than Gooch. They were down-to-earth, practical and enormously helpful and yet never over-stepped the mark. It was their genes that helped shape Gooch the man and, of course, Gooch the batsman although they almost never tried to influence his views. Their son was a paradox. He was anti-establishment, yet he voted Tory and personified Essex Man. Money attracted him and he was determined to make the most he could out of what was inevitably, in the grand scheme of things, a short period of time. He was once asked by David Acfield, an Essex team-mate who had fenced for England while at Cambridge, what he intended doing when he retired from cricket. Gooch's answer was, 'Nothing,' and he meant it.

All of us who were lucky enough to see Gooch bat will have our favourite memories of him. England's tour to the West Indies in 1980/81 was one of the more unfortunate cricketing adventures in recent times. After being kicked out of Guyana because of the South African connections of Robin Jackman, who had joined the tour as a replacement for Bob Willis, the party moved to Barbados for the Third Test match. On the second evening of that game, England's coach, and trusted friend of all the players, Ken Barrington had a heart attack and died on returning to his hotel after dinner. Under Ian Botham's somewhat idiosyncratic captaincy,

England had been on the receiving end of it against the West Indian fast bowlers. It would be impossible to imagine a greater blow to the side than the sudden death of their much-loved coach, who remains the best they have ever had. The England players were, not surprisingly, shot to pieces when they arrived at the Kensington Oval the next morning. The dressing room could only have been like a morgue and yet Gooch found it in him to go out in England's second innings, which began later that day, and score a rousing 116. His drives left the bat with a noise that combined angry defiance with the notes of 'The Last Post' in honour of a man whom Gooch both loved and respected. When he was out he will have come back to the antiquated dressing room at Kensington, slumped into a seat and felt a drained nothing. Yet, in the circumstances, it had been the greatest tribute one cricketer could have paid to another. No one would have understood it better or have been more delighted than Barrington himself. Gooch may have played and missed a number of times along the way and have incurred the criticism of Geoffrey Boycott, but few batsmen would have been able to show what they were made of as Gooch did that day.

I shall always remember the 154 not out he made when captain against the same opponents at Headingley in 1991, which took England to victory in the First Test of that series. England batted first and were bowled out for 198 and the West Indies then could only muster 173 in conditions that allowed considerable movement both in the air and off the seam. For a while, England did little better the second time round and the only hope when the scoreboard read 124/6 was the gallant captain. Gooch had survived a confident appeal for a catch behind and subsequent West Indian displeasure, in that slightly impatient way of his which seemed to say, 'Come on, let's get on with the game.' Heavily moustached and with a dark, three-day growth, a fashion he had made his own, he batted as if he was a combination of an unshaven RSM Britten and the Pirate King in *The Pirates of Penzance*. The drives flowed from his bat with that same primeval crack and his impeccable defence had the answer to any question it was asked. Gooch batted for seven and a half hours as he, single-handedly, took England to a platform from which they won by 115 runs. The ultimate accolade is left to John Woodcock who, although he had retired as *The Times* cricket correspondent four years before, still burst into print when the situation warranted it. 'Since World War II,' he wrote, 'no innings by an England captain has surpassed this. It stands out not for artistic merit, but for skill and courage against a very formidable attack in awkward conditions at a crucial time.'

Gooch played 118 times for England between 1975 when he began with that dreaded pair against Australia at Edgbaston, and 1994/95. These were difficult times for England. The West Indies ruled the cricketing world, taking over from Australia in the second half of the seventies. They held sway until the nineties when Australia again climbed back to the top of the ladder where they have remained ever since. Gooch was consistently batting against disciplined bowling of the highest pace and class: Michael Holding, Andy Roberts, Malcolm Marshall, Joel Garner and all the other West Indians before it was the turn of Craig McDermott, Merv Hughes, Glenn McGrath and just a touch of Shane Warne thrown in. In between times, to keep him on his toes, he was up against Imran Khan, Richard Hadlee, Kapil Dev and a few other fast bowlers well up in the list of wicket-takers. Under that familiar, gleaming white crash helmet life was never easy for him and yet he managed to score more runs in Test cricket, 8,900, than any other Englishman, for an average of 42.38. These are figures that hint as little of uncertainty as that booming cover drive. In scoring runs with such consistency, Gooch had to live with, and indeed sit upon, the doubts that bestraddled him.

He made the decision early on in his career to play cricket for money against white South Africa. He was pilloried for it and banned from playing for England for three years and he probably never forgave those who outlawed him like this. He could see nothing wrong in what he did, which, in essence, was working to provide for his family when his cricketing days were over. It was naïve of Gooch to think that he would be able to fly in the face of world opinion when it came to South Africa. He went to the Cape and gave of his best, in spite of the pressures that were on him. Some of his colleagues on this tour seldom seemed to have much more than half their minds on the job in hand. One of Gooch's most admirable traits was the ability to raise his game as the pressure upon him increased.

Gooch's cover drive, like his moustache, bristled through the eighties, but in the second half of the decade a good many of the old uncertainties came flooding back accompanied by one significant new one. His form with the bat was nothing like as consistent as he would have liked. South Africa and his keenness to play during the English winters for Western Province were to pull and push him in different directions; the Essex captaincy, when Keith Fletcher first passed it on to him, caught him more unprepared than he had expected and it did not help his batting; his three daughters made him feel that he should spend more time at home and, as a result, he missed the tour of Australia in 1986/87, the last time England won the Ashes. In 1988 the England captaincy came to him by default; then his love for Western Province and his resulting reluctance to confirm his availability for the tour to India in 1988/89, twice caused the selectors to delay in making a decision on the captaincy. Gooch's dithering irritated John Woodcock in *The Times*: 'A good batsman, uneasy with the mysteries of captaincy, Gooch is being treated at the moment with the deference that might have attended a "WG" in his heyday. It seems to me that our administrators have gone mad. Either that or I have.' When eventually he accepted the invitation of the selectors, the Indians cancelled the tour because of his South African connections.

Then there was Terry Alderman. In England in 1989, Alderman had tormented and haunted Gooch. At not much above medium pace, although his long run probably made him seem faster, Alderman comprehensively out-thought Gooch. He continually persuaded him to play round his front pad as he tried to drive the ball into the gap between mid on and midwicket. Bowling from close to the stumps, he swung the ball away from the right-hander and Gooch was many times lbw as he played across the line. He made only 183 runs in five Test matches and, when the Ashes had been lost, agreed to stand down for the Fifth, although he returned for the Sixth at The Oval where he was yet again lbw to Alderman for nought.

It always seems extraordinary when as good a batsman as Gooch gets himself into such a pickle, although it has happened to almost all the best players at some stage of their careers. It said a great deal for his character that he was able to fight his way out of this without changing his style of batting or becoming a more intro-spective and less eye-catching performer. The curious part about it was that one of the apparent causes of his uncertainty, the England captaincy, provided the hook that enabled him to pull himself free and enter into the second and final stage of his career, which was more glorious than anything that had gone before. England's administrators had been all over the place in 1988. Mike Gatting captained England in the First Test against the West Indies at Trent Bridge. A much publicised romp with a barmaid then cost him the job in one of the most absurd and reprehensible decisions England's much vaunted cricket administrators can ever have made. John Emburey took over and lost the next two Tests. The selectors turned to Chris Cowdrey who may have brought a breath of fresh air to the dressing room but he still presided over a massive defeat at Headingley. He was then injured and unable to play in the last Test of the summer, at The Oval. Micky Stewart, the England coach, had a considerable influence from within the England dress-ing room and the 'amateur' implications in Cowdrey's appoint-ment will not have suited him. His cricketing ethic was based on unremitting hard work, as was Gooch's, and his appointment as captain for the last Test against the West Indies at The Oval will have won Stewart's heart-felt approval.

The paradox was that Gooch batted like a hirsute amateur from cricket's Golden Age and yet captained the side like an unforgiving contemporary bureaucrat. Hard labour was now the order of the day and free-range extravagances were destined for the Traitors' Gate. It was sad that Gooch's intransigent attitude should have precipitated him into a head-on crash with David Gower, which effectively brought the career of this wonderfully uninhibited free-range artist to a premature end.

Their final clash came on the 1990/91 tour of Australia. Serious net practice was anathema to Gower who had always waved his bat about as if it were a magic wand and dined as if he was a wine correspondent in mid-taste. Gower had started the series well, even if Gooch could never quite bring himself to watch his predecessor bat without wearing an expression that suggested he was a vicar who had just spotted one of his choirboys sucking a boiled sweet. It all began to come to a head during the Sydney Test match. England had had a bad first day and Gooch presided over a vibrant team-talk in the middle before the start of the second day. As it continued, Gower suggested that England should be thinking more positively. 'I'm the captain here, so shut up and listen,' was the response he elicited from his leader. RSM Britten might have said something similar, but one can only wonder if it was wise of a captain to neutralise a talent such as Gower's. After that, their relationship went from bad to worse on that tour of Australia.

Michael Atherton, who was not given to going over the top, was reasonably complimentary about Gooch's captaincy.

Graham Gooch led England firmly by example between 1990 and 1993. I thought he was a much better captain than he has since been given credit for and he was much admired and respected by his team. Under him the team performed creditably, save during the India tour (1992/93) and the early part of 1993 when he knew his time was up. He demanded a strict work ethic. He was a near obsessive trainer himself and could often be seen going for a lengthy run when he had been dismissed. I remember seeing him running with weights up and down the many flights of stairs of our hotel in Delhi, just a few hours after we landed. He pushed himself to levels of fitness few could match.

Gooch captained England in thirty-four Test matches winning ten and losing twelve. He was a captain who led from the front by personal example. England have never had a more devoted patriot or a more determined cricketer. Gooch scored 3,582 runs while captain of England for an average of 58.72, compared to his average of 35.93 in the seventy-five Tests when he was not in charge. He was never better value as a batsman than when he was captain. It suited him to impose his own persona on the side and to run things in just the manner in which he ran his own cricket. It was all based on relentless hard work and perish any backsliders. Knowing that he was the boss gave him more confidence than he had had at any other stage of his career. His loyalty to his country was such that Western Province was not an issue while he was England's captain, which removed a nasty, nagging doubt. He was also backed up by the ideal foil in all that he did. Micky Stewart saw things in precisely the same way as Gooch himself and this will also have helped his peace of mind.

Runs poured off his bat against all-comers and it never paid to turn up late if there was a chance of seeing Gooch open the innings. Those blazing cover drives continued to split the field from the very first ball of the match, although he felt himself that he was now a more sensible and reliable player than when he was younger. This may have been a reflection of the sense of responsibility that the captaincy gave to him. 'Now I am a steadier, more consistent all-round player. I take fewer chances, play more percentages and am not so much of a destroyer as in the first part of my career.' The change was perhaps more imagined than real. 'I'm proud I've been able to outlast some younger players. If anybody's going to take my place, he's going to have to play bloody well.'

No one who was there will ever forget the First Test match against India at Lord's in 1990. England were sent in to bat and soon

Gooch's driving made everyone sit up. When he had reached 36 he drove at Sanjeev Sharma and behind the stumps Kiran More dropped a sitter that will haunt him for the rest of his days. From that moment on, against a pretty motley attack, he was supreme. He played all the strokes, hitting the ball with thunderous power, and it was simply a question of how long he could keep going before tiredness took over. If it had worried him – or maybe he simply didn't think about it – he could have scored another 35 and beaten Garry Sobers' record of 365 as the highest ever individual Test score. A tired drive against Manoj Prabhakar cost his wicket when he had batted for 633 minutes for his 333 and had hit three sixes and forty-three fours. As if this was not enough to be going on with, he put together a small matter of 123 in the second innings off just 113 balls. This may have been gluttony on a grand scale, but it was not boring for a single second, even if these runs stood no comparison whatever with the 154 not out he made the following year against the West Indies at Headingley. Throughout it all, his expression never changed and his moustache never wobbled. The RSM would have been proud of him.

Gooch and Stewart ran the England dressing room exactly as they wanted, outlawing romance, emotion and all forms of free-range attitude and behaviour. It was efficient and effective rather than glamorous. All went reasonably well until England's visit to India in 1992/93 when all three Tests were lost, although Gooch himself was fit enough to play in only two of them. The following summer against Australia he began with 65 and 133 at Old Trafford. In the second innings he became the fifth batsman in Test cricket to be given out handled the ball when he played a ball into the ground and, with a rare mental aberration, knocked it away with his hand when it appeared to be bouncing back towards his stumps. Another hundred followed in the Third Test when he batted at number five, but when Australia had won the Fourth at Headingley and retained the Ashes, Gooch resigned the England captaincy. The half volleys were still leaving his bat with that lovely mellow crack of sophisticated thunder, but this was one defeat too many for him and the poisoned chalice was passed on to Michael Atherton.

Gooch continued to play for England for another thirteen Test matches and in one, against New Zealand at Trent Bridge in 1994, he made 210. When his white helmet and his black moustache had made their final bow for England in Australia in 1994/95, he left an enormous gap. For years, Gooch had made it compulsory for England supporters to be in their seats well before the first ball was bowled in order that they should not miss that first rasping cover drive. He now plays his strokes from the commentary box and, dare one say it, lets his hair down just a little more than he did in the days when he took the field with England, and is the better for it.

IAN BOTHAM

THERE was a wonderful earthiness about Ian Botham's genius. He played cricket in a way that reminded one of those medieval hewers of wood and tillers of the soil. No wonder one of his more eccentric agents planned to take him to Hollywood and turn him into a latter-day Errol Flynn. There was boundless energy, an all-consuming enthusiasm, a flop of unruly hair, a massively cheerful self-destruct button, a warming sense of humour, a devil-may-care generosity, an ability to hit a cricket ball harder and further than anyone else, then to pick it up and go and bowl out the best batsman in the world, and in between to catch swallows in the slips. The one thing he never got round to was acting and Hollywood will never know what it missed. There was nothing too complicated about Botham the man or Botham the cricketer. He was all upfront and you knew what you were going to get. A hard, rugged exterior covered up a soft, caring centre. He espoused the cause of research for the cure of leukaemia and to raise money set himself to walk on two occasions from John o'Groats to Land's End and then to emulate Hannibal in his trek across the Alps, although 'Beefy', as Botham became universally known, left the elephants behind. No one could have gone into these efforts to raise money more wholeheartedly and leukaemia research has profited by at least a million or two.

Ian Botham has never done anything by halves and this is one of his great attractions for it makes him so compelling and irresistible. When he was at his prime in the late seventies and early eighties he was almost as well known a figure as David Beckham is today. The only other cricketer the country has taken to its heart in the same way was Denis Compton in the immediate post-war years when that famous advertisement for Brylcreem beamed down from so many huge advertising boards. This is how Peter Roebuck, a Somerset contemporary, put it: 'Really Ian is a character from Smollett or Fielding. He doesn't give a damn: he wants to ride a horse, down a pint, roar around the land waking up the sleepers, show them things can be done. As it is he has to play cricket all the time and worry about newspapermen, a Gulliver tied down by the little people.'

Botham's deeds of derring-do in county and Test cricket were endless. The feat that will be remembered longest and will be talked about as long as the game is still played was his innings of 149 not out against Australia at Headingley in 1981, which led to perhaps the most remarkable result in any Test match when England won by 18 runs. Australia made 401/9 declared and England were then bowled out for 174 with Botham making exactly 50. They followed on 227 behind and when Botham came in to bat in the second innings, they were 105/5 and this later became 135/7 when the deficit was still 92. Botham went for the Australian bowling from the start and it was one of those days when everything came off in brilliant fashion. Dennis Lillee was hooked for sixes and driven over extra cover and there was nothing the Australian bowlers could do. Botham reached his hundred off only eighty-seven balls. In all he batted for 219 minutes, hitting one six and twenty-seven fours in a virtuoso performance that will never be bettered. It was not so much dynamic as cyclonic. With sterling help from Graham Dilley, Chris Old and Bob Willis, he took England to 356 when he was left with 149 not out.

Australia were left to score 130 to win and there was no obvious reason why this should not be a simple enough task. But the momentum had swung irrevocably towards England. After Botham himself had taken the first wicket in Australia's second innings, Willis took over. In an inspired spell of fast bowling he took 8 for 43 and Australia were bowled out for 111. This was the occasion when Rod Marsh and Lillee took advantage of the generous odds of 500/1 that were offered against England by none other than their former wicket keeper Godfrey Evans who, in his old age, had become a bookie's consultant. He may not have done much for their cash flow but he did a great deal for their celebrity.

This incredible innings by Botham revealed another admirable side to his character. He had succeeded Mike Brearley to the England captaincy at the start of the 1980 season in England when the West Indies were touring. The following winter England followed them back to the Caribbean. Both series were lost and Botham's captaincy was heavily criticised. Australia then won the First Test in England in 1981 and, although they were held to a draw at Lord's, Botham himself made an inglorious pair. At the end of the match he resigned the captaincy, a minute or two before he was to be sacked. This happened on 7 July and the following weekend Brearley agreed to come out of retirement and captain England for the remaining four Tests of the summer. The selectors kept Botham in the side and when the Headingley Test began the following Thursday, nine days after he had resigned, he began by taking 6 wickets in Australia's first innings, which he followed with 50 and 149 not out.

Much has been made of his relationship with Brearley and how the future psychoanalyst managed to put his all-rounder back into the right frame of mind to tackle the Australians little more than a week after his world had seemed to collapse around him. To move in little more than a week from a pair at Lord's to 50 and 149 not out at Headingley against the same attack was extraordinary and there can be little doubt that Brearley did a great deal to try to sort out Botham's thinking. But when it came to it, it was Botham himself who allowed Brearley to convince him. Brearley put it this way: 'He needed an adviser, especially after Barrington died. Who was there to listen to? Viv was not around and no one else was

Alan Knott's keeping to Derek Underwood's bowling was extraordinary. Knott catches Clive Lloyd at Lord's in 1976 with the grey-haired David Steele at backward short leg.

Ninety-five batsmen were caught Marsh bowled Lillee. Derek Randall is the victim in the Centenary Test at Melbourne in 1977, but in the second innings he made 174.

Was there ever a more charismatic cricketer than Imran Khan? A brilliant bowler, an underestimated batsman, a fierce Pakistani patriot, now a politician and husband of Jemima.

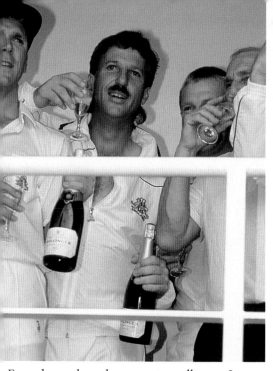

Few players have been as compelling as Ian Botham, both on the field and, as in this picture, off it.

Vivian Richards, the most delightful of men, was the greatest batsman in the world for more than ten years.

Graham Gooch leaves the field at The Oval, without any apparent emotion, after becoming England's highest scorer in Test cricket, against Australia in 1993.

David Gower starts as he means to go on against Pakistan at Edgbaston in 1978. Almost inconsequentially, he pulls his first ball in Test cricket to the boundary.

Unidentical twins – Steve (*left*) and Mark Waugh, whose characters are as different as their batting styles, are two wonderful cricketers.

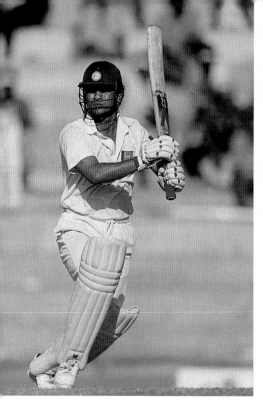

Sachin Tendulkar often has to carry the whole weight of India on his shoulders. His genius is blessed with a steely core of determination.

The unpredictable genius of Brian Lara can be as joyous as it can be irritating and frustrating.

The ball of the century – Shane Warne's first ball in a Test match in England, at Old Trafford in 1993, turns prodigiously and dumbfounds Mike Gatting.

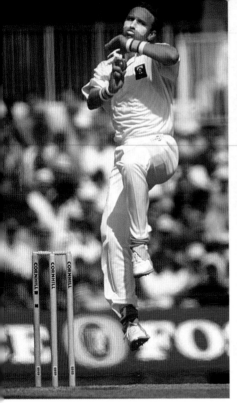

There has been no more fearsome sight for batsmen than South Africa's Allan Donald. The zinc cream can only add to their worries.

Jonty Rhodes, the greatest fielder in modern times, swoops on another in the covers. He alone was always worth the gate money.

Contemporary cricket's greatest enigma – Muttiah Muralitharan, with that deformed arm and double-jointed wrist, has over 400 Test wickets to his credit.

Phil Tufnell, a fine left-arm spinner with the quirkiest of temperaments and cheekiest of smiles, has found fame and fortune in an Australian jungle.

Australia's exuberant wicket-keeper Adam Gilchrist's withering strokeplay at number seven has brought a new dimension to the game.

The ever-ebullient Darren Gough is congratulated by his captain, Nasser Hussain, after defeating yet another West Indian at The Oval in 2000.

Michael Vaughan, England's latest captain and their best batsman, on the way to his third century of the 2002/03 Ashes series.

The Sage of Longparish – John Woodcock, the best cricket writer of them all, and the Cricket Correspondent of *The Times* from 1954 until 1986, in typically benevolent mood.

Only the glass of wine and the Hampshire burr are missing. John Arlott, surely the best commentator the game has known, at home in Alderney.

The humour of *Test Match Special* personified – Brian Johnston up to some prank in the old box in the pavilion at Lord's with a youthful Vic Marks alongside.

really on his level. If I did anything, it was to restore his confidence, to release him from trying too hard and playing too tentatively.' Brearley then made sure that Botham's mind was thinking along the right channels, and, of course, he had the courage – a quality he never lacked – to go out and bat as he had never done before.

This match was not an isolated incident either. In the Fourth Test at Edgbaston, Botham came on to bowl with considerable reluctance when Australia, who needed 151 in the last innings, seemed to be winning in a canter, and took 5 wickets for 1 run in twenty-eight balls, enabling England to win by 29 runs. The series now moved up to Old Trafford where Botham made 118 off 102 in England's second innings, this time reaching his hundred in eighty-six balls, and England's victory meant that the series and the Ashes were theirs. In the Sixth Test, which was drawn, he contented himself with taking 6 wickets in Australia's first innings and 4 in the second. These figures are worth repeating for the excellent reason that they must never be forgotten. They also tell us a huge amount about the character of Botham himself.

Botham was the very essence of a natural cricketer. Nothing had been imposed on his natural instinctive game and I would think that even the young Botham would have given any coach who tried to change what nature had so plentifully handed him pretty short shrift.

I've only had about six hours of coaching in my career. They even gave up coaching me when I was at Lord's. It was the old story. They would ask me where my feet were and I would ask them if they had found the ball yet. There wasn't much anyone could do. Coaches rely upon a fellow being aware of his faults. I've never worried about that, because I've never tried to play perfectly. Some cricketers try to master a technique, so that every muscle in their body is absolutely under control. That isn't my way. They are like classical pianists who spend hours every day practising, whereas I'm like a jazz saxophonist who has a pretty good technique and wants to go into orbit.

Human nature being what it is, we all tend to remember where we were when we first heard the news of earth-shattering events such as the assassination of President Kennedy. The first time I saw Botham remains equally firmly engraved upon my mind. It was on 12 June 1974 at the county ground in Taunton where Somerset were playing Hampshire in the Benson & Hedges Cup. We had heard murmurings of Somerset finding a pretty formidable young all-rounder. Hampshire had been bowled out for 182 and the young Botham had picked up 2 wickets, including that of the redoubtable Barry Richards. Number nine was his modest place in the batting order that day and he made his appearance when the scoreboard showed that Somerset were 113/7, which later in the same over became 113/8. Soon afterwards, Botham faced Andy Roberts who was as quick and nasty as anyone around. With a happy and courageous disregard for the probable, he soon tried to hook a bouncer. He was late with the stroke and the ball crashed into his mouth. He was soon spitting out blood and help was frantically summoned from the pavilion, but Botham stood his ground and wouldn't hear of going off. He shook himself, looked around and prepared to face Roberts again.

He began to produce a few of those withering strokes with which we became so familiar over the next few years. He put on 63 for the ninth wicket with another West Indian, Hallam Moseley, who made him a stalwart partner, before a beauty of a yorker from Roberts ended Moseley's involvement. Botham had already built up his own momentum and, in company with the last man, Bob Clapp, who held a bat only because he had to, he at once smote two fierce sixes. A couple of overs later one of those searing, no-nonsense cover drives took Somerset to victory by 1 wicket. Here was a young man no one could afford to ignore, even though it was three more years before the England selectors embraced him.

From this first moment, Botham was a cricketer who made things happen. Another of his infectious qualities was that he was so obviously enjoying himself every moment of the day and nothing communicates itself quicker to spectators. It was never a surprise when he took a wicket in his first over of a spell. Then he would be standing conversationally in the slips or leaning with his hands on his knees before suddenly uncoiling and holding a superb catch. There were not many bowlers who ran in when he was batting with any sort of confidence unless they were West Indian fast bowlers who usually got the better of him. It was all done with gusto and good humour too. He was fearless when it came to facing fast bowling, just as he had been on that first occasion against Roberts. He was also more than prepared to do the unthinkable if it was in the interest of his side or would give everyone a good laugh.

His first tour was to Pakistan and New Zealand in 1977/78. Mike Brearley, the captain, had broken his forearm in Karachi and Geoff Boycott had taken charge for the New Zealand leg. New Zealand won the First Test in Wellington and in the second, in Christchurch, England needed quick runs in their second innings in order to be able to declare and bowl out New Zealand a second time. The innings was in grave danger of becoming bogged down around the captain, who appeared not to realise the need to hurry the score along. Botham, who had made a hundred in the first innings and then taken 5 wickets, was promoted to number four. He saw it as his first duty on arriving at the crease to run out his captain, which he proceeded to do with some ease. When England declared at 96/4 he was 30 not out and, in the end, England had time to win by 174 runs. Unhappily, the conversation in the dressing room between Botham and Boycott when the declaration was made has not been handed down to posterity. It is fair to say, too, that they never became the best of pals and no two cricketers could have had a more different approach to the game.

Looking back on his Test career more than a dozen years after it ended leaves one with the delightfully easy job of picking all the best plums out of the Botham pie and, of course, of reliving them at the same time. In 1978 at Lord's against Pakistan he cleared his throat in making 108 in 104 balls in England's first innings, batting at number seven. Then, when Pakistan followed on, he produced figures of 8 for 34 and was unstoppable with both bat and ball. He made 137 from 152 balls against India at Old Trafford in 1979, including five sixes and sixteen fours, with the sort of display that gives bowlers recurring nightmares and makes firework manufacturers feel inadequate. He made 99 in the morning session on the second day and, being unaware that he was about to make a hundred before lunch, he blocked the last two balls of the session.

India again felt the full power of Botham in the Golden Jubilee Test in Bombay in February 1980. In a superhuman display he took a total of 13 wickets in the match for 106 runs and in between he scored 114 in England's first innings. At The Oval in 1982, India were again put to the sword when he made 208, reaching 200 in 220 balls, which made it the quickest double century in Test cricket in terms of balls faced. There were also, of course, those astonishing performances against Australia in 1981, which was his apogee. He never mastered the West Indian fast bowlers as he did the rest and it was not until the Fifth Test at The Oval in 1991, which was his last against the West Indies, that he found himself on the winning side and it was his twentieth Test match against them. Nonetheless, for sixteen years he towered over England's cricket and few cricketers have brought so much pleasure to spectators as Botham did in this time.

> I've played three or four innings which I'll remember with pride, innings to tell my grandchildren about if I live so long [he has]. I'll name them. One was in Sydney when I stayed in for ninety minutes and hit 6 runs. Another was for Somerset in a cup semi-final at Lord's: I scored 90 under pressure that day. Then there was the 1981 innings at Old Trafford, which was much better than the Headingley hundred the previous month. We were roaring with laughter at Headingley. The match was lost so we decided to have a go. We'd booked out of the hotel and my golf clubs were in the boot. It inspired a lot of people, the noise was demented, especially when Willis bowled Alderman to win the match. I watch that video sometimes and still it seems make-

believe . . . But mine wasn't a great innings, it wasn't really an innings at all – just an almighty heave. I didn't put anything into it. I didn't walk out and say, 'Right, we're in a mess, and I'm going to sort it out.' That's why Old Trafford was far superior. There I went out with the purpose of winning the game.

Good, honest, uncomplicated stuff!

I have not so far touched on that self-destruct button, which he kept well polished through most of his career. When he decided to kick over the traces he did so in the grand manner. He was accused of snorting drugs off Mick Jagger's bathroom tiles; a steamy session with a former Miss Barbados is purported to have ended with them destroying a formidable wooden double bed; there was an expensive failed libel action he brought, with Allan Lamb, against Imran Khan. He shrugged them all off with a smile that seemed to suggest that we would all probably have done the same thing ourselves. His sense of guilt never appeared to be that highly developed and it was almost impossible to be angry with him, although I daresay that during it all he has had one or two interesting discussions on the home front. Here is Botham's own view on being under the public gaze.

I don't believe sportsmen are any different now from the way they've always been. They are presented in a different way that is all. Actually I suspect for the most part we are a nicer lot altogether. There are some terrific men playing cricket for England, really outstanding characters, fellows worth ten times as much as the cheap snakes who condemn them, not as cricketers but as people . . . I'm sorry that cricketers are presented in such a damning way. I think a lot of journalists regret it too – none of them wanted to write about the business in Pakistan [the drug story which followed them from New Zealand] – they are trapped in a web of hard selling. What we need is a Press Council that has the guts to demand fair play. Our papers – our tabloids – are not the best papers in the world, they are the worst.

Nowadays, his cheerful smiling face, his robust patriotism and that good, honest, down-to-earth common sense on television keeps us very much in mind of Botham the cricketer. If only we could see the like of him again on the cricket field playing for England, crowds and sponsors would be falling over themselves and England might be winning the odd Test match or two.

Perhaps his biggest regret was his inability to make a go of it as captain of England. He had the crucial bad luck to take over just as England were approaching back-to-back series against the West Indies, which was something that not even Mike Brearley had to cope with. Often Botham's instincts were right, but he did not always handle people in the right way and, being the genius he was, may not have been able fully to appreciate the problems that other lesser mortals had with their own game. He captained England for twelve Test matches and lost four of them, which was not that bad and certainly not as bad as it was to become for his successors when it came to playing the West Indies later in the eighties. The captaincy may have come to him too soon, but he desperately wanted it. When Brearley retired after the Golden Jubilee Test match in Bombay early in 1980, he was not only the logical successor, but also he carried his predecessor's ringing endorsement. He found his brief tenure of office extremely unhappy because it coincided with his own loss of form, which will have made him feel even more insecure. It is purely conjecture, but I wonder if it had been given to him several years later when his form as a block-busting freak was just on the wane, it might not have steadied him down and given him the impetus to want to continue as a Test cricketer for longer than he did. It would have given him something else to prove, not least to himself, and might therefore have rekindled a waning interest. Timing is so important in life and the England captaincy may have come to Botham at the wrong time.

DAVID GOWER

DAVID GOWER was the latter-day Anglo-Saxon equivalent of Ranjitsinhji. There was a boneless insouciance about his gloriously instinctive and effortless strokeplay as well as his lithe, fluid fielding. He made it all look so easy and carried it out in such a matter-of-fact sort of way that there seemed to be an Oriental wizardry about it all, even though he may not have invented a stroke of his own. Gower came into the England side for the First Test match against Pakistan at Edgbaston in 1978. Even then, he appeared to be nerveless and after taking guard in his own languid way, he swivelled unhurriedly and pulled his first ball, a long hop from the left-arm seamer Liaquat Ali, to the backward square leg boundary. He played the stroke as if he had not a care in the world and went on to make 58 in much the same vein.

Of course, the downside to this carefree way of playing was that whenever he was dismissed it all seemed so eminently avoidable. This was a complaint that was to follow Gower throughout his career and in the end cost him his Test career when England's cricket was presided over by the humourless and intransigent combination of Graham Gooch as captain, Micky Stewart as coach, with a pinch of Peter Lush thrown in as manager. When Gower made runs it was glorious, when he failed it was unforgivable. When he sauntered off, for that was his way, in the middle of a Test match, having perished as the result of a stroke that his very unconcern made appear even more reprehensible, to the humourless it seemed almost a treasonable offence. But that was his nature.

Transparent hard work was not for Gower. Hard grafting net practice was not his way and was an insult to his extraordinary natural talents. At times in his career, those in charge of English cricket were too limited to be able to understand this. The mere fact that in a career that lasted for 117 Test matches, he scored a small matter of 8,231 runs for an average of 44.25, showed beyond doubt that he was a heavy duty Test cricketer. There was nothing more joyful in the last thirty years than going along to watch Gower play an innings. There was a joyful infectiousness about his batting that communicated itself to the spectators. He made all those lovely strokes seem so absurdly easy, and if there was a public-school arrogance about the way in which he played, it mattered only to the most prejudiced. The fact that Gower had the enemies he did is a reflection of the humourless bureaucratic world in which we increasingly live. Conformity is all-important and individuality a sin. It was as if the fact that his preferred drink was champagne and not pints of bitter was held against him.

The ultimate absurdity was reached in Australia on Graham Gooch's tour in 1990/91. England played Queensland before the First Test at Carrara on the Gold Coast about fifty miles from Brisbane. There was a small airport next door to the cricket ground that provided the holidaymakers with aeroplane rides in Tiger Moths. Gower and John Morris, who had made a hundred, both got out early on the third morning. After lunch, Gower and Morris went round to the airfield and after a wait and the payment of a £27 fee, each boarded a Tiger Moth and convinced their pilots of the need for a spot of low-level flying. Allan Lamb and Robin Smith were putting together a sizeable partnership over the hedge when suddenly they found themselves being buzzed by a couple of low-flying Tiger Moths. Gower had warned Lamb, the vice-captain, and he and Smith pretended to shoot down the Tiger Moths with their bats. Of course, word got out at once and when Gower and Morris returned to the ground, the tour management suffered in a big way from sense of humour failure. The manager,

Peter Lush, accused them of seeking publicity. The two players were summoned to a meeting of the tour management, which consisted of Lush, Gooch, the captain, his deputy Lamb, who did not know where to look so hard was he laughing, and the coach Micky Stewart, at 8.45 the next morning. They reserved their judgment and the two players were eventually fined £1,000 each as the most colossal mountain was made out of a highly entertaining molehill. Lush had the gall to tell them not to comment on the punishment and, later, that they had no right of appeal.

It was a sorry episode for those who ran England's cricket and it reflected little credit on anyone concerned that there was no attempt to put things right at a later stage. A little bit of humour is what England cricket has so badly needed at times during the last twenty years. It is sad when harmless bits of fun like this end up being stifled by the dead clammy hand of self-important bureaucracy. Most people's estimation of Gower and Morris will have risen by leaps and bounds after this incident and what harm did it do to England's cricket? I wonder if those who appointed themselves as judge and jury ever appreciated what a laughing stock they became.

Later in the tour, during which Gower had already scored hundreds in the Second and Third Tests, he appeared to be too casual for his own good. It was on the third day in Adelaide, just before lunch, that Gower had come in to join his captain, Gooch. He was soon into his stride with a drive or two and a couple of those lovely easy flicks off his legs. He now faced Craig McDermott in the last over of the morning. The ball pitched on or a fraction outside the leg stump and without a care in the world Gower, using his bat like a wand, flicked it away behind square on the legside. But this time the trick went wrong. The ball was slower and shorter than he thought and it curved in the gentlest of parabolas to deepish backward square leg where Merv Hughes waited and gleefully clasped the ball to his chest. Gower departed for the pavilion as he had come, without an apparent care in the world, and it would have been in character if he had lunched well. At the other end, it was all too much for Gooch who shuffled off with a deep frown etched across his forehead. Neither he nor Micky Stewart will have been quick off the mark with the 'Bad Luck, Lubo' as the miscreant bent to take off his pads. Of course, it was the nature of the man to play this stroke and to play it when he did, just as much as it was the nature of the other two to consider that it had been something up with which they could not put and jolly nearly a treasonable offence. No one will have realised the folly of the stroke more than Gower, but it was not as if he had failed to produce on the tour and nor was he an evil influence on the rest of the side, either. His genius, like most others to whom that exalted word applies, had its moments of waywardness. Those who were unable to tolerate them in Gower's case might have asked themselves if their attitude was beneficial to the general good.

Gower's own opinion in his autobiography is full of common sense:

On Bob Willis's tour several years earlier, when we had again failed to qualify for the one-day finals, the gap left in the itinerary had indeed been given over to recreation, and while I admit that the rewards and pressures in international cricket had grown considerably in the intervening years, I could still not see the requirement for a different approach. It is impossible to maintain a peak of fitness day in and day out without some form of release. The occasional late night and a lie-in, or a trip out on a yacht, is far more beneficial than the constant cracking of the whip, and I personally believe that the results on this tour [Gooch's in 1990/91] go a long way towards proving it . . . I think, like most average cricket watchers who did not know me, that they were all under the impression that I had always found the game easy, and perhaps felt that this explained why I did not (or appeared not to) treat the game as a matter of life and death. In fact, it had been many years since I thought the game easy. I found it bloody hard, in fact, physically and mentally, and whatever I did that was perceived to be against the system was only my way of keeping myself as fresh and alert as possible. I hate to use the old cliché about being misunderstood, but in this area, I think I have been.

Gower's pet hate in life are the two words 'laid back'. If he had been paid a pound for every time they have been used to describe him, his cellar would be more impressive even than it is. A wide-eyed innocence, curly fair hair and the illusion that even when hurrying he is strolling along in his own time, all combine to create an impression that nothing matters too much. When he hit a ball for four, it was done in a way that suggested he could have hit it to any part of the ground he wished. When he was out, it appeared to be an affront to the laws of nature. The lack of any outward appearance of shock or horror on his face made it all seem an incidental and rather boring inconvenience. It was almost as if the Almighty had the two words 'laid back' on his mind when David Gower was conceived. Appearances can be deceptive, though, for Gower was certainly capable of strong feelings, even if he controlled them better than most. For all that, it was a description that was not wholly wide of the mark. He skated through life with a greater ease, fluency and matter-of-factness than most of us could have managed with a lifetime of trying. When Gower was out, it was almost impossible to tell from his face on the journey back to the pavilion whether he had made a hundred or nought.

Gower burst on the scene in the seventies. He had been born in Tunbridge Wells, educated at King's School, Canterbury ('where I had done little more than give it a swish') and had spent much of his early life with his parents in East Africa, a continent full of animal life with which he has always had a love affair. Gower was taken on to the staff at Grace Road, Leicester for the 1975 season when Leicestershire went on to win the County Championship for the first time. He made his Championship debut against Lancashire at Blackpool and made 32. His first two scoring shots were edged drives between first and second slip. He was eighteen and played only three matches that year, but it was a start and the experience helped him. 'I was a very shy person when I joined Leicester. It would be true to say that my cricket was more confident than my personality. I said little, and took time to make new friends.' He played six games the next year and made his first hundred, 102 not out, against Middlesex at Lord's. But county cricket was never really Gower's thing. In fifteen seasons for Leicestershire he reached 1,000 runs only twice. His threshold of boredom on the smaller stage in particular was low. His class was always abundantly clear and for the workers of the world it must have been immensely irritating that he appeared to find it all so easy. In spirit, Gower was a batsman who belonged to the Golden Age. Just imagine him putting on a couple of hundred with Ranji or Victor Trumper or C.B. Fry!

Gower came into the England side in 1978. From his very first ball, as we have seen, he entertained and tantalised just as he did for the next seventeen years while scoring more than 8,000 runs for his country in Test cricket. In 1992, when a hugely entertaining 73 against Pakistan at Old Trafford took him past Geoffrey Boycott's aggregate, he became England's highest scorer in Test cricket. Not bad for someone who apparently had the attitude of a recalcitrant schoolboy. His methods, like his approach, never changed. Outwardly, at any rate, he played cricket for fun, although I have no doubt that deep down within him there were moments of doubt, even of despair, and certainly of anger as things went wrong, and particularly in his last days as a Test cricketer when he was regarded as a social outcast. It is a sad reflection on the age in which we live that a player of Gower's ability, charm, charisma, entertainment value and attitude could not be accepted into the England side by a management that was so stubbornly inflexible. Gower was a true artist. By their very nature, it is essential to allow the genuine artist a certain leeway and understanding if the best is to be got out of him. Rules that apply to mere mortals do not apply to the likes of Gower and Ranji. Just think what a rigidly inflexible choreographer might have done to Rudolf Nureyev or indeed Nijinsky. Even John Gielgud and Laurence Olivier sometimes made their producers hold their breath or gasp and if, in the long run, they turned their hair white, it was still for the general good of their art. All art, however instinctive, needs a certain amount of discipline as well as humour. The need is for those who preside over it to shape it to their advantage, not to knock it angrily and obstinately over the head.

Gower's record doesn't show him to be a reckless dilettante who was not prepared to put his head down for the general good. When the situation needed it, he could hold himself back as well as the next man. I shall not forget the exemplary manner in which he batted in the second innings at Sabina Park in the last Test of the series in 1980/81. The West Indies, who batted second, led by 157 in the first innings. When England lost their sixth second innings wicket they led by only 58 with four hours remaining. Gower and Paul Downton saved the day with Gower batting for seven and a half hours for his 154 not out. In 1983/84 at Faisalabad, Gower captained England for the first time after Bob Willis had been taken ill. Besides bringing a greater sense of direction to events on the field, Gower settled in for just over seven hours to make 152 after the Pakistanis had put together 449/8 declared. There are plenty of other examples too, even if they did not produce the same bulk of runs. Nonetheless, whenever Gower found himself involved in a lengthy rearguard action he was still enormously good value to watch. The same supple litheness and fluency were there, both in attack and defence.

Gower could not play a boring or an ugly innings and the same was surely true of Ranji, even if he did have more accommodating people around him. Of all the people I have seen bat for England, Peter May, Denis Compton, Ted Dexter, David Gower, with a few drops of Ian Botham thrown in, are the pick of the bunch. With the exception of May, they all may have had their maddening moments, but to have left any of them out of the team would surely have been as incomprehensible as it would have been unwise.

PART FIVE

1988–2003

IN the last fifteen years commercialism has finally and unasham-
edly taken over. International cricket has multiplied almost to the
point that players are expected to be in two places at once and
the domestic game has become a tiresome necessity. The one-day
game is the chief culprit. Spurious tournaments have sprung up all
over the place, mainly, it would seem, to make money for television
companies and their agents. India has become the biggest cash-
generating country of all and the TV companies that supply the
subcontinent appear to be all too anxious to come forward with
their daily dose of cricket. This means that the four teams in the
neighbourhood, India, Pakistan, Sri Lanka and, to some extent,
Bangladesh are in big demand. So too are their African neighbours,
Zimbabwe and South Africa. The West Indies are always strapped
for cash and can easily be persuaded to join in. That leaves England,
Australia and New Zealand to play their own games if they do
not want to take part. As well as bringing riches to television

companies, these one-day competitions also have something to do with an unceasing power struggle within world cricket.

Realising their strong financial position, the President of the Indian Board, Jagmohan Dalmiya, an extremely rich and ambitious man, appears to have set himself to move cricket's headquarters from Lord's to the subcontinent and preferably his home-town of Calcutta. His dislike and mistrust of English cricket has never festered far below the surface.

The biggest single scandal to have affected cricket, perhaps in its entire history, is the match-fixing and betting scandals that have overrun the game in this period. Betting has always been a part of cricket. In the early days, the bookies lined the pavilion rails at Lord's and, although they lost that elevated perch and were shooed away from cricket, they have been lurking in the background. Betting is one of the fundamental instincts of man. Illegal betting will always have gone on around cricket and even in the Golden Age I am sure there were dark forces in action behind the scenes. Punters grew more adventurous as the twentieth century progressed and the appearance of spread betting has increased the temptation to try to steal a march on the bookies and *vice versa*. There is nothing more comforting than to know you are betting on a certainty. The main trouble in recent years has been the illegal bookmakers in Bombay. They have stopped at nothing to gain inside information and indeed to ensure that the result they want is achieved.

I have no doubt that it would cause immense consternation if the names of all those who have been involved in illicit gambling with cricket could miraculously be revealed. If, before Hansie Cronje's admission of guilt, one had been asked to write down the names of half a dozen players who would never have allowed themselves to be involved in such shenanigans, Cronje would have been top of everyone's list. The moment that his involvement was exposed, it was abundantly clear that no one's word could be relied upon. In spite of Lord Condon's optimistic view that the problem has been rooted out, it would be surprising if the ungodly were not still at work. Soon after his lordship, the former policeman who is now the ICC's trouble-shooter in this department, made this pronouncement, the South African bookmaking fraternity couldn't wait to tell him how wrong he was. Let us hope he can contain it and by his brooding presence deter other cricketers who might have been persuaded to go down the Cronje route. The sad point has now been reached that whenever there is a surprising result, especially in one-day competitions, which are the most vulnerable, the automatic reaction is to wonder who gave the brown envelopes to whom. Match fixing *per se* is not the only problem because those involved in spread betting can make a fortune if, for example, they know that a certain team on a certain day will not reach 150 or not be out for less than 200 or that a certain player will not exceed an agreed amount. When a couple of surprisingly bad overs come along in the middle of an innings and produce 30 or so runs, eyebrows shoot up to the ceiling. It is something that brave words will not conquer and with which the game is going to continue to have to live.

One-day tournaments are now being played in unlikely places. Sharjah in the United Arab Emirates was the first of these to come on board, but Singapore, Toronto, Nairobi and Morocco have all followed. They are hosting yet more demanding tournaments, and the playing community, although it may be daily nearer terminal burnout, at least has the satisfaction of knowing that the money keeps coming in. The quality of the cricket, sadly, seems to be one of the least important aspects of it all. Tournaments have also been thrown into confusion, like the recent World Cup in South Africa when New Zealand and England refused to visit Kenya and Zimbabwe because of concerns about the players' safety.

One item on the good side has been the return to the fold of South Africa after their government released Nelson Mandela from prison at the same time as denouncing and abolishing apartheid and introducing free elections. But South African cricket is, like

Zimbabwe, having its own internal political problems. Cricket in both countries has long been a white man's game. Although the West Indian example speaks loudly for the African's natural aptitude for the game, the gospel has so far been slow to spread. The ruling politicians in each country, therefore, demanded a quota system whereby every national team must contain a certain number of coloured players whether they are up to standard or not. This is seen by some as acting against the best interests of the two countries and has subsequently been abolished in South Africa.

The overwhelming authority of the West Indies lasted until the early nineties when, once again, their administrators paid the penalty for not looking ahead and suddenly they had to find too many new young players all at once. The lack of experience cost them dear. By now, Australia had picked themselves up and, under the captaincies of Allan Border, Mark Taylor and Steve Waugh, they strode through the next decade, leaving the rest of the world far behind. They lost the odd Test match and the South Africans ran them closer than anyone, but they kept producing world-class players and their eminence was never seriously challenged.

The Australian players were undoubtedly the best value for money around. You can drop Border, Taylor, the two Waughs, Healy, McGrath, Lee, Warne, Gilchrist, Hayden, Langar and Martyn into a bag and pull out whoever you like and settle down to a happy afternoon with your binoculars and sandwiches.

The body politic of the game is forever expanding. Sri Lanka made their entrance into Test cricket in 1982 with a game against England in Colombo. Zimbabwe did likewise just over ten years later and at the turn of the century Bangladesh became the tenth Test-playing country, some years perhaps before they were ready for it. Their rise has so far meant little more than cheap runs and wickets for their opponents.

It is against this background that every bright spark on the field of play should be seen and appreciated. Allan Donald at full tilt,

Jonty Rhodes in the covers, Darren Gough looking as though he was about to take 10 wickets with one ball, Brian Lara thrashing the ball past cover, Muttiah Muralitharan weaving his spell and convincing one or two curmudgeonly Australian umpires that his deformed arm and double-jointed wrists are myths and that he chucks every delivery that comes out of his hand, Sachin Tendulkar forcing off the back foot and Michael Vaughan pulling, are worth their weight in gold. It is what they do on the field that provides the joy for those of us who have the luck to watch them. They are the coinage in which we want to deal.

STEVE AND MARK WAUGH

UNTIL Steve and Mark Waugh came along, the best-known cricketing twins were Alec and Eric Bedser who were almost as famous at The Oval as the gas-holders. The Bedsers, still acute and informative cricket watchers, have not always been in favour of every path down which the modern game has wended its way. They have also not fully applauded all those who have taken cricket to these different pastures. Nonetheless, they will have undoubtedly appreciated the formidable skills of the Waugh twins and their value to Australia. In one respect the Bedsers have it over the Waughs: they are near enough to being identical and give many people who have known them separately a few nasty moments when they confront them together. The Waugh twins cause no such problem for which cricket commentators around the world have to be eternally grateful.

Steve and Mark Waugh are plainly different, not only to look at, but also in character. It is this that makes it a remarkable coincidence that they should both have played more than a hundred Test matches for Australia. When they are looked at in a long-term perspective, Steve fully deserves to be called a great cricketer for this takes into account his batting, which in my book deserves the accolade on its own, his bowling, which was useful, his fielding, which was exemplary, and his captaincy, which was superb. Mark has his batting, bowling and fielding with which to try to claim the same adjective. We shall never know about his captaincy, but whereas watchfulness and patience were Steve's trademarks, passion, impetuosity and an urge to gamble were streaks running through Mark's batting, not to say his life as well. It would have been a surprise if he had made such an effective captain as his elder brother – in the delivery room in Sydney on 2 January 1965, Steve beat Mark by four minutes, probably the gynaecological equivalent of the shortest of short heads. Mark's batting was brilliant on occasions and more aesthetically satisfying than Steve's. No batsman has been better able to play a great innings, but what sometimes happened in between means that one must leave it at that. He was perhaps the best of all slip fielders and a serviceable off spinner besides. Their father and mother were both considerable sportspeople in their own right, but nothing was as considerable as the genes they handed down to their twin sons. The chance of watching a day's cricket involving the Waugh twins was not to be missed. One of the reasons Australia has been such excellent value for money in recent years has been not only the presence of the twins but also the sharp contrast between the two of them. They set each other off so well.

Steve's focus on the pursuit of victory has always been sharp and relentless. He has allowed nothing to stand in his way. There has never been room for sentiment, emotion, romance, gimmicks, unnecessary risks or allowances for human weaknesses, unless they can be ruthlessly exploited. Steve's purpose in playing cricket for Australia has been to beat the opposition and from the moment he steps on to the ground his only objective has been to 'get the job done'. The opponent who thinks that his Charlie Chaplin walk that takes him strutting around the field while he directs operations is a conscious development, and therefore indicates a man itching to have a laugh, is making a costly error. No fiercer patriot than Steve can ever have pulled on the baggy green cap. He wore his first Test cap through to the end of his career by which time, tattered and torn, it had become a talisman. In the Old Testament, Samson, who used his no doubt well-oiled jawbone of an ass with as much ruthlessness as Steve used his bat, set similar store by his flowing locks

232

of hair. To those who do not know him, Steve may seem cold and humourless with the approach of a calculating automaton. While he has built up an impression of being ice-cold, silent and extremely competitive on the field and, maybe to some, remote, he is talkative and approachable off it. His ability to compartmental-ise himself in this way is why he has such enormous respect from his players. When controversy looms he defends his team to the death, just as he has always defended the integrity of his players. They know he is behind them and is prepared to listen to them and they will follow him in the clinical pursuit of victory. When Steve leads his side out, there are eleven players who are all up for the fight ahead and it is this that makes them both formidable and intimidating.

Steve had to fight for everything he got. It did not help that he did not give a great deal. He was terse with people and, as a young man, kept the lighter side of his nature under impenetrable wraps. He came into the Australian side in the mid-eighties when their cricket was at as low an ebb as it ever can have been. He put noses out of joint, especially among those who played for Australia in the seventies and still thought they ruled the game. Steve strove fran-tically to get out from under their shadow and show that he had what it takes and that he owed nothing to anyone. To begin with he was successful only in one-day internationals. He simply could-n't hit his straps in Test cricket and each failure left a profound mark. His critics were delighted and, although Steve feigned indif-ference, their laughter was torture. Another pressure point, which sharpened his already fierce competitive instincts still further, was his twin brother Mark. Talking of his childhood, Steve said: 'We were in the backyard and highly competitive. Being twins made us more competitive because we were always being compared. People were asking who was the best. If one scored runs one week, the other would try to match him the next week.' I wonder if this sense of filial competitiveness ever left Steve or, indeed, how much it ever touched Mark.

In interviews Steve speaks in measured tones, seldom giving away more than he has to and never embroidering. That unproductive start to his Test career drove him back in on himself to try to find the answer.

> When you're losing as we were in the mid-1980s, you have to find some sort of mechanism to survive. It was no fun playing the way we played and myself getting twenties and thirties, looking good and getting out. I wanted to make the most of my abilities and to play well for Australia, and the way to do that was to change my game. I had to work it out for myself. Bob Simpson [the coach] was great but there wasn't a lot of help around in those first few years. Everyone except Allan Border was in the same position, playing for their places. Also there wasn't a lot of support staff as there is now. It was sink or swim.

It did not happen at once. Steve had to wait twenty-seven Test matches and forty-two innings before he scored his first hundred for Australia, at Leeds in 1989. It was an innings of extraordinary power and certainty and never even hinted that its maker was having trouble with that first Test hundred. Steve's square cutting that day at Headingley will long be remembered, and just for good measure he went on to reach 177 not out. A fortnight later at Lord's he clocked in with 152 not out to show that once the dam had burst, there was not the slightest chance of it running dry. Yet strangely, Steve was back in the doldrums a couple of years later. In 1990/91 he was dropped in favour of his brother, for three Test matches in the West Indies and for the whole series of five matches against India in Australia in 1991/92. It was now that he got to work on the business of cutting out all risk from his technique. He did so with an effectiveness that made his wicket as hard to come by as Geoffrey Boycott's. As usual, he rationalised it with brevity and common sense, qualities he had in abundance.

> After being dropped in 1991 I did that. It was forced on me, facing the West Indians at their peak, four great fast bowlers. Unless you're the best hooker in the world, it's going to get you out regularly. I saw blokes

getting out all the time and thought 'That's not for me.' So I cut it out and it's hard to restore it because it's not in your way of thinking . . . It doesn't matter how pretty you look, it's how many runs you get. I don't mind getting hit on the hands (defending the short stuff) because it gets me fired up.

As far as he was concerned his re-emergence from this bad spell came at Trent Bridge in 1993 when he made 47 not out in the First Test of the series. He puts this relatively small innings among the best four he played for Australia.

If I had a turning point it was that 47 not out at Trent Bridge. I didn't score for an hour, which I'd never done before. I'd always wanted to save a match through my batting. A lot of times as a stroke-maker you can win games, but you don't often save them. We were struggling to save this Test. Everyone kept saying how AB [Allan Border] was the man to do it and no one else could. I felt it was time someone else put their hand up. I really worked hard on that innings . . . It gave me an amazing amount of confidence to go out there and know I could handle any situation.

When batsmen cut out the hook, word goes round that they do not care for fast bowling and this was so with Steve. In 1994/95 Australia went to the West Indies and by then, in addition to cutting out the hook he had remodelled his back stroke so that he could safely defend against the short stuff of which he was well aware that he would receive more than his fair share. Steve's extraordinary character again won through. On the first day of the Third Test in Port of Spain he was brought face to face with fear for the first time on a cricket pitch. Curtly Ambrose, seldom consumed by geniality when the ball was in his hand during a Test match, sent a bouncer far over Steve's head and, as he liked to do, continued on down the pitch in his follow through. Then, standing there, hands on hips, he subjected Steve to one of those Clint Eastwood stares. Steve was not slow off the mark. 'What the **** are you looking at?' His tone of voice said it all. Steve takes up the story:

Ambrose began to move close to me and mouthed the words 'don't cuss me, man!' His eyeballs were spinning and as he edged to within a metre, he seemed ready to erupt. At this point I gave him a short but sweet reply that went down as well as an anti-malaria tablet. Fortunately Richie Richardson moved in swiftly to avert what could have been my death by strangulation, and the game continued.

Although Steve hung on to make 63 not out in that first innings, Curtly Ambrose and Courtney Walsh took full advantage of an underprepared and uneven pitch to bowl West Indies to victory by 9 wickets.

The final match was at Sabina Park in Kingston. After the West Indies had been bowled out for 265, Australia lost their first 3 wickets for 73 before Steve joined brother Mark. They proceeded to put on 231 for the fourth wicket, only the second century partnership between the twins in the thirty-two Tests they had so far played together. Mark was then caught off bat and pad at short leg when he had made 126. As far as Steve was concerned, the job was not yet done and he again dropped anchor. It was not until Australia's last man was in with him that he reached his double century before a vicious lifter had him caught in the slips. He had batted for nine and a quarter hours, facing 425 balls, hitting one six and sixteen fours from a combination principally of drives, square cuts and sweeps. It was an innings that enabled Australia to beat the West Indies for the first time since Greg Chappell's side had beaten Clive Lloyd's 5–1 in Australia in 1975/76. Unsurprisingly, Steve also included this in the best four innings he had played for his country. It was an heroic achievement that spoke so much for the man and his determination. He was hell-bent on putting the West Indies in their place after all those years at the top. He had changed his technique to cope with the short stuff and the final word must be left to Australia's wicket keeper, Ian Healy, in his description of Steve later that night in the team hotel. 'To see those Charlie Chaplin legs of his walking down that corridor was priceless. Tugga was still in his whites, spikes and baggy green cap. We found him stretched out the next morning, still in all his gear, complete with baggy green firmly on his head.'

It was said of Steve that he wasn't able to play spin bowling either. He could have been forgiven for developing a persecution complex. He had taught the seam bowlers in helpful conditions in England a thing or two; he had given the West Indies fast bowlers a drubbing in their own backyard. Now it was the Indian spinners who were going to show him up. Australia went to India for one Test match in 1996/97 and Steve must have felt that his neck was on the line once again. He didn't do himself any favours when he was caught behind off Ashish Kapoor for a duck in the first innings. It was now that all of his formidable resolve came through. He worked out in his mind exactly how to play the spinners and put together a masterpiece in the second innings. He was unable to save Australia from defeat, but once again he had routed his critics. Peter Roebuck watched this innings:

> In Delhi he contributed one of the finest exhibitions of defensive batting it has been my privilege to watch. Anil Kumble was bowling at the peak of his powers, ball upon ball dipping into an area of broken ground about the size of a kitchen towel, and each ball different in some special and hidden way. Repeatedly Kumble uses his height and wrist to persuade the ball to dive into the pitch and to jump as if its bottom had been burnt. And Waugh stood still and watched, not handcuffed to the crease like some comrades but choosing his stroke – or no stroke at all – at the last possible moment. Repeatedly Waugh stunned the most dangerous deliveries, patting them as if they were gentle cats, whereas in fact he had entered amongst tigers with their hunger and their snarls both somehow stifled . . . he left the field undefeated and, as ever, unapologetic. Here is evidence of the power of Waugh's cricketing brain.

Both these innings were typical of the man and his character. Everyone who has seen him play will have their own special memories of this remarkable cricketer. His innings against South Africa at Headingley in the World Cup of 1999 in the last qualifying match of the Super Sixes remains as one of the more remarkable for me. Australia had made a bad start to the tournament, losing to New Zealand and Pakistan. They had to beat South Africa in this last match to find their way into the semifinals. South Africa won the toss and made 271/7 and before long Australia were 48/3 in reply. It was now that Steve came out to join Ricky Ponting. They put on 126 and Steve went on to the end. Caught up in the fantastic excitement and with adrenalin coursing through him, he played just about the best-ever one-day innings. Only one more wicket fell but Australia were fast running out of overs and there were just two balls left when he saw his side home by 5 wickets. He finished with 120 not out from only 110 balls in surely the most pressurised situation in which even he can ever have found himself. He was allowed one dramatic let off which South Africa and Herschelle Gibbs will never forget. When Steve had made 56, he played a ball at comfortable height to Gibbs at short midwicket. It was a simple catch and Gibbs could not believe his luck. So much so that he began to throw the ball in the air before he had completed the catch and it slipped agonisingly from his fingers. 'How does it feel to drop the World Cup, Hersch?' was Steve's withering comment to Gibbs.

As luck would have it, these two sides met again in the semifinal at Edgbaston. Now, it went even closer. Australia were all out for 213 and when the final over of the match began South Africa needed 9 runs with 1 wicket left. Lance Klusener scythed the first two balls of Damien Fleming's over to the cover boundary and only a single was needed from the last four balls. The third ball was a yorker that Klusener could only stun to mid on. The fourth ball he pushed past the bowler's stumps to Mark Waugh at a straight mid on. Klusener, whose nerves were all over the place, set off at a fearsome pace for the bowler's end. Allan Donald, his partner, was a reluctant starter and set off very late, losing his bat in the process. Waugh's throw came in to Fleming who, with Donald stranded, rolled it underarm down the pitch to Adam Gilchrist and Donald was run out by half the length of the pitch. Australia were through to the final by a superior run rate of 0.19. Australia's nerve had held until the end and there was no one ensuring that this was so more than their captain, Steve Waugh. South Africa had a reputation for choking in these tight situations at the end and he made sure they did not lose it. Australia went on to wallop Pakistan in the final. Steve's last Test century, against England at Sydney in January 2003, was another typical effort. The media were talking him out of the captaincy of the Australian Test side. His splendid reaction once again was, 'I'll show them.' And he did too, even though Australia lost the match. This was his 157th Test match and I don't suppose he minds very much when he goes, but I bet he would like to do it when he wants and not when they want.

Being the affable, equable sort of chap that he is, Mark won't mind if he has to go on living in his twin brother's shadow. Mark himself played in 128 Test matches, which means that he can throw a pretty hefty shadow of his own. There was nothing in the least austere about Mark, either in his character or his cricket. He has always enjoyed life to the full. He is an extrovert who is constantly chatting away in the slips as he chews gum. He bats with a lovely, resounding expansiveness and the only irritating thing about his cricket has been an inconsistency that perhaps by rights should not have been there. Yet Mark gives the impression of wanting to live by the seat of his pants. There was no way in a million years that Steve would ever have been involved with the Indian bookmaking fraternity, but it was no great surprise when Mark's name came up. He is a gambler by nature and the Indians had done their homework. He could never have lived the disciplined life that suited Steve. He had the greater natural flare for the game without the temperament or the desire to take the mechanism to pieces bit by bit and put it together again in a different way to turn it into something more fireproof and efficient. He sank or swam as he was. His rule was that when he was out he allowed himself two expletives in the dressing room, but definitely no bat throwing, and then he got on with life.

I was lucky enough to be at the Adelaide Oval in 1990/91 when he made 138 not out against England in his First Test match. It was appropriate that this innings should have been played in Adelaide for it suited the most picturesque of all the Test grounds. Mark gave a wonderful exhibition of classical strokeplay. From the first ball nothing was out of place and he seemed certain to make a hundred before he had reached even 20. His bat gave off that lovely mellow sound, the product of perfect timing; his footwork was a joy and he has a most satisfying array of strokes. This innings was an object of grace and beauty. He was not one to indulge in lengthy exercises in defiance for they were against his nature, although he could if he had to. At Port Elizabeth in 1996/97 he took Australia to victory over South Africa with a superb innings of 116 on a deteriorating pitch. Then, the following year at Bangalore he made 153 not out, allowing Australia to get back on level terms with India. Steve would have liked to have played both of these two. As a rule, Mark played as if he was batting for his own amusement and trying to bend the will of the bowler to his way of thinking. It was his quick hands that gave him the advantage. Those hands also brought him no fewer than 181 catches in Test cricket, which is 24 more than his nearest rival who is his former captain, Mark Taylor. He never had the concentration to become a double of Steve's. Probably it would not have interested him to have done so. Peter Roebuck, who knows the Waughs pretty well, writes that Mark 'has the same gift [as Steve] but after an hour or two he starts thinking about the horses'. Mark may have been born only four minutes behind Steve but he has been playing catch-up in so many ways ever since. The nice thing about Mark is that he will never have held this against Steve for a single second and it won't have worried him that he has not caught up. They brought different characters to the same natural ability and they both developed their art accordingly. The game would have been immensely the poorer without either of them. To have them both, as Australia has, has been an unimaginable luxury. In some ways, their presence may even have lessened the ignominy of defeat for their opponents.

SACHIN TENDULKAR

IT is not easy to live with the title of the 'Best Batsman in the World'. It is part of Sachin Tendulkar's charm that you would never guess that he does have to live with it. His charming demure smile and his slightly shy manner suggest a man who would have trouble in persuading himself of the need to crush a beetle, let alone dismiss the most dangerous bowlers in the world to all points of the compass. There is never even a hint of brutality in his batting. In cricketing terms, small is effective and often beautiful too. Don Bradman, who himself had special words of praise for Tendulkar, Sunny Gavaskar, Rohan Kanhai, Hanif Mohammed, Neil Harvey and, of course, Tendulkar himself, have all been not a great deal more than knee high to a grasshopper. Yet they have all been more than just wonderful strikers of a cricket ball; they have all been true artists who have taken their chosen art to its limits while considerably embellishing it along the way. Tendulkar is probably the most natural of them all.

His strokes today are still connected to those he was playing two decades ago in the small, thirty-square-yard playground of the Sabitya Sabawas housing complex in the middle-class Bombay surburb of Bandra East. For eleven years, his nanny, Laxmibai Ghije, who was the first person to bowl to him, looked after Sachin. When he was two-and-a-half years old she used a plastic ball, while he did his best with a *dboka* or washing stick. For one who has always seemed so gentle, it is strange that as a young boy he loved to fight and show off his strength. If ever a new young face appeared at school, Sachin would clench his fists. He was not used to being on the losing side, either. Maybe he had an important element of surprise on his side for he had a cherubic face and a beguiling look of wide-eyed innocence. As a six-year-old he was capable of beating up boys who were two years older than him. He feared no one and perhaps it was good training for the battles against Malcolm Marshall, Glenn McGrath, Allan Donald and the rest in the years to come.

By the time he was eleven he was obsessed with cricket. He even moved to live with his uncle so that he did not have so far to go for cricket practice before and after each day at school. His brother, Ajit, who was eleven years older than Sachin, was the first to spot his unusual ability. Ajit brought him to the notice of Ramakant Achrekar, known as 'Achrekar Sir', who had a great reputation for finding and bringing on young cricketers in their part of Bombay. Nearly twenty years later, Achrekar was still excited by the thought of the young Tendulkar. 'Everything was just right,' he said. 'He was a natural cricketer. I did not have to change much. By the time he was twelve or thirteen I knew he would make the big time. If I told him something, he would be diligent and persevering. I would have to tell him something only once and he would stick to it.' Achrekar had no doubt that it was the solid structure of the Tendulkar family that provided the basis for his career. 'His father was always behind him and Ajit would accompany him to the nets. This was essential for the youngster.'

After spending two weeks in the nets with him, Achrekar brought Sachin into his first organised matches. He began with two ducks but was soon scoring fifties and then hundreds. In the 1987/88 season there was a not-out double century followed by three not-out triple centuries in club cricket. In the second he was partnered by Vinod Kambli, the future Test batsman, and they put on an unbroken 664 for the third wicket. 'Achrekar Sir's assistant ran all round [the boundary] trying to attract our attention so that he could tell us to declare,' said Kambli years later. 'Sachin kept telling me not to look at him. We even started singing.' They were finally persuaded at the lunch break, but by then their stand was a world record for any wicket in any form of cricket. Kambli was 349 not out and Tendulkar 326 not out. Before the end of the season, Sachin had made his first-class debut in the Ranji Trophy, for Bombay against Gujarat, and, almost inevitably, had scored a hundred. A year later he was to play his first Test match for India, in Pakistan when he was sixteen years and 205 days old.

There is nothing emotive about Tendulkar at the wicket. He despatches the ball with an effortless grace that combines a remarkable technical correctness with an almost clinical and dispassionate efficiency. He plays his stroke and then gets on with the business of playing the next ball. He has never been given over to extravagant outbursts of joy while batting. After acknowledging the applause for a century or a double century, which, in India, can at least bring the roof down, Tendulkar will step away from the wicket and wait for the noise to quieten down. Then he will get ready for the next ball. He keeps his feet on the ground in every sense. In appearance, he always manages to look neat, dapper and in control. You do not see him endlessly wiping away the sweat and when he raises his bat in appreciation, it is a simple, modest gesture rather than the sort of windmill effect that some batsmen seem to strive for. It is the same when he has been dismissed. If he has made a hundred, he walks off as quickly and as undemonstratively as if he has been out for single figures.

There is not the smallest visible element of side in anything that Tendulkar does; there is rather a slight impression of embarrassment and the feeling that he wants to get it over, whatever it may be, as quickly as possible. It would be difficult to imagine a more self-effacing genius. Yet, in spite of all of this, when he is at the crease his genius radiates around him and one is left in no doubt that one is in the presence both of greatness and humility. He is probably the richest cricketer there has ever been, but he will no more throw his wealth about than speak unkindly to an opponent or throw his bat around in the dressing room.

In one-day internationals Tendulkar opens the batting for India and he almost invariably gets them off to a cracking start. Yet Tendulkar's method, which is supremely classical, could hardly be further away from the concept of pinch-hitting, although the result may be the same. He brings the coaching book to life in a way that perhaps no other batsman has ever done. He gives to all his strokes a grace, a fluency and a panache that gives them all the look and feel of consummate artistry. By an extraordinary coincidence, when I was in the middle of writing this essay, I saw Tendulkar open the batting for India against Pakistan at Centurion in the qualifying round of the World Cup in South Africa in March 2003. That day on the loveliest of cricket grounds, Tendulkar took the art of batting to a pinnacle even he had never before reached, and beyond which no batsman in the history of the game has ever climbed. It was a good pitch, and the Pakistani bowling, led by Wasim Akram, Waqar Younis and Shoaib Akhtar who, earlier in the competition had become the first bowler to be measured at more than 100 mph, was fearsome. Added to that, this was a game between India and Pakistan who, because of politics, had not met on the cricket field for almost three years. For countless millions it was nothing less than a religious battle. The pressure on Tendulkar will have been huge as he strode out to bat with the hopes of every Hindu in the world weighing down upon him. Pakistan had already made 273/7, a score that will win more matches than it loses.

During the next hour and three-quarters the full genius of Tendulkar was revealed. Wasim Akram opened the bowling and his third ball was fast, just short of a length and outside the off stump. Tendulkar moved like lightning. His right foot moved back and across to the off stump. Unlike most contemporary batsmen, he uses the full width of the crease to give him that extra split second and a fraction more room for manoeuvre. Tendulkar is a short man while Wasim is tall with broad shoulders and an unusually quick arm action that gives him pace and bounce. It did not seem geometrically possible that Tendulkar should now have done what he did to a ball that was lifting on him. Standing on his toes to give himself an extra inch or two and playing with a straight and perpendicular bat, Tendulkar drove Wasim off the back foot past cover's right hand for four with both power and timing. It was perfection itself and Tendulkar, who is not given to boasting about his prowess, said afterwards that he knew, as that ball sped away for four, that he was going to play a good innings. In cricketing terms, that stroke was the equivalent of an atomic explosion.

Shoaib Akhtar bowled the second over. He runs in like a sprinter and his arm action reminds one of nothing more than a windmill caught in a hurricane. Tendulkar received a short ball lifting above his shoulder outside the off stump. With calm deliberation, he upper cut it over gully and fifteen rows back in to the crowd at backward point. Tendulkar stood there, stock still, as if he had done the most natural thing in the world. Shoaib pitched one a little further up on the line of his body. Tendulkar waited for it – he moves his feet so quickly into position that this is the impression he creates – and turned it backward of square leg for four. It was not a deflection; he hit the ball out of the middle of the bat, imparting power to the stroke and not just using the pace of the ball. All the fielders could do was go and fetch it. Shoaib now produced one on the middle and leg stumps on a good length. Tendulkar came firmly forward in defence and yet he timed the ball so well that it sped away between mid on and the bowler to the boundary. The fastest bowler in the world went for 18 runs in his first over and had to be taken off. India were 27 for no wicket.

Grasping his experience to him like a coat of armour, Wasim's next over cost only a single. Then it was Waqar's turn. He loosened up with an offside bouncer to Verinder Sehwag who upper cut it for six to much the same place that Tendulkar had found for

Shoaib. A single brought Tendulkar into strike and Waqar bowled him one slightly short on his body and he played an identical stroke to the one he had produced against Shoaib in the second over. It was Wasim's turn again. A good length ball on the off stump was driven on the rise through extra cover for four. When Wasim bowled at his legs Tendulkar did not just push to mid-wicket for singles; three times he played the ball straight of mid-wicket for twos. After four overs and five balls had been bowled, India were 50 for no wicket. Tendulkar went on and on.

He gave three hints of mortality. First he drove Wasim to mid off where Abdur Razzaq leapt high, but reached the ball only with the tips of his fingers; he played forward to Shahid Afridi, who on another day might have stuck out a right hand and caught the ball as Tendulkar's uppish forward stroke flew past him; and then he was laid low with a thigh strain, which worried him increasingly. When he was 2 runs short of his hundred, the team's physiother-apist came out and gave him a good going over. In the next over Shoaib produced a nasty bouncer. It followed Tendulkar so that he could only fend at it and the ball lobbed deep to the gully where Shahid Afridi dived forward and held a good low catch. For what it is worth, Tendulkar had faced sixty-nine balls and had hit twelve fours and one six, although genius can never be measured in figures.

Tendulkar and his bat are as free of emotion as Michael Schumacher and the engine of his Ferrari. Theirs are jobs that are equally well done and neither indulges in flamboyant celebratory excesses. When Tendulkar plays a particularly special stroke, he watches it go to the boundary and then waits at the crease, appar-ently unaware of the madly waving Indian flags all around the ground. He appears to be able to shut his ears to the constant and swelling cacophony of sound. Tendulkar bats for India and never for Tendulkar. It is sometimes said that he does not win enough matches for India, but this does not take into account the effect that his mere presence in the Indian side has upon the opposition;

nor does it allow for the inspiration he gives to his fellow players. During his innings at Centurion against Pakistan, he was joined by Mohammad Kaif, who was uneasy at the start of his innings. It is not easy to bat at the other end to Tendulkar when he is in mid-season form. No one was more aware of this than Tendulkar who soon had a couple of chats in the middle of the wicket with Kaif. When Kaif hit his first four, past cover, Tendulkar was quick to go down the pitch and congratulate him. This is an illustration of the man Tendulkar is and what he gives to the team.

He scored his first hundred for India at Old Trafford in 1990 when he was not far past seventeen. This was not the flamboyant Tendulkar of Centurion, but an innings of astonishing maturity in one so young, full of concentration and application and it showed a splendid technique. In 1991/92 he took his talents to Australia where he made hundreds in the Test matches in Sydney and Perth, which are still spoken about with wonderment. They were innings that mightily impressed Sir Donald Bradman. He went on to score seven Test hundreds before his twenty-first birthday, an incredible achievement that may never be beaten.

The first of two blips on his escutcheon, at the age of barely nineteen he came to play for Yorkshire as their first-ever overseas player. He did his best to enter into the spirit of it, but he never managed to produce his best form for the Tykes and scored only one century for them. Nonetheless, it was an important part of his cricketing education. The second was that when elevated to the Indian captaincy in place of Mohammad Azharuddin at the age of twenty-three, it did not all fall into place as it will have been hoped that it would. He was not the first to find that Indian cricket is hopelessly bedevilled by politics, or that India's progress overseas can only be handicapped by the lack of genuine pace bowling. Now that the job is in the relatively successful hands of Sourav Ganguly, Tendulkar probably draws quiet sighs of relief. It leaves him to get on with the job of scoring runs in his own wholly irresistible and uncomplicated way. One can only dream of seeing

Tendulkar and Brian Lara sharing a long partnership after Michael Vaughan has set the innings off with a supremely elegant hundred. The happy thought is that Tendulkar is only thirty and so there is lots more to come.

BRIAN LARA

B RIAN LARA is an eternal paradox and intensely human. There is no contemporary batsman who quickens the pulse and starts the adrenalin coursing through the body at a greater pace. There is no one capable of contemptuously dismissing a bowling attack in such an elegant, cultivated and joyful manner. There is no one who, on his best days, brings more joy to his batting or who is able to so mesmerise bowlers and spectators alike. There is a supreme suppleness and elegance about his strokes and a gloriously uninhibited West Indian elasticity to all that he does. He sees the ball earlier than most and when he decides to go on to the attack his footwork is so fast that it is almost as if he is able to dissolve his body into thin air and to reassemble the relevant bits and pieces half a split second later in the perfect position to carry out the extravagant and flourishing execution he has in mind. He is one of those rare players who do not seem able to make an ugly movement or to play an ungainly stroke. On his best days, he dances with the gods on Mount Olympus.

But, alas, in the way of the world, there is a side to his character that is all too intensely human and tempers all of this. On a good day he is sublime, on others he allows himself to be an insult to himself and his god-given ability. When Lara arrived on the scene, the West Indies must have felt that they had been sent another Viv Richards. To be honest, there were times when he looked as if he might almost have been better than Richards, although this may have had something to do with his left-handedness, which often brings an aesthetical advantage with it. For some strange quirk of nature, the ball seems to flow more seamlessly off left-handers' bats than it does from those of their right-handed colleagues. But when Lara was fashioned, an unfortunate dollop of the Garden of Eden found its way into the mixture. Lara loved the shining red apples that were the fruits of his success, and he ate plentifully therefrom. Success went to his head and he became spoiled. The Trinidad government gave him a plot of land on a small hill at one corner of the Savannah in Port of Spain. He built himself a palace of luxury and relished all the baubles that came with it. Sadly, but inevitably, he took his eye off the reason he had been put upon a pedestal in the first place. For periods that were all too long, cricket seemed to become irrelevant and those big scores became increasingly less frequent.

Worse than that, he tantalised. Once in a while he would show us his full bag of tricks, usually when the situation could hardly be bleaker both for the West Indies and for himself. We would all sit up and think and hope that now that he had refound his touch things would return to normal. The hedonistic side of Lara would soon regain the upper hand, however, and we would be left to watch him scratch around in the crease as if it was all a mystery even to him. He will never quite live in the bracket that embraced George Headley, Everton Weekes, Clyde Walcott, Frank Worrell, Garry Sobers or Richards. Yet, on this day, Lara may still be the best of them all to watch. Of course, he has never had the same supporting cast as Sobers or Richards, not that they necessarily needed it, while the three Ws were their own supporting cast. The trouble with Lara has been that he has not been able to suppress human nature, never an easy task. When he has hit the heights, he has stood in front of a mirror and preened himself. He forgets how important it is to keep on working at his art; he feels he can indulge himself to the limit, put on his pads and, *hey presto*, deliver at will. For those who adopt these attitudes retribution is swift to follow. He would then run away from the pitch and from public life and draw the curtains against the outside world, but when you have revelled in the glamour as he has, withdrawal symptoms soon set in. It has never been that long before he is to be seen peering round the edges of these same curtains looking longingly at the life he has cherished but could not find the will permanently to grasp.

The most eye-catching West Indian batsmen do not, as a rule, come from the slow turning pitches of Trinidad. Barbados is their natural home, although Jamaica produced George Headley and Guyana nurtured Rohan Kanhai and Clive Lloyd, and Antigua sired Richards. At the age of twenty-one, Lara was an established member of the Trinidad side. In the 1990/91 season he scored 627 runs for them in five matches and this included six successive scores of 50. Trinidad visited Jamaica and found themselves playing on an awkward pitch at Sabina Park. Lara's contribution was 122 and 87 and Michael Holding, who was working for a local radio station, was moved to say, 'I'd pick Lara first for the Test team, then look for ten others.' There was a poetry and a beauty about his batting even then and his destiny was plain to see.

His career progressed like a piece of patchwork: intermittent brilliant peaks of colour with dreary areas of greyness in between. In 1992/93 in Sydney he made 277 against Australia in an innings that Sir Donald Bradman earmarked as one of the best he had ever seen. A year later, England visited the Caribbean and Lara followed a small matter of 167 in the Test match at Georgetown with 375, the world record Test score, in the game at the Recreation Ground in St John's, Antigua. The ever pragmatic Mike Atherton, England's captain, summed that one up in a couple of sentences, 'He had looked a brilliant player at times [earlier in the series], with a touch of genius, but he had always looked the type of player to give a chance. In Antigua, on the flattest of pitches it was almost as though he realised from the start that a giant score was in the offing. He played faultlessly; I can't remember him giving one chance.' When he passed 365, Sir Garfield Sobers hobbled out to shake his hand. For 1994, he took Allan Donald's place in the

Warwickshire side and smote 501 not out against Durham at Edgbaston, which remains the highest ever first-class score. A visit to England with the West Indies in 1995 produced scores of 145 at Old Trafford, 152 at Trent Bridge and 179 at The Oval.

It was now, though, that he began to allow signs of the dreaded *ennui* to creep in. He allowed the boring rigours that go with playing cricket for a living at this level to get on top of him: the travelling, the airports, the bus journeys, the endless game of cards with his team-mates. Or, to be more exact, he wanted the six-star glamour that he felt should be the constant companion of his kind of success, but he did not care for the hard work, the discipline and the self-denying ordinances, which have necessarily to go with it. Lara had had a taste of the good life and he liked it. When he returned home to that house on the hill, he opened the doors and glamour and hero-worship and its attendant goodies came tumbling in. Then he would gratefully turn his back on the need to score runs and the necessity of constant practice to make sure he could deliver the next time.

After three relatively barren years, which included losing a series 5–0 in South Africa when he was captain and West Indies cricket coming near to an all-time low, Lara felt the need to peep round the corner of that curtain once again. Australia came to the Caribbean in 1998/99 when he was still captain. In the First Test, at his own Queen's Park Oval in Trinidad, the West Indies had been bowled out for 51 and lost by 312 runs. The house on the hill was draughty that night. The caravan then moved on to Kingston's Sabina Park. The seriousness, not only of his personal situation, but also of the predicament facing the West Indies hit home to Lara. After dismissing Australia for 256, the West Indies found themselves in familiar territory at 34/3 when Lara was joined by that most determined and doughtiest of cricketers, Jimmy Adams. They put on 322 for the fifth wicket with Lara playing an extraordinary innings of 213, and the West Indies won by 10 wickets. Only a batsman blessed with genius could have turned it on as

Lara did that day and by the time he was out his reputation had been restored. The small boys in the West Indian islands had given up ideas of becoming famous basketball players in America. They were gripping makeshift bats and wanting to be Lara all over again.

Bridgetown, Barbados was the next stop on the treadmill. Lara had been returned to his throne, was trusted by everyone and was enjoying it immensely. For more than three days in Barbados, Australia had much the better of things. Courtney Walsh then bowled out Australia for 146 in their second innings and the West Indies were left to score an improbable 311 to win. At 105/5 all seemed lost but once again Jimmy Adams strode steadfastly out to join his captain who was carrying on from where he had left off at Sabina Park. They put on 133, but the last 4 wickets still needed 73 more runs. Thanks to Lara they got them after Walsh, the last man, had stayed firm while the final 9 were scored at the other end. This was how Peter Roebuck described Lara's innings of 153 not out:

> Brian Lara has played one of the greatest innings in the history of the game. Certainly his match-winning and mouth-watering 153 not out at Kensington Oval was the best innings of its type it has been my privilege to watch. Perhaps it was the best of any sort. Throughout a long, hot fifth day, played in a frenzied atmosphere against fierce opponents and before a packed and expectant crowd, the Trinidadian kept his head and his wicket. He showed impeccable judgement and remarkable calm as he took his team for a famous victory in the most exciting and draining Test I've seen. Lara's efforts surpassed his magnificent 213 in Sabina Park since this time the Australians were on their toes – besides which it was a fifth-day pitch and there was a match to win.

The West Indies arrived in Antigua for the Fourth and final Test 2–1 up in the series. This time the Australians' ruthless determination was not to be denied. But before they strode home by 178 runs to level the series, Lara gave them and his West Indian friends and enemies a final reminder of who he was and what he was about.

After Australia had been bowled out for 303, he came to the wicket with the West Indies 20/2 and proceeded to play an innings that brought him exactly 100 in eighty-four balls and that only he could have conceived. It was not enough runs or a long enough innings to deny Australia victory, but as an exhibition of one man's ability, it was staggering, much more so than the 375, which was above all an accumulation contest.

Eighteen months later Lara, was with the West Indies in Australia and was again tiptoeing that invisible line between care and concern on the one hand, and couldn't care less and to hell with it on the other. Since the bonanza in the West Indies he had been busily embracing the affairs of mammon and the captaincy had passed to Jimmy Adams. The West Indians arrived in Adelaide for the Third Test having lost both the first two in complete disarray at Brisbane and Perth. Adams won the toss and the West Indies were 52/2 when Lara emerged from the pavilion. He now threw off his shackles as only he can and made 182 runs as only he can. He was again watched by Peter Roebuck who, with inimitable skill, put his finger on the spot.

> Lara stood out like a strawberry on a plate of plums. Nowadays he seems to produce his best when his fortunes are at their lowest. Last year, in the Caribbean, he was about to lose the captaincy and his dignity, and promptly saved both with a string of innings that combined the power of Sanath, the mastery of Sachin and the grit of Steve Waugh. And then he went back into his shell. Lara was reluctant to tour England and flopped badly. Perhaps it works this way. Lara must summon immense willpower to produce a great performance. No longer do runs appear like water through a tap. Moreover, his mind has become distracted and tired as his life has widened. He needs a long period of rest and some particular motivation to produce those scintillating innings that win matches and delight spectators.

As long as Lara is within their ranks the West Indies are a hard side to assess. If he is interested, anything is possible; if he is not, anything else is. It was not easy to know what to make of their side for the 2002/03 World Cup in South Africa. Under Carl Hooper's shrewd and firm leadership, they had become a more reliable entity. The mercurial Lara was still there. The question everyone wanted to know the answer to was what was the state of his mind? They did not have to wait long for an answer. The first game of the competition was played at Newlands in Cape Town. Hooper won the toss against South Africa and Lara was walking to the middle when the score was 7/2 and there were still some empty seats. He was not at ease and for quite a while it was all he could do to survive the hostile South African opening attack of Shaun Pollock and Makhaya Ntini. That he tried so hard to do so provided the answer to the question. Gradually, the freedom returned and then runs began to come.

The old warhorse, Allan Donald, desperate for one more glimpse of the sun and one more tilt at all the old enemies, came on as first change at the Wynberg End. Table Mountain was at its most solemn and unforgiving as it looked down severely on these two brilliant cricketers. Lara took guard and Donald bowled. The ball was up to Lara, he came forward with that memorably lovely flowing arc of the bat and hit the ball, perhaps not quite as perfectly as he would have liked, but near enough to make no matter. It flew up, up into the air far over mid off and landed with a crash among the members in their enclosure behind long off. It was a stroke that told a sad story for Donald and a joyful one for Lara. Without meaning to be disloyal, Table Mountain nodded knowingly. Lara went on and on, visibly growing in stature all the time. Those shots all returned, first as if from memory and then with an immediacy that was full of wonderful and beguiling West Indian improvisation.

Lara gave the World Cup the start that the entire cricketing world will have been hoping for. He showed, too, that the West Indies were more than just a good outside bet. His 116 took his side to 278/5 and eventually victory by 3 runs in the craziest and best of finishes. Sadly for the West Indies, he could not maintain his concentration and maybe his interest, too, and he was unable to take the West Indies through to the later stages of the competition. But on returning home he found himself appointed for the second time in his career as captain of the West Indies and for the most daunting task of all, a series against Australia. He made a good start with a hundred in the second innings in the First Test, played in Georgetown, even though Australia won by 9 wickets. As always, though, one could only wonder for how long his concentration span would last this time, but his good form continued to the end of the series. Nothing has come much better in contemporary cricket than a glimpse of Brian Lara at his best.

PHIL TUFNELL

PHIL ('I'm a Celebrity') Tufnell has recently undergone the most dramatic transformation since Mrs Lot had a cheeky look over her shoulder as she and her husband fled from the might of Sodom and was turned instantly into fodder for the salt cellar. Served her right. Tufnell has always been value for money, largely in the most recalcitrant and rebellious of ways, although usually with a mischievous twinkle in his eyes. For years, he kicked over the traces like nobody's business and yet at the same time managed to convey one or two rather endearing and innocent-looking characteristics to go with his floppingly youthful brown hair. Those whose job it was to captain him on the cricket field could be excused for not entirely agreeing with this. Tufnell is a left-arm spin bowler of considerable talent who has bowled England to victory in three of his forty-two Test matches. At times, though, those who have had the job of trying to channel his energies and his spinning attributes into the right avenues, will have felt that they would have been better served if he had been drowned at birth. The apparently all-powerful duumvirate of Nasser Hussain and Duncan Fletcher that has been presiding over England's misfortunes in recent years have kicked Tufnell firmly into touch and turned their backs on him. This, of course, made no sense and was an appalling reflection on their inability to understand the basics of man-management, which only served to handicap England still further.

Tufnell was born a maverick. The establishment was not his thing and if he could cock a snook at them he would. It added to the fun that he was born in Barnet and therefore plied his trade at Lord's where cocking a snook tends to make bigger news than in some other parts of the realm. The fag drooping from the lips, the half drunk pint of bitter, the sloppy clothes that all their lives had been deprived of the luxury of an iron and, I daresay, the flip-flops on the feet will have raised rather more than the odd eyebrow or two in that stateliest of pavilions. In a way, 'Tuffers' was cricket's Charlie Chaplin. Even the walk was an unmistakeable slouch, which seemed to say 'Up yours' in a loud and clear voice. The eternal paradox of clowns is that they can be as loveable as they can be infuriating. Tufnell's persona came from a fundamental insecurity, which in turn led to a cover up that manifested itself in an aggressive form of chippiness. He was the *enfant terrible* in both the Middlesex and the England dressing rooms.

His ability to bowl was never in doubt. The only question was whether or not the ability and its owner could be safely harnessed. Tufnell came into the England side for the Second Test match at Melbourne on England's tour of Australia in 1990/91 under the captaincy of Graham Gooch whom one would not instinctively pick as Tufnell's greatest natural supporter. Yet Gooch was his captain when he bowled out and beat the West Indies at The Oval in 1991 and New Zealand in Christchurch the following January. Michael Atherton was in charge when Tufnell was selected for his second tour of Australia, during which his turbulent private life spilled over into the public domain, and later when he took eleven wickets against Australia at The Oval.

There is no point in going into all Tufnell's tantrums and problems. Suffice to that, for all his skill, he was not an easy chap to have around. Yet, in spite of it all, Gooch and Atherton, who are two hard taskmasters, had an underlying sympathy for him. Intrinsically they did not dislike him and regarded him as a character who, insecure or not, was good for cricket. The regime of Hussain and Fletcher was a great deal more unforgiving and humourless. They were not prepared to go the extra mile to try to get the best out of Tufnell. Small wonder that he should have decided at the start of the 2003 season to chuck it all in when the offer came along to go out to the Australian jungle with the curiously disparate group chosen for *I'm a Celebrity . . . Get Me Out of Here*. Middlesex were now being run on the field by the younger generation and he must have begun to feel a little bit out on a limb, and the likelihood of a return to the England side, regardless of his 121 Test wickets, had virtually disappeared.

Somehow he was persuaded to leave the chippy, thorny side of his character in England when he flew out to take potluck in the antipodean jungle. For ten days he showed only that part of himself that Gooch and Atherton had liked. He was charming, extremely funny and allowed nothing to faze him. When, in the final round, I watched him force himself to eat all those creepy-crawly denizens of the jungle and come up with a smile afterwards, I admired him enormously. I also couldn't help wondering what Messrs Hussain and Fletcher would have done in a similar situation. Before that, for nearly a fortnight, he had been an excellent team man showing great concern for the problems of his camp-mates. I shall be surprised if victory in this particular contest does not remove most of those insecurities that have dogged him and held him back for years.

The powers-that-be at Middlesex have said there is no reason why he should not come back and bowl for them if the situation warrants. If he is given that chance, his Middlesex colleagues will almost certainly find a very different Tufnell in their midst. He will now have the confidence to give the ball more air, to become a more attacking bowler, and he should take plenty of wickets. If he does, who is to say that he will not before long be back in the England side as a reliable performer rather than one who has to have a close eye kept on him. I am sure he would then bring his *I'm a Celebrity* persona on to the cricket ground with him and we would all be able to enjoy wholeheartedly watching him for some years as he tried to take his tally of Test wickets past 200. The problem might be that he will be wanted for more of these television extravaganzas and cannot, therefore, spare the time. But what a transformation and let us keep our fingers crossed that it has lifted the scales from his eyes. If he now goes back to his old ways, he can jolly well buzz off and join that brazen hussy and devil-may-care backward glancer, Mrs Lot, as another well-known pillar of salt.

SHANE WARNE

IN modern times, no cricketer has been more intriguing or compelling than Shane Warne who has not only revived, but has also
reinvented the beguiling art of leg spin. Wrist spinners, by the
nature of their trade, are the jokers in cricket's pack. The crafty
ones, led by Warne, are able to perform all manner of tricks and
seem to laugh at the batsman while doing so. From time to time
they get it wrong and then the joke is on the other foot. No one
has done this better to Warne than the Indian, V.V.S. Laxman,
when he made 281 against Australia in Calcutta in 2001 and
turned a match around almost as Ian Botham had done against
Australia at Headingley in 1981. No other leg spinner in the history
of the game has had such a bewildering variety of tricks up his
sleeve as Warne. His exaggerated mop of fair hair, his infectious
enthusiasm, his ruddy complexion, his bounding stride and his
sparkling eyes tell a story even before he begins to flex those
famous fingers.

When he first toured England with the Australians in 1993, the
usual load of advanced publicity, at which the Australians are so
good and which might easily be mistaken for propaganda, preceded
him. All eyes were upon him and the tabloid journalists sharpened
their pencils the moment this genial blond with a reputation for
being something of a beach bum stepped off the aeroplane. He had
already made his mark in Test matches against the West Indies and
New Zealand, but when he arrived in England, he did not hit the
ground running. The Australians made their customary early visit to

Worcester where Warne suffered a purposeful and destructive assault at the hands of Graeme Hick. This was a real test of character for Warne because Allan Border, his captain, had instructed him not to bowl anything other than his leg break at Hick, who was bound to play in the Test series. Border wisely did not want Warne to give away any of his secrets. It was for the same reason that he was not included in the one-day internationals, which were played before the Tests. It called for remarkable coolness from Warne not to slip Hick a single googly or even just a solitary flipper.

Australia batted first at Old Trafford; on the second day, 3 June, it was England's turn. With his very first ball he bowled Mike Gatting with a leg break that seemed to turn about a yard and a half. It pitched well outside the leg stump and hit the top of the off. It was described in accordance with one's loyalty as either 'the ball from hell' or 'the ball of the century'. The sequence of events began with the Australian captain Allan Border: 'Warnie, you're on next over.' Warne himself takes up the story:

> For some reason I've always been able to land my first few balls fairly accurately. Some spinners start with a few innocuous deliveries just to get into a rhythm. I usually start with my stock ball, the leg break, and I usually try to spin it fairly hard. That's the way I bowl so that's the way I start. With the ball to Gatting all I tried to do was pitch on about leg stump and spin it a fair way. As it left my hand it felt just about perfect. When a leg break works really well it curves away to the leg-side in the air before pitching and spinning back the other way. The curve in the air comes from the amount of spin on the ball and in this case I had managed to put quite a lot of purchase on this delivery. That is why it dipped and curved away so far and then spun back such a long way. I knew I'd bowled Gatt and I could tell from the look on Ian Healy's face behind the stumps that the ball had done something special, but it was not until I saw a replay during the lunch break that I fully realised just how much it had done. After stumps Gatt came into our dressing room for a drink and looked up at me and said, 'Bloody hell, Warnie. What happened?' I didn't have much of an answer for him.

It was an astonishing delivery and must join forces with that other one, the googly with which Eric Hollies bowled Bradman for nought in his last Test innings, at The Oval in 1948.

This description of that freak dismissal by Warne tells of a formidable perkiness. It is an account, too, that shows how hard he has worked at his game and how thoroughly he understands the art, which he has perfected as the result of a huge amount of disciplined practice. Warne was born with a vast reservoir of self-confidence, which is half his charm and makes him such an irresistible performer. His meteoric career has only faltered because of the inevitable injuries to his fingers and his shoulder and also because of a not-to-be-sniffed-at ability to self-destruct. Even so, it took him just nine years to beat Dennis Lillee's record of 355 Test wickets and become Australia's leading wicket-taker.

Warne burst upon the scene from middle-class Melbourne. He had played in only seven Sheffield Shield games for Victoria in which he had taken 13 wickets at 51.62 apiece. These were hardly earth-shattering figures, but there were people in important places who saw at once that he was something special. He was thrust into the Australian side in place of off spinner Peter Taylor for the Third Test against India at the Sydney Cricket Ground. It was now that Sachin Tendulkar and Ravi Shastri took it upon themselves to rediscover their form and Warne's only wicket cost 150 runs. It was hardly better in the next Test in Adelaide when his figures were 0/78 and he was dropped for the match in Perth. The selectors kept faith with him, however, and took him to Sri Lanka in 1991/92, and in the First Test his 3/11 at the end enabled Australia to win a close match. In the following Australian season he owed a good deal to Allan Border, who handled him carefully, but even Border could not prevent the mauling he received from Brian Lara at Sydney. It was Border who was largely responsible for Warne going to New Zealand later in the same Australian summer. His 7 wickets took them to victory in the Test at Christchurch. He finished the series with 17 wickets and never looked back.

In the mid-nineties Warne began to have trouble with his spinning finger and his right shoulder. It was now that he showed real character as he fought his way back and this must never be forgotten in any final assessment of Warne. Although the advice he received from other members of the leg-spinning fraternity was almost unanimously against it, Warne took himself off to the United States for the offending limbs to be operated on. The finger was the principal generator of the astonishing amount of spin Warne was able to impart to the ball. It was the thrust of the shoulder that gave the ball its energy and, like the spinning finger, it had protested at the overtime that had been forced upon it. In series against the West Indies in Australia and then in South Africa, Warne was comfortably below his best and by no means all his usual options were available to him. Nonetheless, his phenomenal accuracy still made him an important member of Australia's attack, even if he was not the awesome prospect of a year or two earlier. But Warne never gave up, his spirits never flagged and his character prevented these injuries from wearing him down. Outwardly, at any rate, his confidence always bubbled and, off the field, he spoke as good a game as he played while on it.

Warne's unquenchable spirit has always been epitomised by his approach to the stumps. First, when he marks out his run, an air of expectancy settles over the ground for Warne is one of those few cricketers who almost invariably make things happen. As soon as he is thrown the ball, the crowd collectively moves forward on to the edge of its seat. Then he is ready. He walks five strides with a bouncing confidence that must make even the surest of batsmen a trifle apprehensive. In those walking strides that are almost a swagger, he combines vibrant challenge, an element of disdain, an alarming certainty of purpose, an air of conspiracy, while, in his right hand, he is carrying more tricks than a conjuror. To the batsman, even his glistening earring seems a threat. It all gives off an air of calculating know-how. He springs into his delivery stride and then the batsman's real problems begin. The arm twirls over and here is the

moment of truth. The batsman has a split second to forget the propaganda and to work out what this particular ball has in store for
him.

Warne's propaganda is as important to him as his control and his
ability to spin the ball. As his confidence increased over the years, so
did his ability to develop the weapons of the mind. Long before they
step on to Australian soil, visiting batsmen first hear distant rumours
of a new ball that Warne has been tucking up his sleeve. As D-Day
approaches, more and more hints fly across the oceans as a gentle
game of Chinese torture develops. There is no hint as to what this
new Exocet might do. Will it turn and which way, will it swing
before turning, is it faster or slower, does it drop at the last moment?
He called one such the zooter, another the slider and then there was
the back-spinner, which should have had boomerang-like qualities.
All of them had one thing in common: they went straight on. But
most batsmen would not have been human if they had not been on
the lookout for fiendish extravagances after all the advance publicity. It seems inconceivable that anything so exotically named as the
zooter could have failed to turn at least two ways and swerve a good
deal as well.

Psychological warfare is one excellent way of making even a
good batsman play all round a straight ball. So far, in Test matches
alone, a small matter of 491 batsman have found these distinctly
tricky questions to answer. Warne does it all with a smile on his face
that is just occasionally tinged with superiority, and at the end of
the day he is ready to have a beer and a chat with anyone. Warne
may be a supreme conman, but it is only because he has perfected
his art in a way that perhaps no one has done before him that he
is able to tell a batsman stories and expect him to believe them. It
is a tribute to Warne's intelligence and to his independence that he
has taken his art to new frontiers.

There are occasions, however, when the the beach bum within
Warne has got the upper hand. This is as much a part of him as the
dreaded zooter. But then this larrikinism has, in some ways, made

him even more appealing to his adoring public who find it easy to identify with a rebellious streak in their heroes, just as happened in England with Ian Botham. Life with Warne is never dull. He got into trouble smoking a cigarette while playing cards outside the dressing room at the brand new WestPac Stadium in Wellington, which is an official smoke-free zone. He had been told he could smoke inside the dressing room, but they chose the fresh air for the card game. Some kids took photographs of him smoking and it all developed into a good tabloid story when it was realised he was being paid to support an anti-smoking campaign. When he played for Hampshire in 2000, he met a girl in a nightclub in Leicester. She gave him her number and a week or two later they had some interesting late-night telephone calls that made the front page of the *Daily Mirror*.

Early in his career in 1993/94 in Johannesburg, he blew his top and completely lost it after he had bowled the South African opener, the mild-mannered Andrew Hudson, round his legs. This cost him about four and a half thousand Australian dollars in fines. In 1999/2000 he was playing against Pakistan in Hobart and an ABC cameraman was heard on air to say, 'Can't bowl, can't throw,' when a newcomer, Scott Muller, fielded a ball on the legside boundary. The remark was attributed to Warne and, even though the cameraman owned up, Muller apparently thinks to this day that it was Warne, and was most unhappy and probably still is. Characters like Warne attract trouble and don't always see it coming, but all the same, there is something wonderfully refreshing about their approach to life. He has been lucky to have such accommodating captains as Allan Border, Mark Taylor and Steve Waugh who all liked to win. No one will have appreciated Warne's importance to their purpose better than they. He had a bit of luck, too, to find such a brilliant wicket keeper as Ian Healy behind the stumps for most of his career, while Healy's successor, Adam Gilchrist, is not all that far behind.

When Warne emerges from the pavilion with a bat in his hand, there is usually some fun to be had, even if it does not often last as long as all that. In present times, I cannot think of a player I would go much further to watch. Part of Warne's charm is his impulsive nature. His wide-eyed reaction to almost everything seems to be saying in capital letters, 'Let's give it a go.' There is a down side to that as Warne himself discovered when he and Mark Waugh both accepted money in Colombo from a distinctly dodgy character called 'John'.

In this well-documented story these two players put their foot on the bottom rung of a particularly slippery ladder. It was not long before they were offered the next rung. The tour had moved on to Pakistan when, on no less a celebrated occasion, these two and off spinner Tim May were offered a huge amount of money by the Pakistani batsman Salim Malik to bowl badly on the last day of a Test match so that Pakistan should not be beaten. Mercifully for them, common sense prevailed and Salim, or the 'Rat' as they preferred to call him, was told where he could put it. As luck would have it, Pakistan saved the day in any event and, as Salim was quick to underline, they could effectively have had their money for nothing. The bookmakers had selected their prey wisely because they must have felt they were always more likely to hear the answer they wanted from gambling, and maybe gambolling, extroverts than some of their more earnest and introspective colleagues. There are those who are sure that every man has his price, but the fact that Warne and co. slammed the door in their faces makes them even more engaging characters. There's nothing like a good old-fashioned piece of farmhouse honesty.

If he never left the straight and narrow and did not occasionally get himself into trouble, he would not be the character and, maybe, quite the bowler he is. He thought seriously about calling it a day after Australia had won the World Cup in England in 1999. Thank goodness he didn't for world cricket would have been a poorer place without him. It looked as if Courtney Walsh's tally of 519 Test wickets would lure him on and the Mount Everest of 600 after that. It would have kept him in business for a few more seasons to come – and maybe the shoulder and finger surgeons as well. Before any of this could be put to the test, however, Warne suffered another shoulder injury, during the series against England in Australia in 2002/03. The World Cup in South Africa followed the Ashes almost at once and Warne could see this as his last. He was determined, therefore, to be fit for the competition. Events now gathered pace. All the good and the bad sides of Warne came bubbling up together: the larrikinism, the give-it-a-go approach to life and the cheerful extrovert whose answer to most things has been to shrug his shoulders and say, 'What the hell.'

Warne played in the finals of the one-day VB series in Australia and, for reasons that apparently had more to do with his vanity than his likely bowling skills, he accepted a diuretic pill from his mother. He wanted to lose weight in a hurry for a TV show. Diuretics are on the list of substances that sportsmen are forbidden to take because they can be used to mask the taking of other less attractive drugs. They can, for example, hide the swallowing of steroids. Having taken the diuretic, Warne was asked to take a standard random drug test by the Australian cricket authorities. He arrived in South Africa with the Australian side and, of course, he was the player the media focused upon as they set about preparing themselves for the competition. Shortly before Australia played their first match, the world was shocked when news came through from Australia that Warne had failed a drug test. He admitted to taking a diuretic and within hours was on an aeroplane back to Australia. It was then announced that he had failed the second test taken at the same time as the first and the Australian body presiding over these things banned Warne from all cricket for a year, putting his future in jeopardy.

His immediate reactions were that he would appeal and, if the worst came to the worst, be prepared to sit out the intervening year. Goodness knows what offers will be made to him, what other pressures he will be under, and if his own enthusiasm to continue in the game can be maintained. A year off at the age of thirty-four is a great deal different from a year off at twenty-four. The lure of Walsh's record may come to burn less brightly but, whether he comes back or not, Warne's record will always be there for everyone to see. He has been surely the greatest leg spinner of all time and a magnificent entertainer, full of a rebellious individualism that accompanied him throughout his career. We will not have heard the last of him by a long chalk, but in what capacity he will turn up next is anyone's guess.

ALLAN DONALD

I**T** is fascinating to speculate on the recent history of international cricket if Allan Donald, one of the most dramatically exciting and effective fast bowlers of all, had decided in the late eighties to make his future in England and play for the country of his adoption. He was, at that point, having a trial with Warwickshire, and Edgbaston was to become his long-term home within English cricket. In his early twenties Donald was already destined to become one of the game's great fast bowlers. He was a shy, retiring young man from Bloemfontein in the heart of the Orange Free State, the headquarters of Afrikanerdom. He spoke English with difficulty and was out of his depths in England except with a cricket ball in his hand. Andy Lloyd, who was captain of Warwickshire at the time, well remembers facing the young South African in the indoor school at Edgbaston before the start of the 1987 season:

> When he came in for a loosener it made me blink a little . . . left handers play and miss a lot outside the off stump, but now it was not the usual free-wristed dabble that brought on the error, it was through my being more than a little late on the delivery. Fifteen minutes later I was concentrating as I had never done before indoors, body preservation being top of the priority list. My present chairman of cricket, mentor and critic, Dennis Amiss, followed me into the same net. When we compared notes afterwards it wasn't long before Dennis was recommending to team manager, the former England fast bowler, David Brown, that we should register this young fellow. 'Brownie' didn't need any

nudging, having seen all the ingredients of what makes a quality fast bowler – and Allan Donald became a Warwickshire player.

Of course, once apartheid had been dismantled, South Africa were readmitted to Test cricket and, at the age of twenty-five, Donald could not wait to get started. He had longed to play for South Africa, but was aware that if the country was not allowed back by the ICC it might never happen. He freely admits that England might have been a backdoor way into Test cricket for him. 'It was in the back of my mind, but Ali Bacher told me that I shouldn't be so silly and that South Africa would soon be reinstated. He was right, as he so often is. He is a very proper person and keeps his word.' This story also shows what a decent man Donald is himself.

Allan Donald had been blessed with all the attributes a truly great fast bowler needs. He was strong, supremely fast and naturally athletic with an underlying suppleness. He was genuinely fast and was blessed with remarkable stamina as well as an ability to move the ball in the air. He also had that other essential requirement for a successful fast bowler, an inbuilt hatred for the man with the bat at the other end. He was forced to spend three years in the South African Defence Force, which were not the most enjoyable of his life. Nonetheless, it was a pretty tough and demanding experience that effectively tuned his body for the hard work that was to come later. The powers-that-were in South African cricket knew all about Donald and he will have been one of the first names the selectors will have written down when they embarked upon their first overseas adventure after being readmitted to the ICC. They travelled to India in 1991 for some one-day internationals. The first was played in Calcutta and cricket has never known a more symbolic moment than when South Africa walked out at Eden Gardens for the first match. Some may have been nervous but Donald was not one of them and he took 5/29, even though South Africa did not go on to win.

His innate modesty is one of the things that marked Donald out from other fast bowlers. He was never a prima donna and the only place Donald ever threw his weight around was out in the middle in the presence of the opposing batsmen. Back in the dressing room or, indeed, outside it, he may have had his own thoughts, but he was never more than one of the team. However, he was always in the batsman's face out on the field when the adrenalin was running, as Michael Atherton would surely confirm after his experiences in Johannesburg in 1995/96 and at Trent Bridge in 1998. Donald sums up his approach simply enough: 'I try to be as any human being should be, there's no reason why I should be any different from anyone else. I've been like that since I was a child. It's good to be the way you really are, and people respect you for that, and of course it's good for public relations.' Donald has left Test cricket with a tally of 330 Test wickets taken in only seventy-two Test matches with a strike rate of 47.02, which has been bettered only by Waqar Younis and Malcolm Marshall of those who have taken over 300 Test wickets. Considering that his Test career did not begin until 1991/92 when South Africa played a one-off Test match in the West Indies – another massive sign of the changing times – that represents a handsome enough return and one with which Donald himself is content:

> I suppose it would have been nice to get 400 Test wickets but, when I think that I only started playing Test cricket at the age of twenty-five, I am very happy with what I have achieved. I am very settled in my own mind that I have reached the right decision [to retire from Test cricket]. The last person I consulted before making my decision was Hansie Cronje and he felt that I had done the right thing.

Perhaps Cronje should have told Donald that the time had come to pack it in altogether.

Donald was the most electrifying fast bowler I have ever seen and in my book I shall put him narrowly ahead of Dennis Lillee and Jeff Thomson, who terrified the life out of Australia's opponents for a time in the mid-seventies. Donald added to what was already a fearsome sight by anointing his lips, nose and cheek bones with white sun cream, which gave him the hair-raising aspect of a cross between a circus clown and a fully paid-up ghost. He is slim and on the tall side with rather gaunt aquiline features and a face that, out in the middle at any rate, was not easily given to smiling. If Long John Silver had been confronted by a glaring Donald after being given the benefit of the doubt that he may not have deserved, I can almost hear him exclaiming, 'Shiver my timbers!'

What made Allan Donald the most dangerous fast bowler South Africa have ever had, and one of the greatest of all time, was his outstanding control as well as his many variations. This gave him more attacking options than any of his rivals. While some fast bowlers have relied on their pace to give them extra bounce and some have the knack of swinging the ball and others rely on movement off the pitch, Donald was able to do everything and anything. This was, of course, the product of unremitting hard work, both in the nets where he perfected his skills, and in the gymnasium where he acquired an astonishing level of fitness that never left him throughout his career. The key person in the development and fulfilment of Donald as a fast bowler was Bob Woolmer, who was to become South Africa's coach. Donald first came across Woolmer when he went to Warwickshire where the former Kent and England batsman was to become the county coach. It was Woolmer's know-how that enabled Donald to bring together and make the best of a rare natural ability. He turned Donald into the most intelligent and shrewdest fast bowler of his time, and one of the quickest as well. No batsman could ever have enjoyed facing Donald, although some were able to disguise their apprehension better than others.

Donald's variations were legendary. Woolmer was, of course, lucky to have such wonderful raw material to work with. One of his main achievements was to teach Donald to bowl the slower ball that stood him in such good stead, particularly later on in his

274

career. Then there were the other variations of pace and the angle of attack as he skilfully used the width of the bowling crease. He had to learn to control both the movement he found in the air and off the seam. On occasions, he would use the bouncer sparingly with devastating effect and, at other times, when he was caught up in the emotion of the moment, as he was when bowling at Michael Atherton at Trent Bridge in 1998, they poured forth thick and fast and that unplayable one was never far away. All this was combined with a formidable natural athleticism; the rhythm he brought to his bowling was a by-product of this athleticism. Donald never simply turned his arm over. He was always involved in a plan of campaign to bring about the downfall of whomever he was bowling at. Of all the fast bowlers in the last two or three decades, perhaps only the West Indian, Andy Roberts, had the same ability to work out and exploit a batsman. There was never an ounce of spare flesh on Donald's body and it was this that was one of the main reasons why he was able to keep going for so long. It was Woolmer who enabled him to harness all these attributes and also to put his mind to the job of working out how best to use them. Even so, it was sad that no one in South African cricket, for Woolmer had long since left the South African dressing room, had the courage to put their hand on Donald's shoulder before he attempted to do it once again in the 2002/03 World Cup in South Africa, and say, 'No. The time has come.' Try as he did off his short run, he found himself suffering the most dreadful indignities, which a bowler of his pedigree should have been spared. It was an embarrassment to everyone, but to no one more than Donald.

Probably the greatest spell Donald ever bowled in his life was at Sydney in 1997/98 when he pitted his wits and his strength against the Waugh twins. For sustained pace, hostility and variation, it was an even more stirring performance than that clash with Atherton at Trent Bridge. That day, Donald silenced a huge crowd at the SCG, which is not something that many visiting fast bowlers have been able to do. This famous spell dignified the first occasion that floodlights were used because of poor light in a Test match in Australia. He had no doubt that Sachin Tendulkar was the best batsman he ever bowled against. The ball that gave him more pleasure than any other was the one with which he moved sharply off the seam to bowl Tendulkar at Kingsmead in Durban in 1996. 'It was one of the best balls I have ever sent down. I will still remember that fondly when I am sixty or seventy years old.' Another wicket that gave him great pleasure was Allan Border's in the extraordinary Test match at Sydney in 1994. Needing only 117 for victory, Australia were bowled out for 111. Fanie de Villiers was his partner then and although it was he who won the main accolades taking 10 wickets in the match and bowling throughout the final morning, Donald probably took the 2 most important wickets when he got rid of Allan Border, third ball, and Mark Waugh soon afterwards. His dismissal of Border was an object lesson when it comes to plotting a batsman's downfall. Kepler Wessels, the South African captain, had told his team before the start that morning that Australia sometimes got into a mess chasing small targets in the fourth innings. He was sure that the key to it lay in the quick dismissal of Allan Border. He told Donald to bowl two balls that moved away from the left-hander and then to bring the third back into him. Donald carried out his instructions to perfection. Border did not play a stroke at any of the three. When Donald had bowled the third, he could not see the stumps because Border was in the way. He heard a noise and instinctively appealed for lbw. He was horrified when the umpire did not respond, but then, as Border moved, he saw that there was no need for the stumps had been hit.

No cricket devotee in England will ever forget those few overs that Donald bowled to Atherton at Trent Bridge in 1998. The fate of a Test match and a series hung on them after England had been left to score 247 in a day and a half to win the match and draw level in the series. The drama of the moment was captured perfectly by Atherton himself in his recently published autobiography *Opening*

Up. He has written two paragraphs with such an immediacy that it is almost as if you yourself are playing the one defining ball that made this passage of play as brilliant as it was. The stark reality of the moment and the devastating hostility of Donald himself are brilliantly captured as well as Atherton's thought processes. It will come to serve as a lasting testament to both these two admirable performers. (The italics are Atherton's.)

[After one ball of Donald's second over of a new spell] Umpire Dunne indicates that Donald is going to come round the wicket – a sign that he is fully loose and ready to step up a gear. *Open up my stance – I don't want a blind spot from around the wicket; careful of the change of angle, the ball going across, rather than into, my stumps; try and leave everything outside of my eyeline and make him bowl at me, and then pick him off through the legside.* He bowls one short and at me, hip height, and I turn it round the corner and get up the other end. *That's good – remember Boycott's advice to rotate the strike against fast bowlers ('the best way to play fast bowling is from t'other end, lad'). He's right – let Nasser take the heat for a while. The trouble is, in Shaun Pollock, they've got a fast bowler at the other end too.*

The barrage begins in Donald's next over. It's short and at me, from around the wicket, and I'm in a tangle and can't get out of the way. Instinctively I try to protect myself with my bat and the ball cannons into my right hand and balloons up to Mark Boucher behind the stumps. Huge appeal – I stand my ground and Donald runs past me, right arm raised aloft in triumph. I dare not look up, but when I do umpire Dunne remains unmoved – *surely he's going to raise his finger any second now.* But he remains unmoved, as do I. I can't believe my good fortune. Donald can't believe his misfortune and he stands in the middle of the pitch glowering at me, and screaming, 'You fucking cheat!' *Don't take a backward step here – body language is important. Keep staring at him – he's got to turn away first.* The moment passes although there's plenty of abuse flying from behind the stumps. *Stay calm now; got to stay composed; there will be plenty of short stuff coming and plenty of abuse too. Don't react. Stay in your own bubble. That's why they call it Test cricket.*

Atherton hung on until the end when England had won by 6 wickets and he was 98 not out. After the match, Atherton visited the South African dressing room. Donald somewhat reluctantly had a glass of beer with him and it was then that Atherton showed the mischievous streak of tungsten that ran through him. 'What would you have done?' he asked, knowing all too well that Donald would have stood his ground if it meant South Africa winning. 'Later, he asked me for that particular glove and I readily gave it to him, my autograph neatly covering the offending red mark.'

This seems a very contemporary story, but I wonder if it was ever much different, especially when fast bowlers had their dander up – except, of course, that the prying eye of television was not there to bring it all into our houses in close-up. One thing is for certain which is that Allan Donald was one of the best of all time and no fast bowler has brought spectators to a more charged state of anticipation. It was just a pity that he was allowed to attempt one World Cup too many, but only the most churlish would let that distort the picture.

MUTTIAH MURALITHARAN

THERE will never be universal agreement as to whether Muttiah Muralitharan is a bowling genius, a witch doctor or, like W.S. Gilbert's John Wellington Wells, 'A weaver of magic and spells'. Down-to-earth Australians, who distrust the occult and are even more uncertain about sorcerers, to say nothing of their apprentices, are pretty certain there is skulduggery afoot when Muralitharan comes on to bowl. He has been called twice for throwing by Australian umpires, Darrell Hair and Roy Emerson, and the *éminence grise* of the profession in Australia, Lou Rowan, who threw his hat in the ring with Ray Illingworth at Sydney in 1971/72, is convinced of an illegal kink in Murali's arm. They think his action looks as wrong as wrong can be and want nothing to do with all the talk about a deformity of the right arm, which Murali is unable to straighten. Nor are they impressed by spin bowling's first-ever double-jointed wrist, which, used with thought and skill as it is, can, in their view, get up to all sorts of naughtiness. It is not made any easier by that mischievous grin that Murali wears with an increasing 'I told you so' sort of confidence. Lancashire's David Lloyd, when he was England's coach in 1998, also found the mysteries of the Orient as manifested by Murali in that famous one-off Test match at The Oval that Sri Lanka won by 10 wickets, altogether too perplexing for his comfort. A trifle unwisely, he effectively labelled the off spinner a thrower in the middle of the match. The truth is that Murali is not a bowler who personifies meat and two veg. He serves up a dish that is altogether too hot and incomprehensible for many Western tastes.

Three years ago, I sat up long into the early hours one night in a houseboat on the Murray River. The boat belonged to the former Australian wicket keeper Barry Jarman, then a match referee. One of the other intrepid sailors was John Reid, who captained New Zealand for many years and was also a referee of the no-nonsense variety. The topic was Murali and our host had armed himself with a number of videos of the Sri Lankan spinner in action. Barry was convinced that Murali threw and, like Margaret Thatcher, he was not for turning, while John, who has a pretty strong-minded approach to most problems, had to admit before we all became square-eyed to the point of extinction that he saw nothing that convinced him that this was so. We looked and looked and looked. The bent right arm was there, the double-jointed wrist was among those present, as well as an action that could not fail to have a curious look about it with those two factors alone in the mix. It was impossible to say whether or not his elbow straightened at or just before the point of delivery. By the end of the evening even Barry, although he did not change his mind, was accepting that John had a point of view. A bowler must not be kicked out of the game on a hunch that something is not quite right. The wrongdoing must be established beyond reasonable doubt and not simply on a vague notion of percentages. I do not think Murali throws and I am convinced, beyond any shadow of doubt, that he is one of the greatest attractions that contemporary cricket has to offer. Is there any better way of spending a summer's day than to be sitting in a deck chair with a punnet of strawberries, a glass or two of hock and a pair of field glasses watching Murali wheel away for over after over?

Murali's range of tricks is phenomenal. He can turn his off break the best part of a yard and that on its own can be disconcerting. That rubbery flexible wrist then allows him to bowl a leg break that he appears to be able to make lift or skid through at will. Then there is the one that he cuts away from the right-hander. Goodness knows where he gets them all from. His doubters will say from a straightened arm, but try throwing a leg break. Then, like the alto-gether more Anglo-Saxon Shane Warne, he has that extraordinary control, which allows him to remain on top of the batsman unless he is prepared to take enormous risks. And all the time that inscrutable smile. Murali is the only Tamil in the Sri Lankan side, an accident of birth that fusses neither him nor his colleagues. His father is a confectioner in Kandy, which sounds more tautological than it is. Murali is a freak in that he has taken full advantage of his unique physical attributes to take an art form that was dying as an offensive weapon to new levels. He has brought a variety to his art that no other off spinner, even Saqlain Mushtaq, has been able to do.

The Western mind has never been good at assimilating Eastern magic. Because they don't understand it with Murali, the tendency is to cry 'foul'. At the turn of the previous century, Ranji's leg glance presented a similar puzzle to English cricketers. Stop eating those strawberries for a moment and concentrate on his action for an over or two and you will find it reasonably smooth. There is no fuel for the chucking lobby here. Not the least fascinating part of his art is watching him develop a plan to trap a new batsman about whom he has thought long and hard. Murali leaves nothing to chance for he is a consummate professional.

He is also a real character who brings passion, unbounding energy and spring-heeled enthusiasm to the game. This vitality embraces smiles and laughter and a sense of fun. He enjoys what he is doing. It is abundantly clear that Murali does not think he is breaking any law and would be horrified if he ever discovered that he was. One of his most important attributes has been his inner strength, which has kept him going in the face of the constant barrage of sniping that has gone on around him. He was lucky that for a long time he was protected by Arjuna Ranatunga who, as Sri Lanka's captain, was never afraid to court controversy and never gave an inch in defending the interests of his country and therefore of his players. When the Australian umpires called Murali for throwing, they had to deal with Ranatunga as well as Murali himself, who is just as single-minded in his pursuit of victory. Murali has coped well enough.

> It didn't affect me much because I thought I was doing a fair thing [he said after being called in Australia]. It was his opinion. It was his decision and I cannot overrule that decision. Sometimes it irritates me but you get harder and harder mentally when you feel that someone is trying to push you out. It has certainly improved me mentally when somebody has tried to push me out because it means that somebody is scared of me. You take it at that point and come harder at him. I have never changed my action from the way I bowled as a small boy.
>
> I am very competitive. I don't like losing. Every time I play I want to give 100 percent and do something special for the team. I am totally focused on what I am doing. I don't even like to give away a single run that is not necessary. At the same time you have to realise that cricket requires you to play a very patient game, particularly when you are a spin bowler. It happens in a match that you can get frustrated and sometimes you end up taking it out on a team-mate. Afterwards, I will say sorry to the guy. It is part of the game. You have a drink together and forget about what happened in the middle.

He is rising towards 400 Test wickets and in time will surely go on to beat Courtney Walsh's record of 519. The moaners will always swear that he throws and will therefore never give him the credit he deserves. Of course, not even Murali can do it every time. When England visited Sri Lanka in 2000/2001, they won the series 2–1 and Murali's 14 wickets cost a fraction over 30 runs each, and this in his own midden. By then, he had played part of a season with Lancashire, and England's batsmen, who had a reputation for being no-hopers against class spin, had had plenty of practice against Murali, Saqlain Mushtaq and Mushtaq Ahmed, all of whom had plied their trade in the County Championship. Familiarity may not have bred contempt, but it certainly led to a much more respectable *modus vivendi* for England's principal batsmen. Two years earlier at The Oval they had been nothing more than innocents abroad when confronted by the wiles of Murali in the solitary Test match Sri Lanka were rather patronisingly granted. This match will remain as Murali's greatest tour de force although Sri Lanka's opening batsman Sanath Jayasuriya, who made 213, did not allow Murali to have it all his own way. This was the match in which Arjuna Ranatunga won the toss and put England in and watched them score 445 on a placid Oval pitch. When questioned afterwards about his decision, Ranatunga said that he wanted his spinner to have a rest between innings. He would not have done if Sri Lanka had batted first and England had followed on. In the entire history of cricket I wonder if a captain has ever given one of his bowlers such an overwhelming vote of confidence. For the record, Murali took 7/155 and 9/65 making 16/220 in all. What more can one add to that?

JONTY RHODES

S INCE their return to the international cricket scene in the early nineties, the reputation of South Africa's cricket has owed as much to Jonty Rhodes as any other individual. He is not especially high in the batting averages and does not figure at all in the bowling. Yet Rhodes' fielding has won him a universal renown that may, rather unfairly, have not come the way even of his fellow countryman, Colin Bland, who was surely *primus inter pares* when it came to the noble art of fielding. In Bland's day the tentacles of television had not stretched so far or so wide and one-day international cricket did not exist. He did not have Rhodes' platform, but against this, he did not have to turn it on with anything like such frequency.

While Bland was measured speed, Rhodes is unpredictable quicksilver. He is worth a long journey to any ground, and six hours or more with the binoculars focused exclusively on Rhodes, the fielder, provides as good a day out as anyone could wish for. His unbridled athleticism is to be marvelled at, his abounding enthusiasm and his huge personal enjoyment of all that he does, is to be treasured. It is as if Rhodes plays all his cricket with a smile on his face. This applies to his batting as well, where he is the cheeky, impertinent chap his fielding suggests he would be. So many of his strokes seem to stick their tongue out at the bowler rather as England's Alan Knott used to do when he was batting. When he came to England in 1998, his Test place was on the line as he had scored only one hundred in thirty Test matches. Now, in the First, at Edgbaston, he went in when South Africa were in a hole at 42/4 and in his new style, which involved driving into the V between mid off and mid on and playing much straighter, he made 95 excellent runs and saved the day for his country. At Lord's a fortnight later, South Africa were 46/4 when he made that lonely journey through the Long Room and out to the middle. Playing superbly after a little early edginess, he made 117 taking South Africa to 283/7 and a winning score. Every stroke seemed jaunty and fun and before long, and to great acclaim, he was plying his wares in the field. Small wonder that most evenings in the car on the way home the talk would be of Rhodes. Nothing communicates itself more quickly to those watching than the evident enjoyment of one of the players; in this instance, the joker in the pack who had been no more than true to himself.

Contemporary cricket has not seen anyone quite like Rhodes and he electrifies crowds wherever he goes after coming into the South African side against India in 1992. He has been in and out of the Test side because until recently he had not scored enough runs to make the number six spot his own, even allowing for the fact that he saves at least as many as 30 in every innings the opposition play. He is, of course, ever present in South Africa's one-day side for in that form of the game, fielding has become arguably the most important of the three main disciplines. He is indispensable. It is all topped off by an inherited and devout belief in Christianity, like several others in the post-apartheid South African side, even if their number did include Hansie Cronje who will no doubt have caused the Almighty to draw in his breath a bit sharpish. Rhodes embraces God with a sense of humour. 'In a team like ours where there is such a variety of denominations . . . we have a bit of fun with it. During the Lord's Test [in 1998] we were getting a bit fretful not having had a wicket for quite a while, and I told Adam Bacher that I would pray for the Lord to show him the right way. Soon after, he left the field with a damaged shoulder, and then wickets started to fall left, right and centre. It gave my God quite an edge at the time.'

The danger with Jonty Rhodes is that one tends to take him for granted. If we can't go and see him in the flesh, he's sure to pop up almost daily on one of the myriad television channels that are ever increasingly within our reach. Another flashing run, another astonishing dive, another marvellous throw and another dry-cleaner's bill – it's all such old hat and a little like watching Fred Astaire dance on a daily basis. In the last few years when South Africa have been touring England, I commentated on two entire overs from Allan Donald with my eyes and mouth only on Rhodes at cover point. There was hardly time to get it all in. He is never still for an instant and if he brings all of us watching to a state of high excitement, one can only wonder at what effect he has on his colleagues.

His first act after the umpire has called over at the other end is to run down to third man to collect Donald's cap and sweater and then to deliver them, at the double, to the umpire who will now preside at the bowler's end. Then he runs off to cover on the other side of the pitch and does a couple of jumps as he turns round to face the pitch. He stands deep, about thirty-five yards from the bat. Then, with another jump and a half hitch of the trousers, he starts running in towards the batsman as Donald gathers pace. When the arm comes over he is about twenty yards from the bat straining at every sinew like an electric bolt that has found itself on its own and doesn't know where to go. If the ball is pushed out on the offside, he is after it with the speed of those boys who lit the street lamps as the gloom of the night descended on Victorian London. If it comes straight to him, he picks it up and whizzes it back to the wicket keeper. If it goes to either side of him, he is off after it like a greyhound that has just spotted a passing electric hare. When Rhodes runs he covers the ground at great speed, although there is something amusingly dishevelled about it all with shirt, trousers and boots flying in all directions as they try to keep pace with him. Then comes the well-judged dive and the hand flicking the ball back just before it crosses the boundary. Then, in a flash, he is on his feet and the ball is thumping back into the keeper's gloves. The batsmen have long since given up the thought of trying to pinch an extra run. When the batsman plays a ball within range of Rhodes he will often say no, even when there is a safe single. This is the value of the man to his side. In the pavilion or wherever he is situated, the third umpire will glare at the replay to see if Rhodes had made contact with the boundary while still touching the ball. He needn't have bothered; Rhodes is too fast for that. Rhodes meantime scampers back to his place in the covers and Donald begins again.

This time the batsman plays no stroke to a ball outside the off stump that smacks into the keeper's gloves. Rhodes continues running in almost until he has reached the stumps. Then he vigorously claps his hands to make sure the keeper throws the ball to him, whereupon he bends over and polishes it vigorously on the stretched trousers covering his behind before running most of the way back to the bowler to make a personal delivery and give a few words of encouragement, which may end with a pat on the bum. Now, he races back to cover and gets there just in time to start all over again. The next ball is cover driven and appears to be going past Rhodes, but in a blur of speed he covers three or four paces to his left before throwing himself at the ball, which somehow his telescopic left arm reaches. Then, lying on the ground and swivelling, he somehow transfers the ball to his right hand and sends a hum-dinging throw into the top of the stumps with the batsman struggling to get back. We are only halfway through the over and almost out of breath with excitement at watching what seems to be one optical illusion after another. This is Rhodes and this why we all come to watch him. It is extremely sad that he has decided to call it a day.

DARREN GOUGH

IF Darren Gough's body could have stood up to the enthusiasm, the punch, the *joie de vivre* and the dramatic physical examination he brought to fast bowling, he might have headed the entertainment board. When he first won an England cap, it was his spirit more than anything that acted as a smokescreen for cold logic. Here, at last, was a fast bowler with the pace and ability, the cheek and the devil-may-care approach that had people rubbing their hands and hoping that another Fred Trueman had galloped on to the stage. For all his zeal, Gough was not a natural fast bowler like Trueman. His run up and action was a thing of arms and legs and dramatic visible effort. On a good day there was a rhythm, but not the kind of intangible purr that was the birthright of Trueman. That was the product of an engine so perfectly tuned and serviced that it kept going long enough for him to become the first bowler ever to take more than 300 Test wickets. Gough's bowling was the product of unremitting hard work while Trueman's was the child of a God-given genius – not that he will have worked any less hard than Gough in developing it to its full. Yet there was something of the same exhilarating combustibility about the two of them. 'It is a tale . . . of sound and fury signifying nothing' as the poet wrote of Lady Macbeth. FST would have congratulated him on his choice of words if his subject had been Gough for he was a hard man to please. After Gough's first Test match, against New Zealand at Old Trafford in 1994, Trueman was purported to have said to Gough, 'Who told you to bowl that rubbish at New Zealand in the second innings?'

'I was trying to blast them out,' was Gough's reply.

'Blast them out, blast them out? Your job is to bowl them out. In future, don't listen to them. I'll tell you what to do.'

Gough commented later, 'It's probably the first time Fred thought he could save my career; unfortunately, it wasn't the last.'

In its splendid Yorkshire cussedness it was a revealing exchange. Yet Gough arrived at a time when England's cricket was badly in need of tangible hope and if too many expectations were piled upon his shoulders, it was only natural, although unfair to Gough.

The young Gough was summed up admirably by David Lloyd, England's emotional and ebullient coach whose heart was never anywhere but on his sleeve. 'The heartbeat of the England team' was how he described him. They needed each other. It will be long debated how good Gough really was and what his eventual place will be in the list of England bowlers who have taken more that 200 Test wickets. In the final analysis, his position has to be compromised by his failure to take four of the first five wickets to fall, the sure hallmark of a fast bowler of class, more often than he did. Against this must be set the uplift and the psychological hold he gave his side when in the first few overs he burst through the defences of an opening batsman. The subsequent histrionics did English supporters good; it also did wonders for the chap bowling at the other end who was made to feel that anything was possible. An early wicket from Gough sent a bolt of electricity through the entire side. There was not an England cricket supporter who did not feel his pulse quicken when Gough marked out his run on the first morning of a Test match with that bouncing certainty that seemed to say to everyone, 'Now, just you watch.' The two batsmen walking out will also have felt their tummy muscles tighten just a fraction. The stage was set and before a ball had been bowled Gough had stolen a small but important advantage for England.

Gough's attitude will have won him friends. In that incredible Test match against the West Indies at Lord's in 2000, Gough went out to join Dominic Cork, his long-time friend, in England's second innings with the score 160/8 with 28 more runs needed for victory. Duncan Fletcher and Nasser Hussain had said a little earlier, 'You can do it.' Gough's thoughts in reply had a comforting, charismatic and compelling ring to them.

> I nodded. I wanted to believe it. Frightening. Yet, believe it or not, I wouldn't have swapped the painful knot in my stomach for anything. There was nowhere else in the world I would rather have been at that precise moment. Situations like that are why I play cricket, international cricket, Test cricket for my country. I was only too well aware of the consequences of failure on this day; another summer of cricketing defeat and shame. Perhaps the last chance of this team staying together, of achieving something, anything.

He and Cork scored those 28 runs with Matthew Hoggard shivering in his pads in the pavilion, and England had won in three days by 2 wickets levelling the series at 1–1. Gough won that one with his bat, but with a cricketer of his spirit and brio, one never quite knew where the next telling contribution was coming from. Gough was always his own man, never slow to perceive an insult or an injustice, or to act upon it. In 1991, 'Fergie' Carrick was Yorkshire's captain and early in the season he asked the twenty-year-old Gough to go up the road to Headingley and do his laundry. The reply was brisk and to the point. 'Bugger off. I may be twelfth man, but I'm not doing your laundry.' On another occasion, when he was twelfth man, Ashley Metcalfe asked him to go and get a bat signed. He received the same no-nonsense reply. Gough himself summed up his attitude to all this sort of stuff succinctly enough. 'I was a young lad who was not going to take any shit. I remember the lads a few years above me . . . thinking I was a cocky little bastard . . . what I will not stand at any price is being bullied.' If spirit alone counted for anything, Gough would always have been near the top of the pile.

Fitness has always been his major problem. He is a man-made and highly physical fast bowler, which has put a considerable unnatural strain on his body. It was part of the boyishness that never left him that he was consistently his own worst enemy when it came to injuries. He was always so impatient to get back into the action that he would try to bowl again often weeks before he was fully fit, and this, of course, set him back still further and was no help either to England or to Gough. His unquenchable spirit was seen in many ways. The Lord's Test against South Africa in 1994 will be longest remembered for the folly of England's captain, Mike Atherton, being caught trying to dry the ball with dirt in his trouser pocket. It is something that has still never been satisfactorily explained. In his autobiography, *Dazzler*, Gough had his say. He called Atherton daft and the authorities, especially the England manager, Ray Illingworth, insensitive. In this match Gough was hit a painful blow on his right forearm by Allan Donald. When he returned to the dressing room at the end of the match after an X-ray had revealed that there was nothing broken, Gough wrote a couple of words on a piece of paper and put it in his cricket bag. Somehow those two words 'Donald Dies' appeared the following Sunday in the *News of the World* – Gough claims not to know how. He explained that it was not meant literally, but was his way of saying that Donald had better watch out. His impulsive nature nearly got him into worse trouble on England's tour to Australia in 1994/95. England played New South Wales in Newcastle and Gough strode out with a board and took on the local surf. It did not bother him that he did not know how to surf. He took a disdainful view of the 'rip', an underwater swirl it can be almost impossible to move out of, and about which he had been warned. He didn't realise he was being sucked further and further out and got into the rip. When a lifeguard came out and asked if he was all right, he said he was fine. It was only when the Tetley's Bitter representative arrived on the scene that he jettisoned the board and was able to swim sideways out of the rip and made it to safety. It doesn't always pay to be headstrong.

There were times when he severely tested the nerve of those

who ran the game. When England went to Zimbabwe in 1996/97 the players were forbidden to take their wives out over Christmas and the New Year. Gough was beside himself with fury and had a lively telephone conversation with Tim Lamb, the chief executive of the English Board.

After Gough's initial outburst, Lamb asked him: 'What would you do if you were in the army?'

'I'm not in the fucking army, Tim. I'm in the England cricket team. I should be allowed to bring my wife out for ten days in the middle of a three and a half month tour. I can't see the problem.'

'Isn't your marriage strong enough for you to go away this winter without your family?' came the reply down the line from Lord's.

This took Gough to the combustible side of incandescence. With his wife standing beside him trying to calm him down, he told Lamb what he thought of him before slamming down the receiver. He certainly stood up for his rights, as he perceived them, just as he bowled – flat out with no holds barred.

But all the time he was fighting a losing battle over those injuries. His periods away from the game grew longer and longer. When he was picked for Australia in 2002/03, an extraordinary decision for he was nowhere near fit at the time of selection, he had not played in a first-class match for more than a year. Before leaving for Australia, he and another selection, Andrew Flintoff, who had not recovered from a hernia operation, had spent some time working on their fitness at Lilleshall, the sports training centre in the Midlands. Flintoff was unable to play a meaningful part in Australia and, like Gough, he was sent back to England well before Christmas. By then, the retiring chairman of the England Cricket Board, Lord MacLaurin, was in Australia. He spoke openly of the lack of single-mindedness in Flintoff's attempts to make himself fit. When Gough, who had returned earlier than Flintoff, saw the comments, he announced thunderously that he was extremely disappointed with his lordship's utterances. It remains to be seen whether he has taken his last Test wicket for England, but even if he manages to come back to full fitness, a remark like this could turn out to be one albatross too far. Darren Gough is quite a character, but it seems, in spite of his miraculous return to English colours in 2003, that his will be a career where we are left pondering on what might have been rather than what was. But it is still great fun while it lasts.

DOMINIC CORK

URING the last decade no English cricketer had it in him to
exert more of a hold over spectators than Dominic Cork. He
has always been well short of top pace, but chock full of energy,
determination and self-belief, which, some days, amalgamated to
give him an electrifying brilliance, and on others produced only
make-believe and bullshit. Happily, in his first series for England,
against the West Indies in 1995, he was more or less permanently
in the former vein. He burst upon the Test scene at Lord's and won
the match for England when he took 7/43 in the second innings
and was constantly at the batsmen's throats. His aggressive attitude irritated the hell out of them; he knew it and loved it. His
homespun batting technique, which has a limited but effective
range of strokes, brought him 30 and 23 important runs. In the
series he finished with 26 wickets, an impressive haul that
included a dramatic hat-trick of lbw decisions in the Fourth Test
at Old Trafford. No human being has ever appealed as Cork did
then. He also made a typically robust and important 56 not out.
Cork, like his great friend Darren Gough, has probably been guilty
all along of taking himself a mite too seriously and if he has a sense
of humour it does not involve laughing at himself – unless things
are going terribly well. He has a temper, too, but even so he has
always had it in him to be Exhibit A as far as value for money is
concerned.

Cork was clearly going to annoy a great many opponents and, at
times, some of his colleagues, but he was made of the stuff that

crowds love. After this first heady series, Cork was determined it was all going to continue.

> I try to keep my feet on the ground and I will keep my feet on the ground. My target for this winter is staying in the Test side. I don't want to be labelled as a one-series wonder. I want to be consistent and in South Africa [1995/96] that will mean keeping on working and keeping on taking wickets . . . So many things went right for me last summer – the debut, making runs and then the hat-trick. I'll never forget them, but I'm daft and I know there will be spells when things don't go so well . . . my life has changed quite a bit since I came into the Test side and did well, but I am getting better at handling the extra pressures that go with it.

If only he had been, for this was a speech that surrendered a hostage or two to fortune, although the South African adventure was another success. Cork took 19 wickets in the series at 25.52 and, with compelling blood, sweat and tears, bowled 84 more overs than any other English bowler. His outswing was usually effective in those days and he found reverse swing easy to come by. The only blemish was his batting for he managed only 69 runs in the series, but the demands on his bowling may have accounted for that. He followed this with 22 wickets in the six Tests in England against India and Pakistan and this gave him 67 wickets in his first sixteen Tests. Cork went into every match certain of his ability to make an impact and gloriously unaware of his limitations. There was no situation that he was not prepared to take on and this is what has made him such an irresistible cricketer to watch. Whenever he picks up a ball or a bat he expects to change the course of the game. When it comes off, he is insatiable; when it does not, he looks at best a chump, at worst an idiot. Not that it seems to worry him, for he tries again in exactly the same way, today, tomorrow, later in this innings and the next, in the following match or next week. He is always the same: arms and legs embroiled with effort, the brisk walk, the exaggerated celebrations when it works, the aggrieved irritation when it does not. Cork is not a man who does things by halves. He chases a ball in the field as though his very life depends upon it, he races in to bowl as if he is engaged in mortal combat, and when he bats, he seems to regard the bowler as a form of personal insult. It is a type of sporting warfare that has an infinite appeal and, of course, he never knowingly shirks any challenge. It is gladiatorial and magnificent. While in many ways he makes the best of the ability he has, in others his arrogant temperament lets him down with a colossal bump.

The only problem, of which Cork must surely be all too obviously unaware, is that the raw materials at his disposal are not heavy duty enough to guarantee other than intermittent success. After his heady start in those first four series, Cork began to try too hard to be himself. He felt it was macho to bowl bouncers, failing to realise that his single biggest asset as a bowler was to produce outswingers. When the ball is bunged in short, it does not have time to swing. When it is bunged in at his pace, the batsmen, especially good hookers, will lick their lips. Still he will strut around the field and give the impression that he is about to cause mayhem, but it is in this situation that he becomes a caricature of himself. He has always relished the big stage and, although he becomes a temperamental question mark when things do not work for him, he has usually managed to pull himself up again.

Problems with his personal life have taken their toll and prevented him from going with England to Zimbabwe in 1996/97. He joined the side for the New Zealand leg of the tour where he batted better than he bowled. A hernia operation caused him to miss the Ashes series in 1997 and he was not picked for the West Indies that winter. He was back in the England side for the successful series in 1998 against South Africa, throwing his weight around in his normal way and taking 18 wickets. The following winter the Australians more than had the measure of him. When it came to Cork's antics on the field, a few well-chosen words by their close fielders soon put him back in his place and it seemed likely that the two Tests he played on that tour would be his last. Yet, when the West Indies were back in England in 2000, Cork forced his way back for the Second Test at Lord's and turned in one of his most inspired performances. He took 4 wickets in the first innings and 3 in the second when the West Indies were bowled out for 54. But his greatest moment came at the very end of a match that was over in three days. England needed 188 to win and were 140/6 when Cork came in. He finished with 33 not out and steered England to victory by 2 wickets at three minutes past seven when he forced Courtney Walsh to the Tavern boundary. Of course, he was at his most charismatic and the crowds adored every moment of him and cheered him until dusk.

Cork was at his abrasive best getting up the noses of the West Indians. His self-belief has never been better vindicated than it was then. He was back at Lord's against Australia a year later, picked on a horses-for-courses hunch by the selectors that did not work. His arm was even lower, his outswinger had disappeared, he pitched the ball too short and even though the bustle and swagger was still there, sadly it was not enough on its own. Some energetic county performances brought him back into the squad on a regular basis in 2002, but, by then, it was a question of that well-known selectorial habit of going backwards instead of forwards. The touch paper may have been lit but when it came to Test cricket, alas, the squib was damp, but what fun it had been while it lasted.

ADAM GILCHRIST

THE Australians could scarcely believe their luck that, after old age had, in 1999, accounted for Ian Healy, their effervescent wicket keeper-batsman, an even more exciting player should have been on hand to take his place. Adam Gilchrist not only had a hard act to follow, but he was also taking over from a player who was enormously popular throughout Australia. His fellow countrymen did not want to see Healy disappear. They made sure that Gilchrist had a hot reception. It probably made it worse that their beloved 'Heals' was now dispensing wisdom from the commentary box. All this animosity only acted as a spur to Gilchrist whose startling performances, especially with the bat, soon had the crowds baying for more. Queenslanders were hoping in 1999/2000 for a farewell performance from Healy against Pakistan in the First Test match at the Gabba in Brisbane. Australian selectors have never been known for their romantic inclinations and the gloves were given to Gilchrist.

However, it is as a batsman that Gilchrist has made his mark on the game. The idea of having a batsman coming in at number seven, who could score runs at such an extraordinary pace and in a novel style, was something completely new. Number sevens had almost invariably been the side's all-rounder who could make useful contributions with both bat and ball without taking either art beyond the known limits. Gilchrist has often said that he does not want to bat any higher than seven. A number six cannot bat in this romantic, swashbuckling manner; he has to bat like a proper batsman. At seven, Gilchrist has the licence to play as he does. If he fails, he will be greeted with a few headshakes and not much else. If it comes off, he transforms a game. He gives his bowlers more time to do their work, he completely demoralises the opposition and he is responsible for the marked increase there has been in the last year or two in the rate at which runs are scored. There may not be many batsmen like Gilchrist, but both Lance Klusener of South Africa and England's Andrew Flintoff, if ever he can fulfil an extraordinary potential, are cast in a similar mould and there will be others. But it was Gilchrist who began it all and turned what is a potentially boring stage of an innings into the most exciting form of theatre.

Shutting his ears to the barracking of the crowd, he pirouetted and flashed his way to 81 in just 88 balls in an exhibition of batting in which his choice of stroke and his timing were as compelling as the spirit of adventure he brought to the crease with him. Gilchrist will take on any situation and that day he made the Queenslanders sit up. His appearance is deceptive. He is open-faced, smiling, slightly built, almost demure and does not look capable of swatting a fly. He is as cheerful as his bat. Healy, on the other hand, had a more rugged look about him that suggested he was always eager to be in the thick of it. As if to prove that his performance at the Gabba had not been something he had specially reserved for Healy's most fervent admirers, Gilchrist turned it on again in the Second Test. Pakistan had left Australia to score 369 to win on the flattest of pitches in Hobart. When Gilchrist joined Justin Langer, Australia were 126/5 and accelerating towards defeat. These two now added 238 with Gilchrist showing the way with a breathtaking display of strokes, and Australia won the match. Gilchrist was 149 not out at the end and he had taken the Pakistan attack apart, playing pure cricket strokes with power and timing and without ever resorting to slogging. After the match, Gilchrist was asked if the Hobart pitch had been the best Test pitch on which he had ever batted. He replied after a bit of thought, 'Well, it's in the top two!' He would be the first to admit that he is not as good a keeper as

Healy, but he is still competent enough and misses very little. He is also able to read Shane Warne, which is a *sine qua non* for present-day Australian wicket keepers. Above all else, and this belies his slightly innocent looks, he is a formidable competitor.

Gilchrist was born in the country in southern New South Wales. His father had played for the state second XI and he has a brother who coaches in a Sydney grade club. Cricket soon became a major focus of attention and he was only ten when his mother gave him his first pair of wicket-keeping gloves as a Christmas present. The first time he used them he broke his nose, but did not regard this as an ill omen. His father taught him how to bat and instilled in him first principles that were always to stand him in good stead. When he took them a stage further, they helped turn him into one of the most exciting batsmen of his generation. The basis of his father's advice was to watch the ball, so that he was able to give himself as much time as possible, and to play naturally. 'I suppose that's the way I have always thought about it. Just try to hit the ball. That's what the game's about,' was his simple, homespun philosophy and, of course, he was blessed with a great natural talent, which enabled him to put it into effect as he does. Anyone who has seen a big innings by Gilchrist will never forget it because he is one of those few batsmen who are able to lift the game to a new and dramatic level.

He was seventeen when he had to make the choice between taking university entrance exams and going on a cricketing scholarship to England. It will not have taken him long to make up his mind and he played a summer's cricket for Richmond in the Middlesex League. He was later a member of the Under-19 Australian side that knocked all opposition from its path in 1991 in England. He first played for New South Wales when he was twenty-one, simply as a batsman. He had thoughts at that time of giving up his wicket keeping, but shrewdly realised that if he did not have a second string to his bow it would put more pressure on his batting. Being a pragmatist, he also realised that he would have to move from New South Wales if he was to realise his ambition of playing for Australia. Phil Emery, a thoroughly reliable keeper, had made the job his at the Sydney Cricket Ground. As a result, he packed his bags and moved across to Western Australia where he soon took the place of Tim Zoehrer, who had kept ten times for his country. Initially, the move was none too popular, but his adventurous batting and his gymnastic wicket keeping meant that the public soon took him to their hearts. He took over the gloves from Healy in Australia's one-day side in 1997/98, by which time he had turned himself into a dashing opening batsman.

His chance came in the five-day game in 1999 when he was twenty-eight years old and he never looked back. There was one slight hiccough in India in 2000/01. After whacking an exhilarating hundred in the First Test, his game, with both the bat and gloves, briefly went to pieces in the last two. Happily for him, there was a reasonable break before the side came to England in 2001 and it was a refreshed Gilchrist who stepped off the aeroplane at Heathrow. What an impact he was to make in that Ashes series! In the First Test at Edgbaston, he strode to the crease when Australia were 336/5, hardly a position of poverty, but not one, in the context of the match, of overwhelming prosperity either. He proceeded to put on 160 in double-quick time with his Western Australian colleague, Damien Martyn. When he was last out, he had hit five sixes and twenty fours in his 152, which came from only 143 balls. Of the 63 he had put on with Glenn McGrath for the last wicket, McGrath's contribution had been a solitary single. In the Second Test at Lord's, he made a rather more fortuitous but nonetheless entertaining 90 in which he was dropped four times. In the Third at Trent Bridge, his 54 out of a total of 190 was crucially important to Australia and before the end of the third day Australia had won by 7 wickets and were 3–0 up in the series. The only blemish on Gilchrist's performances that summer came in the Fourth Test at Leeds when he took over the captaincy from the injured Steve Waugh and was not as incisive as he might have been,

allowing Mark Butcher to take England to victory with a remarkable innings of 173 not out. By the end of the series, English
crowds, resigned to the inevitable, were coming to watch Gilchrist
bat as they might have turned up for a Punch and Judy show. While
Gilchrist is around, Australia will always provide more than usually
worthwhile entertainment.

MICHAEL VAUGHAN

GENERALLY speaking, Yorkshire cricketers have not often been suggested as possible candidates for the role of James Bond. A great many of them would have had a healthy suspicion about 007 in the first place, regarding him as a lounge lizard from south of Watford. Michael Vaughan not only fits the bill, but in 2002 when he made seven Test hundreds, he batted as Bond might have done if Ian Fleming had wished to make a cricketer of him. Diehard Tykes would probably shrug their shoulders and say that that is what happens if you allow chaps who come from the wrong side of the Pennines to wear the White Rose – he was born in Lancashire. Vaughan is the most delightful, charming and relaxed of men and yet, as he has shown in becoming far and away England's best batsman, he has a backbone of steel and a razor-sharp mind, and thinks nothing of repeatedly pulling bowlers of the pace and ferocity of Glenn McGrath and Brett Lee through midwicket.

Like his opening partner, Marcus Trescothick, Vaughan captained the England Under-19 side and was always on a secure path towards the upper reaches of English cricket. He was an upright, elegant strokemaker who sheltered behind a more than adequate defence. He was twenty-five when he first played for England, in Johannesburg in 1999/2000, in what must have been a most unnerving experience. He walked to the wicket for the first time in an England cap with the scoreboard showing 2/4 and Allan Donald breathing fire through both nostrils on a dreadful pitch. These were the sort of odds that 007 faced on a regular basis. Vaughan may not have slayed the dragon on that occasion, but he made a most composed 33 and showed that both technically and mentally he was up for it. He did not go on to establish himself in the side beyond doubt during that series because he was affected by what was to be the first in a string of injuries. His highest score in seven innings in that series was 69.

He was back in the England side for the Second Test against the West Indies, at Lord's in 2000, and played an important part in taking England to an extraordinary victory. He came into the side for Nasser Hussain who had broken yet another bone in his hand and had been badly out of form. After bowling out the West Indies for 54 in their second innings on an increasingly uneven pitch, England needed 188 to win. Vaughan came in third after the experiment of opening with Mark Ramprakash had yet again failed, and Curtly Ambrose and Courtney Walsh were on the rampage. Feeding off Michael Atherton's inspiring example at the other end, Vaughan put his head down and fought. Both bowlers continually beat the outside edge, but the batsmen kept their sense of humour and had a good laugh about it between overs. Atherton reckoned that the 45 runs he made then comprised one of the best and most important innings he played for England. Vaughan's contribution was 41 and, just as it had been in Johannesburg, his composure was most impressive. His dedication to the business of wearing down Ambrose and Walsh was as dedicated and as capable as his illustrious partner's.

It was a fascinating defensive operation that went a long way towards drawing the fangs of these two formidable bowlers. Vaughan, like Atherton, played the ball late with hands that gripped the bat lightly and for over after over he dropped the ball at his feet frustrating the grasping hands of the close fielders. Vaughan made an important contribution that day to England's success that was sealed so dramatically later on by Dominic Cork's flailing bat. The following year, Vaughan made his first Test hundred when he put on 267 for the third wicket with Graham Thorpe against Pakistan at Old Trafford. It was a wonderfully composed and attractive innings by Vaughan, the logical conclusion to the preparations that had been progressing for the last two or three years. Sadly, a knee injury then kept him out of the five-match series against Australia in the second half of the summer. It says a great deal for Vaughan's temperament and humour that, in spite of his knee, that hundred against Pakistan should have been the springboard to his *annus mirabilis* in 2002.

When the England season began in 2002, Vaughan was still seen as a good technician with a sound temperament, even though he was not going on to make the big scores of which he so often suggested he was capable. There was also his injury record. One cannot blame a player for being injured, but it is curious how some players seem to attract more injuries than others. In some instances, this suggests a lack of resolve and too great a willingness to give in when a niggle should appear. It is no good having the best batsman in the country on your side if you can't get him out to the middle. Vaughan will have been aware of this. Clearly, when he embarked upon the season in 2002 he had done a good deal of thinking for he was a much more determined character. One reason was surely that he realised that he was now twenty-seven and it was high time that he made sure of a permanent place in the England side. He had realised that he needed to play his strokes and to show that he could take control of any bowlers in the world. He knew, too, that he had to take the attitude of 007 in to bat with him and to dominate where, hitherto, he had been content to survive.

The effect of this was remarkable. Almost overnight, Vaughan had transformed himself into an attacking batsman who was not afraid to play his considerable repertoire of strokes. He was now batting in a manner that was as pleasing as Sachin Tendulkar's. Sri Lanka and India's bowling was obviously nothing like as demanding as Australia's was going to prove the following winter. But Vaughan's success against the new ball gave him the confidence to think that he could bat the same way against the Australians. He also handled the spin of Anil Kumble and Harbhajan Singh most effectively and this particularly impressed no less a critic than Sunil Gavaskar. Before the end of the summer he had passed 1,000 Test runs within the year and had become the most exciting England batsman since the days of Gooch, Gower and Botham. Not only had he managed to make batting look much easier than he had before, but now he was evidently enjoying it all so much more.

His summer, with three Tests against Sri Lanka and four against India, which brought him four centuries, was the perfect preparation for what lay ahead in Australia. Injury had prevented Vaughan from playing in the series against Australia in England in 2001 and he did not know much about the Australian bowlers. Before he went to Australia, he had faced only one ball from McGrath, when McGrath had played for Worcestershire, and it had been too good for him. Yet it was an Australian who had had a good deal to do with the change that had come over Vaughan.

> Ironically, it's [Darren] Lehmann to whom I'd give part of the credit for the strides I've made of late. At Yorkshire he kept on at me about running hard between the wickets, and that seems to have energised my whole game. That's been coupled with the technical work I've done on my batting with Duncan Fletcher and I'm also a great believer in the old adage that the harder you work, the luckier you get.

In the First Test in Brisbane, which Australia won by a distance, McGrath got rid of Vaughan in both innings. In the second match in Adelaide, he went a long way towards putting that particular record straight when, on the first day, he made 177 before being out in the last over. In the second innings he perished to a wonderful catch on the square-leg boundary by none other than Glenn McGrath. At the time, Vaughan reckoned his 177 was the best innings he had ever played.

> That innings will bolster me for the rest of my career, because I will always be able to say I got 177 against the Australians when they were

at their peak. But, boy, did it get under their skin! After Brisbane, which was pretty quiet out in the middle, I think they had reassessed their approach to me and I was getting plenty of stick from the start. Following the well-documented incident with the appeal for a catch when I had scored 19, the volume only increased, particularly from the direction of Justin Langer. It is fair to say we had some frank exchanges that went on through the day. I believe that, even if you are relatively mild-mannered like I am, it is important to give some back and not let these Australians intimidate you. In fact, I take it as a compliment that I was frustrating them so much that they felt it necessary to sledge me.

There is a much tougher and more relaxed and entertaining Michael Vaughan in those words. There is, too, something distinctly Australian about it. This innings gave him the confidence to go and score two more centuries in the series, 145 at Melbourne and 185 in the final Test at the Sydney Cricket Ground. Three big hundreds in a series that was lost by 4–1 speaks for itself, as does the fact that it was Vaughan who was given the Man of the Series award, something the Australians like to preserve for one of their own in a series in Australia. When Vaughan left Australia it was with the reputation of being one of the few batsmen in the history of the game to have played the pull so magnificently. The manner in which he despatched the Australian quick bowlers through midwicket whenever they pitched anything at all short was miraculous. His reactions were like lightning and his footwork was remarkable. Vaughan is, too, the nicest and most modest of men and it did not require a massive amount of crystal-ball gazing to divine that before long he would become captain of England in Test as well as one-day cricket. He has a mind that is as nimble as his footwork and, who knows, if given the chance would surely be as quick on the draw as 007.

PART SIX

A Watching Brief

O UR enjoyment of all these cricketing entertainers comes to us either in the columns of our daily newspapers, which try their best to make breakfast a more agreeable feast, or over the air waves. I, like everyone else, have my favourite writers and commentators and this book would not be complete if I did not include at least a couple of each. The inimitable Hampshire burr of John Arlott still rings in one's ears almost on a daily basis. The humorous and eternally cheerful voice of Brian Johnston does much the same. I have also written briefly about Alan Gibson who had a foot in both camps and became a good friend when he wrote those unforgettable essays in *The Times* about his day at the cricket and his means of getting there. Personally, it has been the greatest piece of luck in the world to be a member of such a wonderful institution as *Test Match Special*. One hopes the fun we have in bringing the cricket into houses, offices, cars and anywhere else communicates itself to listeners.

Sydneysiders had the luck to be the first to listen to a chat on the wireless about a day's cricket. The Australian Broadcasting Commission sent one Lionel Watt to the Sydney Cricket Ground in 1921 to tell listeners what had happened during the day's play. Out of small beginnings . . . The Bodyline tour in 1932/33 was broadcast to England from a studio on the first floor of the Eiffel Tower. It was not that the French had more powerful binoculars than the English, but that a French station spotted the chance of fascinating the English and arranging not only for an Australian summariser, Alan Fairfax, but also for cables to be sent from Australia after every single ball. The commentary captured the imagination in England. There were then the synthetic commentaries by the Australians during their tour of England in 1938 when cables flowed on the same ball-by-ball basis into a studio in Sydney. They were received and put out over the air by Alan McGilvray and company. A wooden pencil was tapped on the table to give the impression of the bat hitting the ball and canned applause was used. The BBC then broadcast England's series in South Africa in 1938/39, but cricket commentary did not really settle down until after the war with the arrival of the assistant poetry producer from the Eastern Service of the BBC.

The written word has always been a source of fascination for cricket lovers. The game has produced more literary offerings than any other. John Woodcock, who was the Cricket Correspondent of *The Times* from 1953 until 1986, has always been my own *primus inter pares* (*pace* Neville Cardus and a host of others) and the writer who gave me more pleasure in book form than any other was Raymond 'Crusoe' Robertson-Glasgow. As a medium fast inswinger, he had bowled for Oxford and for Somerset. After one unsuccessful morning at The Oval bowling at Jack Hobbs and Andy Sandham, he said that it had been 'like bowling to God on concrete'. I rest my case.

'CRUSOE' ROBERTSON-GLASGOW

O NLY cricket could throw up a name like 'Crusoe' Robertson-Glasgow, and then produce a character to live up to it. Raymond Charles Robertson-Glasgow was born in Aberdeenshire in 1901 and was Scottish to the bottom of his boots. He was then translated, by way of Charterhouse and Corpus Christi, where he picked up four cricket Blues between 1920 and 1923, to Somerset and became as redolent of cider as he had once looked like being of Scotch whisky. There is an innate humour about cricket in Somerset and no other county would have suited Crusoe half as well. Amid solid endeavour and much eccentricity he plied his wares with 'a high, rollicking action' at a brisk pace, which was well short of truly fast. He took enough wickets with his inswing to look nervously more than once at the morning papers to see if he had caught the selectors' eyes. Alas, it was never to happen, but worse bowlers than Crusoe have been selected to play for England. Maybe, even in those days, Somerset was too unfashionable a county. While Crusoe strove manfully on their behalf, they never finished top of anything – they had to wait for Ian Botham and the others for that – but they were always a sharp thorn, which, if pointed in the right direction, was likely to prick the ego of any aspiring county.

Crusoe was a jolly cricketer who always did his utmost and enjoyed every moment of it; he loved to laugh and had a loud, raucous and unforgettable laugh to match. He might have got into these pages as a player and he has got into them as a writer instead.

He wrote as he played: with an unsinkable gusto, a huge sense of fun, the shrewdest knowledge of the game and a tongue that was always in and out of his cheek. Before the war, he wrote for the *Morning Post*, which was then absorbed by the *Daily Telegraph*. At the end of the hostilities he found his home at the *Observer* and they also served each other well. His short idiosyncratic weekly essays on any sporting idea that caught his imagination were required reading.

There were many rich characters in the Somerset side with him and Crusoe adored them all. David Foot beautifully summed up his feelings: 'He liked the pastoral calm of Somerset, he liked, almost without exception, the players. He marvelled at the stroke-play of Jack MacBryan, Dar Lyon – brother Bev was in the same Oxford side as Crusoe – and Randall Johnson. He put the taciturn Jack White ahead of everyone as a left-arm exponent of flight. He chuckled that slogger Guy Earle didn't even know the way to play back. He chatted too much with Len Braund in the slips and saw that wonderful catcher put one down. "It's a bit like fishing, Raymond. I can afford to let the little ones go."'

He also enjoyed the ageing and rather less mobile C.C.C. ('Box') Case who had once been felled by a bouncer from Voce. When he at last rose unsteadily to his feet he staggered off carrying a stump rather than a bat. It was the sort of impromptu farce that Crusoe loved and that reminded him of his beloved Crazy Gang at the Victoria Palace. Nervo and Knox, to say nothing of Naughton and Gold, would have made a good opening pair for Somerset.

Crusoe, playing for the university, was among the wickets one day when Somerset were playing Oxford in the Parks, and John Daniell, at different times captain, secretary and president of the county, said to him, 'Why don't you join us – we could do with another bowler?'

'But I'm Scottish, no links at all with the West Country,' Crusoe replied.

Daniell was ready for him. 'That's where you are wrong. Been

312

looking into your background. Aren't you a cousin of this Foxcroft chappie, the MP for Bath? Family seat at Hinton Charterhouse? Can't get more Somerset than that, you know.'

He could not have been better suited, either, by his nickname of 'Crusoe', which he acquired when Oxford played and beat Essex in 1920. As he tells it, 'I acquired a nickname which has stuck ever since. Charlie McGahey and A.C. Russell had put on some 60 runs at the start of their second innings when I bowled McGahey with a full pitcher, which he later referred to as a yorker. In the bowels of the pavilion, Johnny Douglas, the Essex captain, asked him how he was out, and McGahey answered: "I was bowled by an old —— I thought was dead two thousand years ago, called Robinson Crusoe."'

Crusoe moved seamlessly from the end of his run to the press box at the start of the thirties. He worked at first for the soon-to-be-extinct *Morning Post* where he found that he was sent on a number of rather disparate journalistic treasure hunts. It was in April 1933 that the editor summoned him and asked him if he would rather report golf or cricket. Mercifully, and one would think without hesitation, Crusoe plumped for cricket. He took over the job of Cricket Correspondent from Plum Warner and was now to entertain his readers with an admirable conciseness that Cardus on the *Manchester Guardian* would have found both heretical and distasteful. His cricket reports were a joy, but so too were his observations on peripheral matters, not least those in and around him in the press box. His description of Old Trafford and its press box should live for ever.

> The turf at Manchester's Old Trafford, unlike the neighbourhood, is a thing of beauty, and has broken the hearts and loosened the tongues of many bowlers. The present groundsman, however, promised and, to some degree, performed a reformation. But the Press Box was surely designed by Einstein, after a Reunion Banquet of Mathematicians. From its rear-most seats on the right, only a castrated version of the match is visible. One umpire, one batsman, three or four fielders,

according to the length and flexibility of the critic's neck. Hardly a quorum. The front row gives a more total view. Here sat Neville Cardus of the *Manchester Guardian*, slim, grey, contained, master of the rhapsodical style, cutting his sharp epigrams from the most amorphous material.

Crusoe was also wonderfully observant when it came to his fellow scribes. After Frank Woolley's sadly unsuccessful recall to the colours for The Oval Test match against Australia in 1934, he wrote of the great Charles Fry:

> Among those who conveyed information on this melancholy match to the enduring public was Commander C.B. Fry R.N.R. In cricket, triumph and disaster will come again; but, in this world, Charles Fry will not. The ingredients for such a dish are lost. I never heard that C.B.F. was much of a golfer, and I believe him to be an uncertain mathematician; but he has fewer things that he cannot do than any other man I know, and even when he cannot do them, he can talk about them with a fluency which descends, clear and free, from the wits and philosophers of ancient Athens.

Here he is looking at the respective merits of Bradman and Ponsford who in 1934 made England's cricket pitches their own personal playground:

> It is the joy of the critics when appraising a great player, to say why he is not quite to be compared with this or that hero of the past. When all else fails, they bring up the question of style. 'Wonderful,' they cry, 'yes, very wonderful, but not so *beautiful* as so-and-so.' So-and-so, in his day, of course, had the same thing said about him. Thus, elusive perfection is chased ever back. Maybe Adam had an off-drive that made the Serpent weep for very delight . . . Bradman's pads and gloves seemed incidental, just a concession to custom; but Ponsford always suggested the old advertisement for Michelin tyres. His pads would have made a summer cottage for little Willie Quaife.

These are just random examples of Crusoe's genius with the pen. The cricket infection was quick to embrace Crusoe. As a small boy, he was a passionate player of what we would probably call dot cricket. By his own admission, he played it in such a way that his favoured team always won. One scorecard from those memorable contests remains in tact. It says simply:

J.B. Hobbs, bowled Me 0

ME, not out (at the end of Latin) 381

JOHN ARLOTT

No name has ever been more synonymous with the game of cricket than John Arlott's. The Hampshire burr grew more resonant, instantly recognisable and fruity as the years went by. Often it sounded gruff and yet it was largely benevolent. By the end, it had reached a point where it had turned into a cross between Ralph Richardson on one of his more rustic days and a large glass of vintage port of an exceptional year. Once picked up, it was hard to put down. The English that flowed out over the airwaves was impeccable; the adjective seemed to appear as if by the command of a conjuror. There was never an unkind remark unless the game's establishment got in the way, and always a lovely after-taste of humour and occasionally an irresistible chuckle. When Arlott settled in behind the microphone, listeners knew something was going to happen, if not out on the field, then out of the wireless set as those compelling tones painted pictures in a way that led your imagination down byways and footpaths that were as glorious as they were unpredictable. But however unpredictable they were, he steered you through them with the safest of hands. You always felt secure listening to commentary by Arlott. You knew you were in the presence of a master and you also knew that he was not going to take advantage of you. It was the perfect partnership.

Arlott had been born in Basingstoke within earshot of that lovely ground so romantically named May's Bounty. Cricket soon became a passion and never went away. His original entry into the commentary box was romantic, too. In 1945 he left the Hampshire police as

a Detective Sergeant and became the poetry producer in the
Eastern Service of the BBC where he succeeded no lesser a person
than George Orwell. In 1946 the Indians toured England and
reports and spells of commentary were required for listeners in
India, in both English and Hindi. The Head of the Service, Donald
Stevenson, asked Arlott to confirm that the Indians were coming to
England to play cricket. Then he remembered from Arlott's interview for his present post that he loved cricket. On the proviso that
he was still able to make his own programmes, he was given the task
of following the Indian cricketers, and he did a good job.

'For me, it was a sort of seventh heaven to be watching cricket
and talking about it and being paid for it,' was how he put it.
Wisely, he did not attempt the Hindi commentary, which was left
to the better-qualified Abdul Hamid Sheikh. The Head of Outside
Broadcasts at once recognised Arlott's talent as an ad-lib broadcaster and the following year, 1947, when South Africa were the
visitors, allowed him to join forces with Rex Alston and Jim
Swanton for the Old Trafford Test match. In those early days his
voice already had a distinctive enough sound. His friend Dylan
Thomas wrote to a friend of his that year: 'I hear John Arlott's voice
every weekend, describing cricket matches. He sounds like Uncle
Tom Cobleigh reading Neville Cardus to the Indians.' Then, in
1948, Arlott became a permanent member of the team for the
series against Australia. After that, he never missed a Test match
until he retired after the Centenary Test match against Australia in
1980, although for five matches, in 1966 and 1967, he was sec-
onded to the television commentary box, which was never his
natural home.

What made Arlott such an interesting man was that cricket, to
him, was only one, and a fairly minor one at that, of an enormous
range of human activities. It was never a matter of life and death
and this enabled him to keep it in a realistic perspective. He loved
the actors on this particular stage. He tried to understand their
problems and always spoke of them as human beings and never as

automatons. He was good at noticing and conveying any special characteristics and it was in this way he was able to bring the players to life. When, at the end of an expensive over, a bowler trudged disconsolately down to third man, Arlott would wonder aloud what was going on in the wretched man's mind. Listening at home, one could sense the feeling of near-despair and hopelessness as he went to his place, wondering if he would ever be allowed another over, let alone be asked to play again. The departing batsman was treated the same way as the nought went up against the Last Player's name on the scoreboard. Arlott did not follow him off the field with criticism and insults, but with sympathy and understanding. A fielder who dropped a catch was never turned into an object of ridicule.

He respected cricketers and, like a good umpire, he always liked to give the players the benefit of the doubt. If he could avoid pointing the finger of blame, he would. If he had a fault, it was perhaps that at times he tended to hero-worship them. His attitude to the game and its participants is beautifully summed up in some of the lovely sketches he wrote of cricketers of his time, and especially those who played for his beloved Hampshire, although Arlott was a better commentator than he was a writer. He had not played the game to any great extent and to see him climbing the steps to the commentary box did not make one immediately think that one was in the presence of a great athlete. There were those who were only too ready to make much of his limitations as a player and accuse him of knowing all too little about the game. But Arlott was an assiduous man who did not leave much to chance. He may not have had a great deal of practical first-hand knowledge of the game, but he loved nothing more than good conversation with cricketers. It was in this way that he picked up a wide knowledge and understanding of the game.

His choice of adjectives was supreme. 'The big, burly Bedser striding in from the pavilion end' conjured up the perfect picture of a genial tidal wave, just as 'the balcony on the first floor of the pavilion with the portly iron railing' left one in no doubt as to the shape of this particular balcony at Old Trafford. 'Portly' was a brilliant choice of adjective and it perfectly described a railing that bulges towards the base and looks like every elderly tummy one has ever seen. If any of the rest of us had thought of it, it would have been in the middle of the following night when the audience would necessarily have been small. It was at the Lord's Test match in 1975 that England's first streaker appeared, a merchant seaman from Marylebone who was enjoying his shore leave more than he should have done. Happily, Arlott was on the air most memorably to immortalise the moment.

> We've got a freaker. Not very shapely – and it's masculine. And I would think it's seen the last of its cricket for the day. The police are mustering; so are the cameramen and Greg Chappell. He's being embraced by a blond policeman and this may be his last public appearance, but what a splendid out. He's now being marched down in the final exhibition past at least eight thousand people in the Mount Stand, some of whom, perhaps, have never seen anything quite like this before.

When England were in South Africa in 1948/49, 'Tufty' Mann, the South African slow left-hander, clean bowled George Mann, the England captain. 'Another example of Mann's inhumanity to Mann,' was Arlott's instant rejoinder over the airwaves. Then there was Asif Mahsood, the Pakistan fast bowler who had a most comical way of pawing at the ground with his feet as he began his run up. He then approached the crease with his knees bent. Arlott described him unforgettably when he said, 'He reminds me of Groucho Marx chasing a pretty waitress.'

Arlott did an enormous amount for the popularity of the game, and probably there will never be another voice so redolent of cricket. It was a mark of the man that he was so respected by those whom he commentated about that he was elected President of the Professional Cricketers' Association. It was an honour of which he was extremely proud. It is a reflection of Arlott's reputation that his voice is imitated as much today as it was when he retired in 1980. He was a great companion and storyteller, a tremendous *bon viveur*, an obsessive lover of good wine and food, he had formidable collections of aquatints, glass and first editions of books and he was a hymn writer. He wrote six hymns in all and one of them is in *Hymns Ancient and Modern* in the upper four hundreds, somewhere between Bradman's 452 not out and Lara's 501. What is more, he wrote all six hymns on the same evening, but history does not relate the name or the year of claret that produced these heavenly outpourings. There was, too, a mischievous incorrigibility about the man and none of those who were lucky enough to work with him will ever forget him or, for that matter, stop trying to imitate him.

He was determined not to stay on too long, but to go when he was at his best. If he had been born twenty years later, he might have lasted longer. As the main grounds have been modernised, lifts have been installed and although most of them, for some strange reason, are the slowest lifts in the realm, they get there in the end. Towards the end of his commentating days, the walk up the interminable flights of stairs to the commentary boxes took its toll of the great man who arrived at the top puffing like an out-of-condition steam train. His final departure was unbelievably low key, but exactly as he wanted it. At the end of his last scheduled twenty-minute spell in the Centenary Test match at Lord's in 1980, he said simply, 'And after Trevor Bailey it will be Christopher Martin-Jenkins,' and he got up and walked slowly to the door of the commentary box, opened it and went out, never to return. Alan Curtis on the public address announced that his final spell with *Test Match Special* had ended. There was huge applause – from the players as well. At the end of the season he was made an Honorary Life Member of the MCC. Then, with his books and as much of his wine as he could carry, he disappeared to the island of Alderney where he lived out his final years, aided and abetted as much by his corkscrew as his memories.

ALAN GIBSON

Aᴌᴀɴ Gɪʙꜱᴏɴ's genius, for it was undoubtedly that, was sometimes as rough at the edges as his appearance and, on occasions, his humour. His ability as a cricket commentator on *Test Match Special* should have left him with as rich a reputation as John Arlott. Towards the end of his working life, the irresistible essays he wrote in *The Times* about his day at the cricket, as he meandered back and forth through the shires, were unique.

Alan was highly articulate on the broadest possible range of subjects. Although he was born a Yorkshireman in Sheffield, he upped sticks to the West Country and became the most wholehearted of Gloucestershire's adopted sons. It was in the West Country that he was best appreciated. It was mostly from the BBC studios in Bristol that he broadcast on myriad regional programmes. In these, in one form or another, he talked knowledgeably about almost every facet of everyday village life, the arts, poetry, archaeology and anything else that struck him. He was hugely well read and almost no subject fazed him. He spoke, too, in a gentle but erudite and enquiring voice with a comprehensive command of the English language and its grammar. He introduced *Sunday Half Hour* and his contributions to *Round Britain Quiz* contained an extraordinarily diverse, interesting and entertaining scholarship. Alan was a man of many parts who should have gone much further than he did.

He loved cricket and rugger. He captained Queen's College, Oxford at cricket and in his commentaries his knowledge of the intricacies of the game was always apparent, although he liked to tackle his commentaries, as he did his writings in later years, with a broader brush. In 1948 he began to commentate about cricket for the BBC in the days when they found time for commentaries on county matches on the old Home Service. Curiously, it was not for another fourteen years, in 1962, that he joined *Test Match Special*. In the winters, he tucked himself into the back of a chilly West Country rugger stand from where he would regale his listeners with all that was going on. Just occasionally, he found himself on a distant Cornish touchline trying to do something similar, although on those draughty occasions the lilt in his voice was harder to detect and his hip flask had a hard day at the office.

Alan's views were unorthodox, to say the least, and it was surely because of this trait, which in his case was always pertinent and amusing, that those in charge at Broadcasting House may have felt that on occasions he was too big a potential risk. He also had an infinite capacity, first for beer, which was probably containable, but when he transferred his affections lock, stock and barrel to whisky, the firmament shook. Alas, this was to cost him his commentating career and in the end his life. But Alan without booze would have been hard to imagine.

I barely knew him in the days when he was a Test match commentator, although I listened with great enjoyment to everything that he said through fourteen summers. Why then does Alan play a part in this book? It was later, in the seventies, that John Hennessey, the Sports Editor of *The Times*, employed him to write about county cricket, and for some years he regaled readers on a daily basis with the most delightfully amusing essays. The following was written at the Garrison Ground in Colchester when Geoffrey Boycott scored a double century for the second year running. This time he opened the batting with Phil Sharpe with whom he added 240 in a stand that was memorable for its noise. Alan first compared Boycott and Sharpe's method of calling with that of Herbert Sutcliffe and Percy Holmes, who moved between the wickets in almost an eerie silence. Gibson had seen them add 555 for the first wicket against Essex at Layton in 1932. He goes on: 'The present Yorkshire system is for both batsmen to shout simultaneously, pause and then shout again. If, as happens about once an over, this has not cleared the situation up, it is considered wise to keep shouting. This is especially the policy of Boycott, whose progress down the pitch is often one long ululation.' Those three sentences capture the essence of Gibson.

The cricket was the vehicle for an account of his day, which usually began at Bristol Station in the early morning and continued with a predictable hiccough at Didcot. This hiatus usually involved him in being sent to the wrong platform by a porter or an inspector who had not done his homework, and caused him to be an exceedingly late arrival at whatever ground he was heading for. His lateness never impaired his ability to write a highly entertaining and stimulating piece for the following day's paper. As he shuffled round the ground, paying homage to each bar he passed, Alan scarcely made a note and if he appeared at all in a press box, it was with obvious and considerable distaste, to find the answer to a problem he had been unable to solve elsewhere. He wrote his pieces with a fountain pen and at the end of the day would tramp back to the nearest railway station and find his way back home to Bristol. He hated staying in hotels.

At the ground, his conversation was unmissable. He was marvellously cynical about much that went on, he insisted on filling you up with quantities of booze and would never allow one to cry 'Capevi.' It was best to meet up with him before lunch and then to tackle a scotch egg or a pork pie with him. One of the great joys of Alan's writings was that he produced *dramatis personae* of his own around the county grounds about whom he invariably wrote when applicable. Puff The Magic Dragon who, in real life, was Graeme Parker, the secretary of Gloucestershire, led the off-the-field characters. This appellation came his way because whenever he was about to make an announcement over the public address system, he always blew forcibly into the microphone to make sure it was live. Two rasping puffs burst across the ground. GRIP was another notable character at Bristol. The Glorious Red-headed Imperturbable Pamela presided over the dispensing of drinks in the Hammond Bar and was therefore an indispensable part of the Gibson lexicon. On the field his opening bowlers would have been the Demon of Frome and the Shoreditch Sparrow. The Demon of Frome was Colin Dredge who ran in to bowl in a slightly mechanical-man-ish sort of way and his pace was distinctly less than terrifying. The Shoreditch Sparrow was otherwise known as Robin Jackman who was here, there and everywhere rather in the manner of a sparrow, and who also had the loudest and most ferocious appeal imaginable.

If Alan hated one type of person more than any other, it was the bore and, I suppose, it is the long drawn out nature of cricket that attracts members of this particular species to the game. Alan, John Arlott and I appointed ourselves as selectors of the Bores XI on our travels around the cricket grounds of England. Each bore selected was given his own name and furious debate would ensue to decide which place in the batting order he should occupy. There was the elderly gentleman at Canterbury who, on even the hottest days of summer, would wear a brown overcoat. He went into the side as Mr B. Overcoat and he was the sort of reliable, if rather dull, number five all sides need who would score about 1,500 runs a season. He talked unceasingly from behind a close clipped moustache with unbounded enthusiasm about the weather and what his wife had said to him that morning. (Mrs B. Overcoat was herself a candidate for any Ladies XI.) Mr B. Overcoat liked to sit beside the press box and this made him even more of a danger. Whenever one of us went there we made sure we gave him a good net to confirm that his form was not slipping away. As it was, we found that, if anything, his form improved with age. The know-all at Southampton was quickly translated into Mr K. All who made the all-rounder's spot his own for as long as he wanted. Mr B. Clips, who would probably have wanted his bicycle clips beside him in his coffin, haunted the

Recreation Ground at Bath. It was exactly like talking to a signpost as he told you by which route he had peddled to the ground that morning. At the Racecourse Ground at Derby there was Mr N.O.T. Trent whose discourse about the delights to be found North of the Trent was unstoppable. It gave us a lot of fun and Alan's imagination put together the most splendid anecdotes about all of them.

If Alan had not had such a large self-destruct button, goodness knows where he would have ended up. As it was, on a good day, he gave me as much fun as anyone I can remember on the circuit and became the greatest and one of the most unforgettable of friends. I daresay his shade is still haunting Didcot station. I do hope so.

JOHN WOODCOCK

No book of this nature written by me would ever be complete without a piece about John Woodcock, the ablest, most discerning and interesting of all the cricket writers it has been my luck to read. It would also be hard to find a pleasanter or more amusing man and he had the misfortune to be the conduit whereby I came into his line of country. He became the Cricket Correspondent of *The Times* in April 1954 and remained in that august post until he retired at the end of the 1986 season in England. Mercifully for those of us who jolly nearly hang on his every word, he allows himself to be persuaded to unsheathe his pen from time to time and give us his views on some burning topic. It is part of his charm that he makes a fierce show of reluctance every time he is asked to pick up the cudgels one more time; it is his great skill that the contribution that follows will put the issue, whatever it is, into a truer perspective than anyone else has so far managed.

Rem acu tetigisti is the phrase Jeeves would have used, which for those who do not have a command of Latin at their fingertips means, generally speaking, putting your finger on the spot. Woodcock's great ability when confronted by a major story was to be able immediately to put it into a long-term perspective. He was also the best watcher of a day's cricket I ever knew. Nothing would escape him and, although one had been watching and writing about the same day's play, one always had that sinking feeling when opening the cricket page in *The Times* the following morning that in his piece there would be at least two highly relevant points that one had oneself completely missed. He writes with a total lack of bombast or pomposity in the most charmingly conversational and readable style.

Wooders's physical problems began at the age of fifteen when he was at school at St Edward's, Oxford and came within a whisker of dying. He was already a considerable games player in embryo when he got a blister on his toe while playing squash. It developed into something, which, thank goodness, he was able to spell, called staphylococcal septicaemia, or septic arthritis to the uninitiated. It laid him low to the extent that prayers were said for him in the chapel of St Edward's and, happily for the game of cricket and for all his many friends, the Almighty was listening that day. Hip replacement had not yet been invented and he had to have three big operations over fifteen years, all done by orthopaedic wizards, but with varying degrees of success. After the first, in Oxford, he had to lie on a frame in hospital for four and a half months without being allowed to move. The second operation, in London ten years later, did not really work and it was in the late sixties that he travelled up to Wrightington and came under a knife held by John Charnley who had pioneered a hip replacement operation. Even though that was successful, there was so much residual damage that he has never walked easily or painlessly. I remember once flying to the West Indies with him when our aeroplane was diverted to New York. While we were there, the security chaps insisted that we walked through various mine-detection machines and the pin in Wooders's hip set one off. It made a lovely noise that suggested it might have won the jackpot. The Americans in charge showed a serious sense of humour shortage and in no time at all they had stripped Wooders down to his pants. No one enjoyed the joke more than he did, even if our trans-Atlantic cousins failed by some way to see the point.

Like so many of our generation of cricket writers, Wooders – the inevitable Johnstonism – began his journalistic career by working for Jim Swanton. This provided a noble training even if one's *sang-*

froid was on occasions severely tested by the great man, who was, not unreasonably, known as *Pomponious Ego* by some of his acquaintances. I also came under the Swanton umbrella on the 1967/68 tour of the West Indies when we had our moments. In 1950/51 Wooders went to Australia, partly to work for Swanton, and partly to make a television film for the BBC, something that had not happened on tour before. Wooders did a BBC course at Alexandra Palace and eventually set sail for Australia accompanied by a television camera and 22,000 feet of film. He filmed each day's cricket and every third day he would take the film he had shot to the airport and it would be flown back to Pinewood or Denham where they dealt with these things. I can't think how Hollywood let him escape their clutches. Then, in 1952, he found himself Cricket Correspondent of the *Guardian*, temporarily succeeding Denys Rowbotham, and in April 1954, there was a certain rearrangement of human resources in the sports room at *The Times* and Wooders was appointed the Cricket Correspondent. It was a position he held with such extraordinary distinction for thirty-three years that Alan Gibson was to christen him the Sage of Longparish.

The greatest qualities Wooders brought to cricket writing were common sense and a complete lack of pretentiousness. He always thought out his position most carefully, be it in terms of writing a match report, taking a view of some earth-shattering decision by the game's authorities or writing about any issue that was controversial or dramatic. On these occasions, Wooders knew his own mind and was always faithful to it. He wrote forcefully, but in such a way that he made almost no enemies, even if he is still waiting for his first Christmas card from Kerry Packer who did not take kindly to Wooders's views about his breakaway circus and World Series Cricket in general. To see the two of them, as I once did, in verbal combat at Waverley Park, where Packer played his first WSC matches in Melbourne, was rather like having a look at David and Goliath on a really bad day. Packer is a huge man with a somewhat rubbery face while Wooders is small, but nonetheless combative because of it. The result did not require a rewriting of the Old Testament matchcard.

No one who has spent a day in the press box sitting next to Wooders could help but be richer for the experience, and a more shrewd observer of the game at the end of it. He would have enjoyed many humorous asides and one or two really good belly laughs. He will have had to have been careful, because Wooders will suddenly decide in the middle of the afternoon, or occasionally even earlier, that he needs to write about something that has already happened. He then gets out his pen and becomes impervious to all conversation and chatter. He is greatly helped in this by being seriously deaf in one ear. If you have the misfortune to find yourself sitting on that side of him, you may feel after a while that you were foolish to have thrown away the chance of a lesson or two in semaphore. If you're on his good side and begin to chatter while he is in mid-season form with his pen, he will caution you with a quick word and a look that will ensure no further interruptions. But a day at the cricket with Wooders is not to be missed and an evening with Wooders is compulsory if given the chance. My own life in cricket would have been infinitely the poorer without the company of Wooders and I would not have had half the laughs I have had. He is one of the great men.

BRIAN JOHNSTON

IN many ways Brian Johnston was the complete antithesis of John Arlott and yet he did every bit as much for the game and its popularity. Johnners was indomitably cheerful, a great comic with a never-ending fund of good stories. He loved puns, saw the humorous side of everything, pulled legs fast and furiously and was the nicest man in the world who never said a nasty word about anyone. He was really a music hall artist *manqué*. He lived most of his life a stone's throw from Lord's until, towards the end, he moved to the outskirts of St John's Wood. On the morning of a Test match he would enlist the help of a bus to propel him down the Wellington Road to the North Gate of Lord's. The infectious chuckle, the brown and white co-respondent shoes, the jaunty walk – here was the man who was always set to have the time of his life, whatever he was doing and wherever he was. In some ways, he was an indomitable teenager until the day he died in January 1994. The guffaws that increasingly emanated from the commentary box were usually the result of his handiwork.

He was a passionate lover of and believer in *Test Match Special* and all that it stood for. There were times in the last fifteen or so years of his life when the future of *TMS* was anything but assured. There was no obvious home for us on any of the networks. When we were on Radio Three medium wave, vast tracts of the country were unable to pick up the signal. When we moved to Radio Four long wave, the dyed-in-the-wool listeners to *The Archers* on long wave nearly had apoplexy, while the cricket devotees never found it in their hearts to embrace the shipping forecast as they might have done. When we broadcast from overseas they tend, too, to regard *Yesterday in Parliament* as a luxury that could be dispensed with. Johnners fought our corner tooth-and-nail. I well remember one evening at the Swan at Bucklow Hill, which for years was *TMS*'s home for Old Trafford Test matches. The new Head of Outside Broadcasts (Radio) visited us and spoke with less than conviction about our future. Johnners was livid and, apart from calling the Head of OBs by the wrong name, showed splenetic qualities we none of us knew that he possessed. He had been a particularly gallant soldier and had won a Military Cross during the Second World War, and he was not to be trifled with. The Head of OBs will have gone to bed that night hoping that he was not going to meet Johnners later in a dark passage.

Johnners could never understand why, and it made him furious, such a successful programme should be constantly forced to look for a new home. But, as I write, we nestle happily under the auspices of Radio Four long wave, threatened by nothing more immediate than the prospect of becoming exclusively digital at some relatively distant date. The popularity of *TMS* owes a huge debt to Johnners, whom we still talk about as though we expect him to be the next man through the door, although he has been dead almost ten years.

He began to work for BBC Radio soon after the war before being lured to television by Ian (later Lord) Orr-Ewing who was Head of Television Outside Broadcasts. He knew Johnners loved cricket and, as the BBC were televising the Test matches against India at Lord's and The Oval in 1946, he thought Johnners would be an admirable commentator. He was not wrong. So, while the Eastern Services poetry producer was sharpening up his talents on behalf of the listeners in India, his future colleague was cutting his teeth on television. Johnners always reckoned that television commentary was far harder than radio, which is how most radio commentators view it. Radio commentators have to keep talking and they have a 360-degree angle of vision to describe. The job of a television commentator is to explain and comment on a picture and not to talk too much. Johnners had other strings to his bow apart from cricket. He did the 'Let's Go Somewhere' spot on *In Town Tonight*. In all, on 150 Saturday evenings, Johnners went somewhere unusual and did a live four-minute broadcast. Once they dug a small trench so that he could lie between the rails on a railway line. He broadcast while the train went over the top of him and he always said that someone pulled the plug at the same time. On another occasion, he hid in a red post box and, when a lady was about to post a letter, he put his hand out and took it and she fainted. Another time he sang in the street, pretending to be a tramp. 'Underneath the Arches', which he once sang with Bud Flanagan outside the Victoria Palace, must have been one of the songs. Later he took over *Down Your Way* from Franklyn Engelmann and retired after doing exactly the same number of programmes as his illustrious predecessor.

Johnners was very much more than just a cricket commentator, although he was one of the regular voices behind the BBC television cricket pictures from 1946 until 1969. Then, early in 1970, he returned home from commentating on South Africa's series against Australia, and found out that he was no longer wanted on television. No one had had the guts or the grace to tell him and he heard the news through a chance conversation in Broadcasting House. He went at once to see Robert Hudson who had just taken over as Head of OBs (Sound) who confirmed the news, but said that he wanted Johnners as a regular for the *Test Match Special* team. Those in charge of television thought that he was too light-hearted and generally trivialised things too much, which was unfair. His irrepressible humour now did an amazing job on radio where Johnners was a pivotal figure. The time had arrived when commentators had to become entertainers in their own right and no one fitted that particular bill better than Johnners.

He not only introduced humour to *TMS*, he also started the

chocolate cake era. He loved chocolate cakes and when one day a listener sent one to the box, Johnners was fulsome in his thanks. He suggested it would be nice if more listeners did likewise and soon the box was awash with chocolate cakes, the stickier and more gooey the better. His enthusiasm, his boyish sense of humour and his pranks created a wonderfully jolly atmosphere in the box, even if it depressed a few inveterate cricket listeners who like their information uncorrupted by such things as laughter, chocolate cakes and sticky fingers. No one has been better than Johnners at conducting those mad conversations that take place in the box when rain or bad light has stopped play. It is then that we talk about anything and everything from deadly serious cricket to intense frivolity. Johnners always brought the best out in everyone, and with his wide and varied experiences he was always full to the brim with wonderfully amusing anecdotes. Listeners began to write in and say how much better *TMS* was when there was no cricket being played.

Johnners was also brilliant on the Saturday lunchtime feature during Test matches, *View from the Boundary*. Someone who was well known with an interest in cricket was asked to the commentary box and had half an hour's conversation with Johnners. He would ask his guest about his interest in cricket and where it came from. Then he would ask questions about his guest's own life in whatever field it was. It involved Johnners in a good deal of homework and with the help of the research department at Broadcasting House he was never short of material. Johnners himself had almost always had some part to play in his guest's previous life and so you could be guaranteed that there would be plenty of laughter and leg-pulling. Since Johnners departed, this feature has continued although now we all take it in turns to interview the guests, but I am not sure we match the *joie de vivre* or the laughter he produced.

He could be dynamite on the air for you never quite knew what was going to come next. In 1976 at The Oval when England's batsmen were making better progress than usual against Andy

Roberts and Michael Holding with the score about 80/6, he suddenly announced to the unsuspecting world: 'I can tell all you cricket lovers at home that the bowler's Holding, the batsman's Willey.' Of course, the rest of us were momentarily shocked that such an experienced commentator, who was a watchword as far as decorum was concerned, should have stooped as low as this. Then we looked up and saw that Michael Holding was running in to bowl to Peter Willey, and breathed more easily. Johnners had clearly worked that one out in the middle of the night because he was the only person in the box who didn't laugh. Whenever he said something funny that came out totally unexpectedly, he would fall about as much as anyone.

Then there was the Johnners mating call, a noise that sounded as much as anything like a human hunting horn and came more from the depth of his chest than from his throat. It had a lively resonance about it and was produced, more than many times on air, whenever something unexpected happened or he saw someone he hadn't seen for ages. It was a call of friendship and amusement and was Johnners through and through. After the departure of John Arlott in 1980, Johnners became *TMS* to a great many people, and his spirit of fun still persists and I hope it always will. If *TMS* is ever allowed to become deadly serious, it would miss the point by a great distance.

There were those who felt that his way of doing commentary trivialised the game, but they were heavily in the minority. He did not profess a great knowledge of the intricacies, taking the view that the experts such as Fred Trueman and Trevor Bailey were there to cope with those things. When he was young he had been a passionately enthusiastic club cricketer who had enjoyed the game enormously. He was a wicket keeper and often told the story against himself about his most famous dismissal. In the days when Sunday was the rest day during Test matches, he was asked to play in a benefit match on the Sunday of a Test match at Old Trafford and he was thrilled to don the gloves. One of the bowlers he had to keep to was none other than Richie Benaud and I daresay Johnners had about as much idea of telling his leg break from his googly or his flipper as all the other lay members of the commentary box. I think Richie was probably kind to him and didn't fizz his googlies or flippers too much that Sunday. Eventually, a batsman went charging down the wicket to Richie's leg break and missed the ball. Johnners gathered it in with all the haste he could manage and removed the bails before appealing for a stumping. The square leg umpire duly raised his finger, the batsman departed and the famous entry 'st Johnston b Benaud' was solemnly inscribed in the scorebook. When the innings ended soon afterwards, Brian was feeling pretty pleased with himself as he walked off the field. The stumping had left a warm glow. He had just crossed the boundary when a spectator came up to him and insisted on shaking his hand. Having done so he congratulated Johnners on his splendid stumping and then added, 'But what made it so wonderful was the sporting way in which you delayed taking off the bails and gave him such an excellent chance of getting back.'

It is safe to say that, sadly, there will never be another Johnners, but his memory will always provide the *TMS* box with the unadulterated adrenalin of true enjoyment and entertainment.